To Chris,

Happy 21st Birthday,

With love

from

Wendy xx

His servants speak

Statements by Latter-day Saint Leaders
on Contemporary Topics

R. Clayton Brough

INTERNATIONAL STANDARD BOOK NUMBER
0-88290-054-4

LIBRARY OF CONGRESS CATALOG CARD NUMBER
75-17101

Second Printing, 1977

Printed in the
United States of America
by

**Horizon Publishers
& Distributors
P.O. Box 490
50 South 500 West
Bountiful, Utah 84010**

To my parents, R. Marshall and
Utahna C. Brough, who inspiringly taught me the
Gospel, and to my loving wife, Ethel,
who righteously helps me
live it.

PREFACE

How The Book Is Arranged

His Servants Speak is a compilation of documented statements
made by Presidents and other General Authorities of The Church
of Jesus Christ of Latter-day Saints, on various topics of contemporary interest to Latter-day Saints today.

The statements are arranged in this book under a series of over
fifty general topics. Official Church Statements* where necessary
and available, are presented first. Statements by Presidents of the
Church appear next, with statements by other General Authorities
and those from *Church News* Editorials** following thereafter.

It is hoped that this compilation will serve as a useful tool for
those who wish to locate expressions by Church leaders on the
topics covered. Many of the quotations cited are not readily
accessible to Church members and this compilation can save them
considerable research time and expense. It should be understood,
of course, that this is a compilation made by an individual and is
not an official publication released by The Church of Jesus Christ
of Latter-day Saints.

It is the compiler's hope and prayer that those who read this
book will seek inspiration from the Holy Ghost in gaining a
testimony of the truthfulness of the statements by the Brethren
contained herein, and apply that knowledge in their own lives and
actions; for the Lord has said:

Wherefore the voice of the Lord is unto the ends of the earth, that
all that will hear may hear; ...

---

*Official Church Statements are those distributed to Church
leaders and members under the sanction and or signature of the First
Presidency, such as: *Circular Letters of the First Presidency, General
Handbook of Instructions, Priesthood Bulletins,* and First Presidency
statements in General Conferences. These statements usually express
the doctrinal position, attitude, and or policy of the Church on the
various topics they discuss.

**Church News* Editorials are written by General Authorities,
usually one of the Apostles, and before any are published they must be
approved by the First Presidency. Thus, *Church News* Editorials are
often considered to express the attitude of the Church on the various
topics they cover.

And the arm of the Lord shall be revealed; and the day cometh that they who will not hear the voice of the Lord, neither the voice of his servants, neither give heed to the words of the prophets and apostles, shall be cut off from among the people; ...

What I the Lord have spoken, I have spoken, and I excuse not myself; and though the heavens and the earth pass away, my word shall not pass away, but shall all be fulfilled, whether by mine own voice or by the voice of my servants, it is the same. *(D&C 1:11, 14, 38)*

And whatsoever they shall speak when moved upon by the Holy Ghost shall be scripture, shall be the will of the Lord, shall be the mind of the Lord, shall be the word of the Lord, shall be the voice of the Lord, and the power of God unto salvation. *(D&C 68:4)*

Expression of Appreciation

Grateful acknowledgment is expressed to those General Authorities who granted reprint permission to the compiler: Elders N. Eldon Tanner, Marion G. Romney, Ezra Taft Benson, Gordon B. Hinckley, Bruce R. McConkie, Henry D. Taylor, Alvin R. Dyer, Theodore M. Burton, Bernard P. Brockbank, Robert L. Simpson, O. Leslie Stone, H. Burke Peterson and Vaughn J. Featherstone.

Statements by several living General Authorities are not quoted herein but, rather, are listed under a summary heading with the locational reference noted. The reason for this is that several General Authorities, when contacted, desired to retain their material for personal use in future publications.

My sincere appreciation is also expressed to Duane Crowther, President of Horizon Publishers, who patiently and expertly assisted the compiler by making many helpful suggestions in readying this book for publication.

Deep thankfulness is expressed to my parents, R. Marshall and Utahna C. Brough, and to my wife's parents, Clark A. and Helen N. Mickelson, for their diligence in teaching their children correct principles of the Gospel and for their encouragement in this project.

And last but most important, eternal gratitude is expressed to my loving wife, Ethel, who more than anyone else has sustained and encouraged me during my many months of research.

R. Clayton Brough

TABLE OF CONTENTS

     The Church Opposes Abortion—19; Abortion And Steriliza-
tion—20; Abortion: An Evil Act—20; The Evil of Premeditated
Abortion—20; Women Who Yield To Abortions Should Remember That God's Retribution Is Sure—21; To Destroy An
Unborn Child Is One Of The Most Despicable Of All Sins—
21; Abortion Is One Of The Most Revolting And Sinful Practices In This Day—21; When The Mother Feels Life, It Is The
Infant's Spirit Entering Its Body Preparatory To Existence—21.

     Thou Shalt Not Commit Adultery—23; Church Courts To
Handle Adulterers—24; No Fine Distinctions Between Adultery, Fornication, And Sex Perversion—24; Marriage Presup-
poses Total Fidelity—24.

     The Superstitions Of Astrology—25; Stars Cannot Control
Your Acts—26.

     Where Husband And Wife Enjoy Health And Vigor It Is Con-
trary To Church Teachings To Artificially Curtail The Birth Of
Children—27; The Desire Not To Have Children Is Based Upon
Vanity, Passion, And Selfishness—28; No Promise Of Eternal
Salvation For Those Who Practice Birth Control—29; Limiting
Offspring Is An Abomination—31; Restrictive Measures Invites
Righteous Anger From God—32; The Only Legitimate Birth
Control—33; Marriage Is For The Purpose Of Rearing A Fam-
ily—33; Young People Who Resort To Surgery To Limit Their
Families Will Find It Difficult To Rationalize Before The
Lord—34; Infanticide Is A Crime—34; The Principles Heavily
Populated Countries Should Adopt To Overcome Poverty—34;
False Reasoning In Population Limitation—35; Concerning
"Family Planning"—35; The Realistic Approach To "Popula-
tion Explosion"—37.

     Death: The Penalty For Capital Crime—41; A Murderer Shall

12

14

Peace Cannot Be Legislated Into Existence—199; Love All Men, Including Your Enemies—200.

KEY TO ABBREVIATIONS

CL	—	Circular Letters of the First Presidency
CN	—	Church News
CR	—	Conference Reports
E	—	Ensign, The
F	—	Friend, The
GHI	—	General Handbook of Instructions
I	—	Instructor, The
IE	—	Improvement Era, The
JD	—	Journal of Discourses
JH	—	Journal History of the Church
JI	—	Juvenile Instructor
MS	—	Millennial Star, The
NE	—	New Era, The
PB	—	Priesthood Bulletin, The
RSM	—	Relief Society Magazine, The

CHAPTER 1

ABORTION
(See: Birth Control)

Church Opposes Abortion

In view of a recent decision of the United States Supreme Court, we feel it necessary to restate the position of the Church on abortion in order that there will be no misunderstanding of our attitude.

The Church opposes abortion and counsels its members not to submit to or perform an abortion except in the rare cases where, in the opinion of competent medical counsel, the life or good health of the mother is seriously endangered or where the pregnancy was caused by rape and produces serious emotional trauma in the mother. Even then it should be done only after counseling with the local presiding priesthood authority and after receiving divine confirmation through prayer.

Abortion must be considered one of the most revolting and sinful practices in this day, when we are witnessing the frightening evidence of permissiveness leading to sexual immorality.

Members of the Church guilty of being parties to the sin of abortion must be subjected to the disciplinary action of the councils of the Church as circumstances warrant. In dealing with this serious matter, it would be well to keep in mind the word of the Lord stated in the 59th Section of the *Doctrine and Covenants*, verse 6, "Thou shalt not steal; neither commit adultery, nor kill, nor do anything like unto it."

As to the amenability of the sin of abortion to the laws of repentance and forgiveness, we quote the following statement made by President David O. McKay and his counselors, Stephen L. Richards and J. Reuben Clark, Jr., which continues to represent the attitude and position of the Church:

> As the matter stands today, no definite statement has been made by the Lord one way or another regarding the crime of abortion. So far as is known, he has not listed it alongside the crime of the unpardonable sin and shedding of innocent human blood. That he has not done so would suggest that it is not in that class of crime and therefore that it will be amenable to the laws of repentance and forgiveness.

This quoted statement, however, should not, in any sense, be construed to minimize the seriousness of this revolting sin.

(PB, February, 1973.)

Abortion and Sterilization

The question is frequently raised as to the policy of the Church regarding abortions. The following is quoted from a statement recently issued by the First Presidency on the subject of abortion and sterilization:

> We have given careful consideration to the question of proposed laws on abortion and sterilization. We are opposed to any modification, expansion, or liberalization of laws on these vital subjects.

The Church takes the view that any tampering with the fountains of life is serious, both morally and physiologically. The Lord's command imposed upon Latter-day Saints is to "multiply and replenish the earth." Nevertheless there may be conditions where abortion might be justified, but such conditions must be determined in each instance upon the advice of a competent, reliable physician, preferably a member of the Church, and in accordance with the civil laws pertaining thereto.

(PB, February, 1971.)

Abortion: An Evil Act

I call upon the Church and all its members to forsake the evils of the world. We must shun unchastity and every form of immorality as we would a plague. We must not dam up the wellsprings of life by preventing childbirth. We must not be guilty of unrighteous and evil acts of abortion.

(Joseph Fielding Smith, President of the Church,
CR, April, 1971, p. 47.)

The Evil of Premeditated Abortion

[Comments on this subject were made by *Spencer W. Kimball,* President of the Church, in the April, 1974, General Conference, and can be found in the *Ensign,* May, 1974, p. 7.]

Women Who Yield To Abortions Should
Remember That God's Retribution Is Sure

[Comments on this subject were made by *Spencer W. Kimball*, President of the Church, in the October, 1974, General Conference, and can be found in the *Ensign*, November, 1974, p. 9.]

To Destroy An Unborn Child Is One
Of The Most Despicable Of All Sins

[Comments on this subject were made by *Spencer W. Kimball*, President of the Church, in the October, 1974, General Conference, and can be found in the *Ensign*, November, 1974, p. 7.]

Abortion Is One Of The Most Revolting
And Sinful Practices In This Day

[Comments on this subject were made by *Spencer W. Kimball*, President of the Church, in the April, 1975, General Conference, and can be found in the *Ensign*, May, 1975, p. 7.]

When The Mother Feels Life, It Is The Infant's Spirit
Entering Its Body Preparatory To Existence

...When the mother feels life come to her infant it is the spirit entering the body preparatory to the immortal existence. But suppose an accident occurs and the spirit has to leave this body prematurely, what then? All that the physician says is—"it is a still birth," and that is all they know about it; but whether the spirit remains in the body a minute, an hour, a day, a year, or lives there until the body has reached a good old age, it is certain that the time will come when they will be separated, and the body will return to mother earth, there to sleep upon that mother's bosom. That is all there is about death.

(Brigham Young, President of the Church, *JD*, July 19, 1874, 17:143.)

CHAPTER 2

ADULTERY
(See: Marriage)

Thou Shalt Not Commit Adultery

One of the ten basic principles of Christian society, and accepted by all worshippers of the true God, came to men at Sinai when God wrote with His own finger: "Thou shalt not commit adultery."

By the laws of Moses, adulterers were stoned to death. *(Deut. 22:24)* God said to Israel: "There shall be no whore of the daughters of Israel, nor a sodomite of the sons of Israel." *(Deut. 23:17)* When God, through Jeremiah, chastened Israel for apostasy, He pictured her loathsomeness by calling her a harlot. *(Jeremiah 3)* Paul declared to the Ephesians:

> For this ye know, that no whoremonger, nor unclean person ... hath any inheritance in the kingdom of Christ and of God. *(Eph. 5:5)*

The Revelator declared that whoremongers "shall have their part in the lake which burneth with fire and brimstone: which is the second death." *(Rev. 21:8)* And when he wished to condemn the great false church and its iniquities that had led the world into apostasy and wickedness, the Revelator called her "Mystery, Babylon the Great, the Mother of Harlots and Abominations of the Earth." *(Rev. 17:5)* Jacob, teaching the Nephites, declared:

> Wo unto them who commit whoredoms, for they shall be thrust down to hell.—*(2 Nephi 9:36)*

To us of this Church, the Lord has declared that adulterers should not be admitted to membership *(D&C 42:76)*; that adulterers in the Church, if unrepentant, should be cast out *(D&C 42:75)*, but if repentant should be permitted to remain *(D&C 42:74, 42:25)* and, He said, "By this ye may know if a man repenteth of his sins—behold, he will confess them and forsake them."— *(D&C 58:43)*

In the great revelation on the three heavenly glories, the Lord said, speaking of those who will inherit the lowest of these, or the telestial glory:

These are they who are liars, and sorcerers, and adulterers, and whoremongers, and whosoever loves and makes a lie.—*(D&C 76:103)*

Heber J. Grant, J. Reuben Clark, Jr., David O. McKay
The First Presidency
(*CR*, October, 1942, pp. 9-11.)

Church Courts To Handle Adulterers

Cases handled by Church Courts include ... Fornication, Adultery, homo-sexual acts, or other infractions of the moral code....
(*GHI*, 1968, p. 122.)

No Fine Distinctions Between Adultery, Fornication, And Sex Perversion

One of the most corrupting and debasing vices rampant in our society today is unchastity. Let us be ever mindful that from Sinai the Lord thundered, "Thou shalt not commit adultery." *(Exod. 20:14)*

The penalty for so doing under the Mosaic law was death. Notwithstanding the fact that in this generation's corrupt permissiveness its violation is tolerated with impunity, under God's divine law it is as it has always been, a soul-destroying sin. Its self-executing penalty is spiritual death. No unforgiven adulterer is magnifying his calling in the priesthood; and, as President Clark used to say, the Lord has made no "fine distinctions ... between fornication and adultery" (*Conference Report*, Oct. 1949, p. 194). Nor, may I add, between adultery and sex perversion.

(*Marion G. Romney*, Second Counselor in the First Presidency, *CR-E*, May, 1974, p. 82.)

Marriage Presupposes Total Fidelity

[Comments on this subject were made by *Spencer W. Kimball*, an Apostle, in the October 1962, General Conference, and can be found in the *Conference Report* for that same month and year, pp. 57-58.]

CHAPTER 3

ASTROLOGY
(See: Witchcraft and Evil Practices)

The Superstitions of Astrology

Astrology has had a new birth in the world, and many normally intelligent people are beginning to study it.

Most of the suggestions made in horoscopes are not only outlandish but actually amusing.

How can the time of your birth determine your character? How can a star a million light years away influence your morning moods and actions?

If you are willing to believe superstition in this form, why not accept it in other forms?

Under Capricorn, do you really believe that every older person will become romantic at a time of life when they should be settling down?

If you are born under Leo, do you really believe that you are predestined to be overworked all your life, but that you may take comfort in the thought that at least you will have something left for your old age?

Or if you were born under Virgo, do you really think it will be easy for you to "polish off household chores in a hurry" so that you can plan escapes and outings any time you wish?

And if you were born under Aquarius do you really think that you, and only you, must not mix love with money?

The horoscope tells you that if you are born under Pisces you should not pick a quarrel if some member of the family objects. Do you believe it?

The stars cannot possibly and do not have any relationship to your actions or to your lives. You are free agents. God himself, who is your Father, gave you self-determination. That is one of the basic teachings of the gospel. Without free agency, there would be only slavery. And are we slaves to the stars? There is no place for predestination in his gospel plan.

What does it matter when Taurus rises in the sky, or when Leo goes to bed? Who is concerned about Scorpio and whether he will give you a new and more interesting romance? Are you not supposed to be true to your own wife or husband and not covet someone else's?

Latter-day Saints tempted to believe in these superstitions should remember some of the basic gospel precepts.

For one, we are children of God, and we lived in a pre-existent life where we developed character traits. What we did in the eternity before we were born can determine our so-called natural tendencies, but not the ascendency of Jupiter or Pisces.

Another point to remember is that God has given us the gospel, with many commandments on how to live and develop Christ-like souls, and doing so, he does not place us under the influence of any star or set of constellations which could take away the right of choice which he has given us.

Our relationships are with the Almighty, not with his stellar creations. It matters not to any of us whether Aries appears on our birthday nor whether the moon is made of cheese or granite, nor whether the astronauts find shining diamonds or pieces of flint in its crevices.

We are related to God and his laws, which prohibit superstitions like astrology.

Think of the astrology mentioned in the Bible. Were not astrologers the enemies of Moses, who was a prophet of God? Did not astrology contribute to the downfall of Saul? The Prophet Isaiah rebuked a superstitious astrology-fortune-telling-spiritualist oriented people with these words:

> And when they shall say unto you, Seek unto them that have familiar spirits and unto wizards that peep and that mutter, should not a people seek unto their God? To the law and the testimony: if they speak not according to his word, it is because there is no light in them." *(Isa. 8)*

It is paradoxical that in this time of scientific advancement, in this enlightened day when we are supposed to be more intelligent than at any time past, this ancient superstition should rise again.

And it is more than fantastic that people who have access to the Prophets of God would give heed to astrologers.

(Editorial, *CN*, May 16, 1970, p. 16.)

Stars Cannot Control Your Acts

The stars can't control your acts any more than the green cheese of which the moon is supposed to be made.

God gave you free agency, and He does not allow even the stars to interfere with it. He is the Creator of the stars but He did not devise the peculiar cult of astrology.

(Editorial, *CN*, October 14, 1972, p. 16.)

CHAPTER 4

BIRTH CONTROL AND POPULATION EXPLOSION
(See: Abortion, Marriage)

Where Husband and Wife Enjoy Health and Vigor ...
It Is Contrary To Church Teachings To
Artificially Curtail the Birth of Children

The First Presidency is being asked from time to time as to what the attitude of the Church is regarding birth control. In order that you may be informed on this subject and that you may be prepared to convey the proper information to the members of the Church under your jurisdiction, we have decided to give you the following statement:

We seriously regret that there should exist a sentiment or feeling among any members of the Church to curtail the birth of their children. We have been commanded to multiply and replenish the earth that we may have joy and rejoicing in our posterity.

Where husband and wife enjoy health and vigor and are free from impurities that would be entailed upon their posterity, it is contrary to the teachings of the Church artificially to curtail or prevent the birth of children. We believe that those who practice birth control will reap disappointment by and by.

However, we feel that men must be considerate of their wives who bear the greater responsibility not only of bearing children, but of caring for them through childhood. To this end the mother's health and strength should be conserved and the husband's consideration for his wife is his first duty, and self-control a dominant factor in all their relationships.

It is our further feeling that married couples should seek inspiration and wisdom from the Lord that they may exercise discretion in solving their marital problems, and that they may be permitted to rear their children in accordance with the teachings of the gospel. Sincerely yours,

David O. McKay, Hugh B. Brown, N. Eldon Tanner
The First Presidency
(*CL*, April 14, 1969)

[Compilers Note: The following five articles on birth control were written by members of the Quorum of the Twelve Apostles during 1916, and appeared that year in the July and August issues of the *Relief Society Magazine*. Within a few months these articles had attracted such national attention to the Relief Society and its Magazine that the Editor of the Magazine, Mrs. Susa Young Gates, felt it imperative to inquire of the First Presidency of the Church if they approved in full of the statements made by the members of the Quorum of the Twelve Apostles on the subject of birth control. The enclosed response, dated December 13, 1916, was sent to Mrs. Gates from the First Presidency:

Mrs. Susa Young Gates, Editor *Relief Society Magazine*

Dear Sister: The July and August numbers of the Relief Society Magazine contained brief articles by some of the prominent elders of the Church on the subject of birth control, and in view of the importance of the subject and the attention it is receiving throughout the nation, you desire an expression from us in writing in regard to the attitude taken by the writers thereof, together with the soundness of the doctrine contained therein, with special reference to the article by Elder Joseph F. Smith, Jr.

We give our unqualified endorsement to these articles, including that of Elder Joseph F. Smith, Jr., and commend the sentiments contained therein to members and non-members of the Church of Jesus Christ of Latter-day Saints everywhere.

Your Brethren,
Joseph F. Smith, Anthon H. Lund, Charles W. Penrose
(The First Presidency)]

The Desire Not To Have Children Is Based Upon Vanity, Passion, and Selfishness

Any effort or desire on the part of a married couple to shirk the responsibility of parenthood reflects a condition of mind antagonistic to the best interests of the home, the state and the nation. No doubt there are some worldly people who honestly limit the number of children and the family to two or three because of insufficient means to clothe and educate a large family as the parents would desire to do, but in nearly all such cases, the two or three children are no better provided for than two or three times that number would be. Such parents may be sincere, even if misguided; but in most cases the desire not to have children has its birth in vanity, passion and selfishness. Such feelings are the seeds sown in early married life that produce a harvest of discord, suspicion, estrangement, and divorce. All such efforts, too, often tend to put the marriage relationship on level with the panderer and the courtesan. They befoul the pure fountains of life with the slime of indulgence and sensuality. Such misguided couples are ever seeking but never finding the reality for which the heart is yearning.

Depriving themselves of the comfort and happiness of the companionship of children, the barrenness of their lives drives the young couple to seek the hollow fads and fascinating excitements of "Society," many of which pursuits are as antagonistic to the real purpose of life as the influence of evil can make them.

As I write these lines, I have in mind a young girl who has substituted for the reality of home and family, the froth of week-end parties and midnight carousals, including the most degrading but fashionable habit of cigarette smoking. She began her married life in honor, and is the mother of two beautiful children; but she was caught in the whirlpool of pleasure and passion, and though flaunting daily the latest fashions, is sinking from respectability to refined degradation. "O what a falling off were here!" I cannot look upon such actions of young husbands and wives without a feeling of pity mingled with contempt. There is comfort only in the thought that in our communities such cases are exceptional.

Love realizes his sweetest happiness and his most divine consummation in the home where the coming of children is not restricted, where they are made most welcome, and where the duties of parenthood are accepted as a co-partnership with the eternal Creator.

In all this, however, the mother's health should be guarded. In the realm of wifehood, the woman should reign supreme.

Man, not woman, is the chief cause of this evil of race suicide now sweeping like a blight through the civilized nations.

Marriage is ordained of God that children might be so trained that they may eventually be worthy of Christ's presence; and that home is happiest in which they are welcomed, as God and nature intended they should be.

(*David O. McKay*, an Apostle, *RSM*, 1916, 3:363-368.)

No Promise of Eternal Salvation For
Those Who Practice Birth Control

In answer to your communication in which you ask me for my views on the question of "birth control," or the limiting of the number of children in a family to one or two, according to the teaching of the day by the so-called elite or fashionable class, I have this to say:

The first great commandment given both to man and beast by the Creator was to "be fruitful and multiply and replenish the earth;" and I have not learned that this commandment was ever repealed. Those who attempt to pervert the ways of the Lord, and to prevent their offspring from coming into the world in obedience to this great command are guilty of one of the most heinous crimes in the category. There is no promise of eternal salvation and exaltation for such as they, for by their acts they prove their unworthiness for exaltation and unfitness for a kingdom where the crowning glory is the continuation of the family union and eternal increase which have been promised to all those who obey the law of the Lord. It is just as much murder to destroy life before as it is after birth, although man-made laws may not so consider it; but there is One who does take notice and his justice and judgment is sure.

I feel only the greatest contempt for those who, because of a little worldly learning or a feeling of their own superiority over others, advocate and endeavor to control the so-called "lower classes" from what they are pleased to call "indiscriminate breeding."

The old Colonial stock that one or two centuries ago laid the foundation of our great nation, is rapidly being replaced by another people, due to the practice of this erroneous doctrine of "small families." According to statistics gathered by a leading magazine published in New York, a year or two ago, the average number of children to a family among the descendants of the Old American stock in the New England states, was only two and a fraction, while among the immigrants from European shores who are now coming into our land, the average family was composed of more than six.

Thus the old stock is surely being replaced by the "lower classes" of a sturdier and more worthy race. Worthier because they have not learned, in these modern times, to disregard the great commandment given to man by our Heavenly Father. It is indeed, a case of the survival of the fittest, and it is only a matter of time before those who so strongly advocate and practice this pernicious doctrine of "birth control" and the limiting of the number of children in the family, will have legislated themselves and their kind out of this mortal existence.

(*Joseph Fielding Smith,* an Apostle, *RSM,* 1916, 3:363-368.)

Limiting Offspring Is An Abomination

The efforts on the part of Eastern magazine writers to educate the people of the United States, particularly parents, to the doctrine that they should limit the number of their offspring to three or four children, and how this can be accomplished, is both pernicious and an abomination in the sight of the Lord; and it robs both man and his Maker of their glory and increase. I view it as a direct fulfillment of what was shown the Apostle Paul by the Spirit, would come to pass. *(1 Tim. 4:1-3)*

It is marvelous how many are departed from the faith and are giving heed to seducing spirits, and doctrines of devils, speaking lies in hypocrisy; having their conscience seared as with a hot iron, some forbidding to marry and others commanding to abstain from meats, and from child-bearing, which God hath created to be received with thanksgiving. The Apostle admonishes Timothy to refuse profane and old wives' fables, and to exercise himself rather with godliness. These may well be called old wives' fables, and a curse will follow those who advocate such doctrines.

My wife has borne to me fifteen children. Anything short of this would have been less than her duty and privilege. Had we received and obeyed the doctrine of three or four children to the home, we would have cut ourselves short of blessings more valuable to us than all of the wealth in this world would be, were it ours. We might never have known in this life what our loss had been but would have been just as great as we now see it, and sometime we would know as we now know. Then consider the joy and value of life to others. What of our eleven children born to us in excess of the four to which such as these magazine writers would limit us? Can the value of such a mission and service be estimated? Will not these our children and their husbands, wives and children, for generations after us, if they are duly appreciative, rise up and call us blessed forever and ever?

As to the danger and hardship of childbearing to the mothers, I have to say that from my observations, I conclude that the answering of nature's laws which are God's laws is far less injurious and dangerous than the efforts made to defeat these laws.

That there is less of anxiety and cost in rearing but few children in the family, is granted, but that children thus brought up are better reared, I do not concede. It is an easy matter to understand how that people would make popular the wrong of which they are guilty and having no thought of repentance, seek to drag others down to their own, low evil level. It seems to take away, in a measure, their reproach. This class, as a rule, are guilty of the double offense of both practicing and teaching a false and abominable doctrine. For such, the patience of the Lord, I fear will cease to be a virtue and His anger will be kindled against them.

(*George F. Richards*, an Apostle,
RSM, 1916, 3:363-368.)

Restrictive Measures Invites Righteous Anger From God

In my opinion the practice of restricting the number of children in the family, as advocated by many people, is sinful. It is contrary to the first great commandment given to Adam and Eve in the Garden of Eden, when the Lord said to them, "Be fruitful, multiply, and replenish the earth," etc.

Woman is so constituted that, ordinarily, she is capable of bearing during the years of her greatest strength and physical vigor, from eight to ten children, and in exceptional cases a larger number than that. The law of her nature so ordered it, and God's command, while it did not specify the exact number of children allotted to woman, simply implied that she should exercise the sacred power of procreation to its utmost limit.

Restricting the family to one or two children, as is often done in the world at large,—more especially among the rich who have ample means to support large families—is a serious evil even to them. It may, and frequently does, lead to grievous disappointment in after life, where death has stepped in and claimed the children as its victims before they reached maturity. Thus the parents are left without the ministrations of loved ones to smooth their pathway down to the grave. The hope of posterity is cut off, and their names disappear from among men. Those who resort to restrictive measures, respecting the number of children in the family, except it be by non-association of husband and wife, trifle with the fountains of life, and will certainly invite the displeasure and righteous anger of an offended Creator, who gave to man and woman this God-like power for the express purpose of bringing the souls of men into the world. The Lord has said, "This is my work and my glory to bring to pass the immortality and eternal life of man." Hence those who are instrumental in bringing children into the world, and doing their full duty by them, help to accomplish the designs of the Almighty Father.

Blessed is the man and blessed is the woman to whom no sin is imputed in the marriage relation, but who carefully observe the law of their natures and keep the commandments of God. To them the future will bring no regrets, and they will not be troubled by an accusing conscience or keen and abiding anquish of the soul.

(*Rudger Clawson*, an Apostle,
RSM, 1916, 3:363-368.)

The Only Legitimate Birth Control

I believe in large families, though I am aware, of course, that it is easier to feed, clothe, educate and rear a few children than many. But these considerations, so conclusive to some minds, have never had weight with me, contemplating as I do the eternal rather than the mere earthly phases of marriage and procreation.

The only legitimate "birth control" is that which springs naturally from the observance of divine laws, and the use of the procreative powers, not for pleasure primarily, but for race perpetuation and improvement. During certain periods—those of gestation and lactation—the wife and mother should be comparatively free to give her strength to her offspring; and if this involves some self-denial on the part of the husband and father, so much the better for all concerned.

"Birth control," under God's law, is a problem that solves itself. I have no faith in the sophisms of those who reject His law, and try to substitute therefore their own vain theories for sex regulation. The eugenists may mean well, but they don't know enough to lead the world out of the wilderness.

(*Orson F. Whitney*, an Apostle,
RSM, 1916, 3:363-368.)

Marriage Is For The Purpose Of Rearing A Family

True motherhood is the noblest call of the world, and we look with sorrow upon the practice here in our own United States of limiting families, a tendency creeping into our own Church.

Some young couples enter into marriage and procrastinate the bringing of children into their homes. They are running a great risk. Marriage is for the purpose of rearing a family, and youth is the time to do it. I admire these young mothers with four or five children around them now, still young and happy.

(*David O. McKay*, President of the Church,
CN, June 11, 1952, p. 3.)

Young People Who Resort To Surgery To Limit Their Families Will Find It Difficult To Rationalize Before The Lord

[Comments on this subject were made by *Spencer W. Kimball*, President of the Church, in the October, 1974, General Conference, and can be found in the *Ensign*, November, 1974, p. 9.]

Infanticide Is A Crime

To check the increase of our race has its advocates among the influential and powerful circles of society in our nation and in other nations. The same practice existed forty-five years ago, and various devices were used by married persons to prevent the expenses and responsibilities of a family of children, which they must have incurred had they suffered nature's laws to rule pre-eminent. That which was practiced then in fear against a reproving conscience, is now boldly trumpeted abroad as one of the best means of ameliorating the miseries and sorrows of humanity. Infanticide is very prevalent in our nation. It is a crime that comes within the purview of the law, and is therefore not so boldly practised as is the other equally great crime, which no doubt, to a great extent, prevents the necessity of infanticide. The unnatural style of living, the extensive use of narcotics, the attempts to destroy and dry up the fountains of life, are fast destroying the American element of the nation.

(*Brigham Young*, President of the Church,
JD, 1867, 12:120.)

The Principles Heavily Populated Countries Should Adopt To Overcome Poverty

Now, again, where there is abject poverty in some heavily populated countries, we declare it is a grievous sin before God to adopt restrictive measures in disobedience to God's divine command from the beginning of time to "multiply and replenish the earth." Surely those who project such measures to prevent life or to destroy life before or after birth will reap the whirlwind of God's retribution, for God will not be mocked.

What is sorely needed is a worldwide movement, with every means possible, to overcome the ignorance to be found among these unfortunate peoples, where the fundamental principles of right living and self-control and sound economic principles, patterned after the Lord's plan of salvation, must be adopted. This Church must be in the forefront in showing the way.

(*Harold B. Lee*, President of the Church,
CR, October, 1972, p. 63.)

False Reasoning In Population Limitation

The precepts of men would have you believe that by limiting the population of the world, we can have peace and plenty. That is the doctrine of the devil. Small numbers do not insure peace; only righteousness does. After all, there were only a handful of men on the earth when Cain interrupted the peace of Adam's household by slaying Abel. On the other hand, the whole city of Enoch was peaceful; and it was taken into heaven because it was made up of righteous people.

And so far as limiting the population in order to provide plenty is concerned, the Lord answered that falsehood in the Doctrine and Covenants when he said:

> For the earth is full, and there is enough and to spare; yea, I prepared all things, and have given unto the children of men to be agents unto themselves. *(D&C 104:17)*

A major reason why there is famine in some parts of the world is because evil men have used the vehicle of government to abridge the freedom that men need to produce abundantly.

True to form, many of the people who desire to frustrate God's purposes of giving mortal tabernacles to his spirit children through worldwide birth control are the very same people who support the kinds of government that perpetuate famine. They advocate an evil to cure the results of the wickedness they support.

(*Ezra Taft Benson*, an Apostle,
CR, April, 1969, p. 12.)

Concerning "Family Planning"

Our late President David O. McKay was a great teacher, as all who knew him understood, and one of his greatest fields of instruction was in family life.

He was a family planner, but not in the sense in which many today think of it. His family planning was for children in the home, proper rearing of those children, living the gospel on the part of all, and mutual love and respect between father and mother, and between parents and children.

And what did he think of the other kind of family planning—the kind which calls for restriction of the number of children to one or two to the family? Did he ever express himself on this subject?

Here is what he said:

Any effort or desire on the part of a married couple to shirk the responsibility of parenthood reflects a condition of mind antagonistic to the best interests of the home, the state, and the nation.

No doubt there are some worldly people who honestly limit the number of children and the family to two or three because of insufficient means to clothe and educate a large family as the parents would desire to do, but in nearly all such cases the two or three children are no better provided for than two or three times that number would be.

Such parents may be sincere, even if misguided; but in most cases the desire not to have children has its birth in vanity, passion, and selfishness.

Such feelings are the seeds sown in early married life that produces a harvest of discord, suspicion, estrangement, and divorce.

All such efforts too often tend to put the marriage relationship on a level with the panderer and the courtesan. They befoul the pure fountains of life with the slime of indulgence and sensuality.

Such misguided couples are ever seeking but never finding the reality for which the heart is yearning.

Depriving themselves of the comfort and happiness of the companionship of children, the barrenness of their lives drives the young couple to seek the hollow fads and fascinating excitement of "society," many of which pursuits are as antagonistic to the real purpose of life as the influence of evil can make them.

As I write these lines, I have in mind a young girl who has substituted for the reality of home and family, the froth of weekend parties and midnight carousals, including the most degrading but fashionable habit of cigarette smoking. She began her married life in honor and is the mother of two beautiful children; but she was caught in the whirlpool of pleasure and passion and though flaunting daily the latest fashion, is sinking from respectability to degradation.

Oh what a falling were here. I cannot look upon such actions of young husbands and wives without a feeling of pity mingled with contempt. There is comfort only in the thought that in our communities such cases are exceptional.

Love realizes its sweetest happiness and most divine consummation in the home, where the coming of children is not restricted, where they are made most welcome, and where the duties of parenthood are accepted as a co-partnership with the eternal Creator.

In all this, however, the mother's health should be guarded. In the realm of wifehood, the women should reign supreme.

Man, not woman, is the chief cause of this evil of race suicide now sweeping like a blight through the civilized nations.

Marriage is ordained of God that children might be so trained that they may eventually be worthy of Christ's presence; and that home is happiest in which they are welcomed as God and nature intended they should be. The principal reason for marriage is to raise a family.

Next to eternal life, the most precious gift that our Father in Heaven can bestow upon man is His children. Our country's most precious possession is not our vast acres of rangeland, supporting flocks and herds; not productive farms; not our forests; not our mines nor oil wells producing fabulous wealth.

Our country's greatest resource is our children.

Before Latter-day Saints submit to the views of uninspired men pertaining to limitation of families, let them give serious consideration to the teachings of President McKay, one of the most beloved and constantly inspired prophets of our day.

(Editorial, *CN*, July 11, 1970, p. 16.)

The Realistic Approach To "Population Explosion"

Someone has said that there is nothing quite like a fertile imagination. Especially is this true when the imagination runs riot on the subject of population control.

A recent issue of "Medical Times" provides a case in point. Here one of the experts, Dr. Louis J. Polskin of Lakeland, Fla. indulges in some speculation on the subject, and quotes certain other scholars regarding their theories.

At the close of his article he describes their findings as "terrifying, fantastic and incomprehensible." And were these postulates correct, or within any kind of reason, he would be right.

Frightened for fear the world's increasing birth rate and decreasing death rate will condemn us all to starvation in the distant future, these experts indulge in the following speculations:

They point out that the world population at present is increasing at the rate of 2 per cent a year, which means that, when "compounded," we will double our population in 30 years. That may be.

Then, to put it more plainly, the experts say that 120 babies are born every minute. In six weeks the number of these infants will equal the present population of New York City. By the year 2,000, the article says, we will have to feed twice as many people as there are now on earth. And then comes the question: "Where will the food come from?"

To further frighten us the learned doctors say that for each

person now on earth there is available about five acres of land.
But by 1986 there will be five persons standing where three now
are and by 2100 A.D. there will be 20 people on those five acres
of land.

The equation is extended then to the year 2180 when the
scholars say each person on earth will have only a plot 33 x 33 feet,
but by the year 3000 A.D. 15 people will have to live on a piece of
earth no larger than a card three by five inches!

But that is not all. Their computations take us much further,
and explain that by the year 5000 A.D. the combined weight of
the human population will exceed the weight of the earth itself,
and by 13,000 A.D. the earth's human population will outweigh all
the planets in the visible universe.

Could anyone devise a better argument for birth control than
that? Imagination indeed can run riot!

But let us remember, even though no one will take these
calculations seriously, that they nevertheless represent the serious
thinking of some, especially scholars who leave God out of their
computations.

What makes the learned doctors think there will be a year
13,000 A.D. on this mortal earth? Or even a 5,000 A.D.?

Have they never heard of God's plans for this planet?

Human beings born on this earth are not creatures of chance.
Every person coming to this world is a child of Almighty God, and
He determines the number who will come here, and when and where.
He has set definite times and limitations for this earth, and He has
decided when mortal existence as we know it will come to an end.

Christ will return in the not-too-distant future. Because of
the wickedness of men, his coming of necessity will be preceded
by a time of cleansing. So great will be this cleansing that Isaiah
says "the earth will be empty," and "few men left." (Isa. 24)

This should give the population "explosionists" reason to
ponder.

We are living in the "Saturday night" of time. The Savior
will come to usher in his millennial reign. But is He to reign over a
filthy earth and godless people?

In a world filled with corruption such as ours is now, we need
not fear the danger of starving because of lack of food. What we
should fear are the "burnings" which will accompany His coming,
for the day that comes "will burn as an oven, and all the proud,
yea and all that do wickedly, shall be as stubble, and the day that
cometh shall burn them up, saith the Lord of hosts, that it shall
leave them neither root nor branch." *(Malachi 4)*

Ours also should be concern over our own worthiness, for although the Lord says his great day will be one of joy and salvation to the faithful, we must determine how faithful we ourselves are.

The population "explosionists" ask us to be realistic and face the future as it will be.

That is exactly our position. Let us be sufficiently realistic to face the fact of the existence of God and the Second Coming of Christ which will introduce His millennium of peace. And let us be realistic enough to believe the revealed word of God.

(Editorial, CN, April 18, 1970, p. 16.)

CHAPTER 5

CAPITAL PUNISHMENT
(See: Crime)

Death: The Penalty For Capital Crime

We solemnly make the following declarations, vis: That this Church views the shedding of human blood with the utmost abhorrence. That we regard the killing of human beings, except in conformity with the civil law, as a capital crime which should be punished by the shedding the blood of the criminal, after a public trial before a legally constituted court of the land.... The revelations of God to this Church make death the penalty for capital crime, and require that offenders against life and property shall be delivered up to and tried by the laws of the land.

Wilford Woodruff, George Q. Cannon, Joseph F. Smith
The First Presidency
(*MS*, 1890, 52:33-34.)

A Murderer Shall Have His Blood Shed

It has been the law of the Lord from the beginning that

...flesh with the life thereof, which is the blood thereof, shall ye not eat.

And surely your blood of your lives will I require; at the hand of every beast will I require it, and at the hand of man; at the hand of every man's brother will I require the life of man.

Whoso sheddeth man's blood, by man shall his blood be shed: for in the image of God made he man. *(Gen. 9:4-6)*

Moreover, Moses reiterated this commandment to Israel as the Lord commanded him, and it has never by divine decree been revoked. The Nephites taught and practiced it. In this, the last dispensation, the Lord has confirmed this penalty upon those who deliberately kill.

President Charles W. Penrose, speaking of capital punishment, has said:

This divine law for shedding the blood of a murderer has never been repealed. It is a law given by the Almighty and not abrogated in

the Christian faith. It stands on record for all time—that a murderer
shall have his blood shed. He that commits murder must be slain.
"Whoso sheddeth man's blood, by man shall his blood be shed." I
know there are some benevolent and philanthropic people in these
times who think that capital punishment ought to be abolished. Yet I
think the Lord knows better than they. The law he ordained will have
the best results to mankind in general....

Is it the prerogative of the Church to inflict the punishment?
No! The Lord has given commandment that all offenses worthy of
death shall be handled by the courts of the land as declared in the
Doctrine and Covenants, "And it shall come to pass, that if any
persons among you shall kill they shall be delivered up and dealt
with according to the laws of the land; for remember that he hath
no forgiveness; and it shall be proved according to the laws of the
land." *(D&C 42:79)*

(Joseph Fielding Smith,
President of the Council of the Twelve Apostles,
Answers to Gospel Questions, 1957, 1:189-191.)

The Eternal Significance of Capital Punishment

It is not uncommon these days for mankind to turn its back
upon Biblical principles, considering them passe, obsolete, cruel, or
based on primitive tribalism.

It is true that there is tribalism in the Lord's work, but it is
not primitive. There are twelve tribes of Israel, but is that bad?
Can anyone say truthfully that tribalism is inseparably connected
with primitive life, illiteracy or decadence of culture?

Abraham was one of the greatest minds of his day, and even
taught the Egyptians astronomy, adding to their already great store
of learning. Yet he was a tribesman.

Moses—himself of the tribe of Levi and therefore a tribesman—
was the greatest lawgiver of all time. All basic fundamental law
today rests upon the principles he taught. So was his tribalism
bad? Was he a cruel man?

Biblical principles are sound, and are as applicable today as
they were in ancient times. One of those principles as taught in
scripture was capital punishment.

As far back as the days of Noah the Almighty gave this law:
"Whoso sheddeth man's blood, by man shall his blood be shed,
for in the image of God made he man." *(Gen. 9:6)* That was no
outgrowth of tribalism.

Capital punishment was practiced under the Mosaic law. It came by command of God, not of man, and was not devised through superstition or to satisfy primitive fears. It was a law of God.

It applied to adultery and homosexuality, to murder, and to other crimes. And, it had its place.

Have the opponents of capital punishment ever thought of it in its eternal sense? Is this one way by which sinful man may atone at least in part, in the eyes of God, for his serious offenses?

(Editorial, *CN*, February 26, 1972, p. 16.)

CHAPTER 6

CARD PLAYING
(See: Gambling)

Card Playing Is A Vice

One's character may be determined in some measure by the quality of one's amusements. Men and women of industrious, business-like, and thoughtful habits care little for frivolous pastimes, for pleasures that are sought for their own sake. It is not easy to imagine that leading men in the Church would find any pleasure that was either inspiring or helpful at the card table; indeed the announcement that a president of a stake, bishop of a ward, or other leading official of the Church was fond of card playing would be a shock to every sense of propriety even among young people who are not seriously inclined to the duties and responsibilities of life. Such a practice would be looked upon as incompatible with the duties and responsibilities of a religious life. Even business men, as a rule, are distrustful of business associates whose inclinations engage them in frequent card playing.

But it may be said that the same objections do not hold good in respect to young people who do not take life so seriously; but the evil is that young people who indulge in the frivolous and vicious pastime of card playing are never likely to take life seriously unless they forsake such questionable pleasures early in life. It is the serious and thoughtful man and woman who are most likely to assume the higher and nobler responsibilities of life, and their tastes and pleasures are never satisfied by means of a deck of cards.

Card playing is an excessive pleasure; it is intoxicating and, therefore, in the nature of a vice. It is generally the companion of the cigarette and the wine glass, and the latter lead to the poolroom and gambling hall. Few men and women indulge in the dangerous pastime of the card table without compromising their business affairs and the higher responsibilities of life. Tell me what amusements you like best and whether your amusements have become a ruling passion in your life, and I will tell you what you are. Few indulge frequently in card playing in whose lives it does not become a ruling passion.

Cards are the most perfect and common instrumentalities of the gambler that have been devised, and the companionship of cards, unlike the companionship of most other games, is that of the gambling den and the saloon. But cards do not stand alone in their enticement to evil. Any game that ultimately leads to questionable society, because it is the chief pleasure of such society, should be excluded from the home. There are innocent games enough to satisfy the required pleasures of the home without encouraging card playing.

> *(Joseph F. Smith*, President of the Church,
> *JI*, 1903, 38:529.)

The Evil of Card Playing

But, you say, we must have recreation; what shall we do? Turn to domestic enterprises, and to the gaining of useful knowledge of the gospel. Let the love of reading good and useful books be implanted in the hearts of the young, let them be trained to take pleasure and recreation in history, travel, biography, conversation and classic story. Then there are innocent games, music, songs, and literary recreation. What would you think of the man who would argue for whisky and beer as a common beverage because it is necessary for people to drink? He is perhaps little worse than the man who would place cards in the hands of my children—whereby they would foster the spirit of chance and gambling leading down to destruction—because they must have recreation. I would call the first a vicious enemy, and refer him to water to drink; and the latter an evil spirit in the guise of innocence, and refer him to recreation containing no germs of spiritual disease leading to the devil!

Let our evenings be devoted to innocent amusements in the home, and let all chance games be banished from our families, and only recreation indulged in that is free from gambling and the gambling spirit. And let excessive card-playing, and the person who strolls about among neighbors at all hours of the night and day encouraging this evil, be put far from us. Just as sure as we encourage this evil it will bring other grievous troubles in its wake, and those who indulge excessively will lose the spirit of the gospel, and go to temporal and spiritual ruin.

Young people in their recreations should strive to form a love for that which will not be injurious. It is not true that only that recreation can be enjoyed that is detrimental to the body and spirit. We should train ourselves to find pleasure in that which invigorates, not stupefies and destroys the body; that which leads upward and not down; that which brightens, not dulls and stunts the intellect; that which elevates and exalts the spirit, not that clogs and depresses it. So shall we please the Lord, enhance our own enjoyment, and save ourselves and our children from impending sins, at the root of which, like the evil genius, lurks the spirit of cards and gambling.

(Joseph F. Smith, President of the Church, *JI*, 1911, 14:735-738.)

The Pernicious Nature Of Card Playing

Card playing is a game of chance, and because it is a game of chance it has its tricks. It encourages tricks; its devotees measure their success at the table by their ability through devious and dark ways to win. It creates a spirit of cunning and devises hidden and secret means, and cheating at cards is almost synonymous with playing at cards.

Again, cards have a bad reputation and they are the known companions of bad men. If no other reason existed for shunning the card table, its reputation alone should serve as a warning. It may be conceded that superb skill is often acquired in this game of chance, but this skill itself endangers the moral qualities of the possessor and leads him on to questionable practices.

Such games as checkers and chess are games more of fixed rules, whose application are open and freer from cunning devices. Such games do not intoxicate like cards and other games of chance.

(Joseph F. Smith, President of the Church, *JI*, 1903, 38:591.)

Card Playing Is A Waste Of Precious Time

It is no uncommon thing for women, young and middle-aged to spend whole afternoons, and many of them, evenings as well, in playing cards, thus wasting hours and days of precious time in this useless and unprofitable way. Yet those same people, when approached, declare they have no time to spend as teachers in the Sabbath schools, and no time to attend either Sunday Schools or meetings. Their church duties are neglected for lack of time, yet they spend hours, day after day, at cards. They have thereby encouraged and become possessed of a spirit of indolence, and their minds are filled with the vile drunkenness, hallucination, charm and fascination, that take possession of the habitual card-player to the exclusion of all spiritual and religious feeling. Such a spirit detracts from all sacred thought and sentiment. These players at length do not quite know whether they are Jews, Gentiles, or Saints, and they do not care a fig.

While a simple game of cards in itself may be harmless, it is a fact that by immoderate repetition it ends in an infatuation for chance schemes, in habits of excess, in waste of precious time, in dulling and stupor of the mind, and in the complete destruction of religious feeling. These are serious results, evils that should and must be avoided by the Latter-day Saints. Then again, there is the grave danger that lurks in persistent card playing, which begets the spirit of gambling, of speculation and that awakens the dangerous desire to get something for nothing.

(Joseph F. Smith, President of the Church,
IE, 1903, 6:779.)

Concerning Card Playing In The Home

But if cards are played in the home and under the eye of an anxious and loving parent, what harm can come from it all? is asked. Most vices in the beginning take on attractive and innocent appearing garbs, and a careful examination of the career of many an unfortunate man will reveal the first step of his misfortune in some "innocent pastime" whose vice rarely manifests itself in its infancy. There are different spirits in the world and the gambling spirit is one of them, and cards have been from time immemorial the most common and universal means of gratifying that spirit. An "innocent game of cards" is the innocent companion of an innocent glass of wine and the playmate of tricksters.

Again, all amusements become pernicious when pursued excessively. No game in the world has been played a thousandth part of the time, aye all the games in the world have not consumed a thousandth part of the time, that cards have taken. The game itself leads to excessiveness; it is the enemy of industry; it is the foe of economy and the boon companion of the Sabbath-breaker. The best possible excuse that any one can render for playing cards is that there is a possible escape from the dangers to which it leads; and the best explanation that people can give for such a vice is the adventurous spirit of man that delights in that which is hazardous to his physical and moral safety.

(Joseph F. Smith, President of the Church,
JI, 1903, 38:593.)

Latter-day Saints Should Stop Playing Cards

I am told that the prevalence of card parties in the homes of the Latter-day Saints is much greater than is supposed by those whom society people never think of inviting to make the card table the source of an evening's pastime. The presiding authorities are not invited to the card parties, and, as a rule, are not permitted to witness them, simply because those who give such parties feel that a deck of cards in the hands of a faithful servant of God is a satire upon religion.

I have heard that some who are called to officiate in holy ordinances have, when absent from the House of the Lord, or when tardy in arriving, excused themselves because of the time occupied in giving or attending a card party. Those who thus indulge are not fit to administer in sacred ordinances. They are no more worthy than others who violate good morals in any respect. They should be excused.

I am told that young people offer as an excuse for such questionable pastime the accusation that cards are played in the homes of certain leading men in the Church. Bishops, however, ought never to be deterred in their efforts to suppress the evil by counter complaints of this kind. The bishop has the same right to inquire, through the means of his teachers, into the pleasures of the homes of the highest authorities of the Church as he has into those of its most humble members. If it be true that card playing is prevalent in the Church, the bishops are charged with the responsibility for the evil and it is their duty to see that it is abolished, or that men and women who encourage it be brought to account before their brethren and sisters for the pernicious example they are setting before the youth of Zion. Certainly no bishop can report his ward in good condition where such a practice prevails.

Presidents of stakes are not without their responsibility in this matter, and at the general priesthood meetings of the stakes they should make searching inquiry of the bishops concerning card parties in the homes of the Saints. It is an easy matter for every bishop to know through the medium of the ward teachers, whether there are any practices in the homes of the people inconsistent with the mission of "Mormonism," and card playing is certainly inconsistent with that mission. No man who is addicted to card playing should be called to act as a ward teacher, such men cannot be consistent advocates of that which they do not themselves practice.

The card table has been the scene of too many quarrels, the birthplace of too many hatreds, the occasion of too many murders to admit one word of justification for the lying, cheating spirit which it too often engenders in the hearts of its devotees.

My frequent and emphatic expressions on this subject are the result of the alarm I have felt over the well founded reports that have come to me concerning the prevalence of card playing in the homes of some who profess to be Latter-day Saints. Upon every officer in the Church responsible in any way for the dangers of the card table is placed, and placed heavily, the duty of doing all that he or she possibly can in prayerful and earnest manner to eradicate the evil. Let us be fully conscious of the old adage which says that "The devil likes to souse whatever is wet," and stop card playing in the home before it reaches the gambler's table.

(Joseph F. Smith, President of the Church,
JI, 1903, 38:561.)

Saints Should Not Use Playing Cards Which Are Used For Gambling

[Comments on this subject were made by *Spencer W. Kimball*, President of the Church, in the October, 1974, General Conference, and can be found in the *Ensign*, November, 1974, p. 6.]

Card Playing Affects Spiritual Sensitivity

Let me tell you about a sister who became literally hypnotized by a deck of playing cards. Eventually, there were not enough hours in the week to fit everything in. Her keen spiritual sensitivity became dulled, and it was easy for the cunning one to help her decide to give up an important Relief Society calling and abandon her wonderful circle of former associates in favor of the non-essential, time-wasting pastime that had captured her fancy. Sisters in the ward continuing their lives of charity and compassionate service are now termed by her as narrow-minded, as hypocritical and do-gooders, but in reality, the only thing that changed was this woman.

(Robert L. Simpson, First Counselor in the Presiding Bishopric,
CR, April 1969, p. 86.)

Innocent Non-Gambling Card Games Not Objectionable

Members of the Church should not belong to bridge or other type of card clubs, and they should neither play cards nor have them in their homes. By cards is meant, of course, the spotted face cards used by gamblers. To the extent that church members play cards they are out of harmony with their inspired leaders. Innocent non-gambling games played with other types of cards, except for the waste of time in many instances, are not objectionable.

(Bruce R. McConkie, Member of the First Council of the Seventy, *Mormon Doctrine,* 1966, p. 113.)

CHAPTER 7

CHARITY SUPPORT

Support The "Red Cross Drive"

During March 1974, the American Red Cross will be conducting its annual membership drive to raise funds while continuing its extensive programs and services which help people in all parts of our nation.

Every year millions of prople in the United States join together under the banner of the Red Cross to help themselves and their neighbors—and people in unfortunate circumstances in other parts of the world.

Red Cross is more than its well-known blood drives—more than its help for thousands of victims in disasters and assistance to servicemen and veterans and their families. It stresses safety and health, providing home nursing, first aid, water safety, and other training vital in daily living. Volunteers also assist in a wide variety of community programs that benefit people of all ages. In this same spirit of neighbor helping neighbor, we urge members of the Church to give their generous support to this worthwhile organization.

Spencer W. Kimball, N. Eldon Tanner, Marion G. Romney
The First Presidency
(*CN*, February 23, 1974, p. 2.)

Support The "March Of Dimes"

During this special month, volunteer workers will visit, as nearly as possible, all homes and businesses in Utah for the purpose of providing each individual the opportunity to assist in the many programs undertaken through the National Foundation--March of Dimes, including education, medical service and research in the areas of prenatal care and birth defects. The National Foundation—March of Dimes has sponsored a Birth Defects Center at the Latter-day Saints Primary Children's Medical Center in Salt Lake since 1962, and is presently sponsoring three grants to the University of Utah Medical School.

We urge our people to be generous in their support of this very worthy undertaking.

Spencer W. Kimball, N. Eldon Tanner, Marion G. Romney
The First Presidency
(*CN*, December 28, 1974, p. 3.)

CHAPTER 8

CHILDREN: NEEDS, RESPONSIBILITIES, AND DISCIPLINE
(See: Home and Family Life; Husbands and Fathers;
Womenhood and Motherhood)

The Three Fundamental Things To Which Every Child Is Entitled

There are three fundamental things to which every child is entitled: (1) a respected name, (2) a sense of security, (3) opportunities for development. The family gives to the child his name and standing in the community. A child wants his family to be as good as those families of his friends. He wants to be able to point with pride to his father, and to feel an inspiration always as he thinks of his mother. It is a mother's duty to so live that her children will associate with her everything that is beautiful, sweet, and pure. And the father should so live that the child, emulating his example, will be a good citizen and, in the Church, a true follower of the teachings of the gospel of Jesus Christ.

A child has the right to feel that in his home he has a place of refuge, a place of protection from the dangers and evils of the outside world. Family unity and integrity are necessary to supply this need.

He needs parents who are happy in their adjustment to each other, who are working hopefully toward the fulfillment of an ideal of living, who love their children with a sincere and unselfish love—in short, parents who are well-balanced individuals, gifted with a certain amount of insight, who are able to provide the child with a wholesome emotional background that will contribute more to his development than material advantages.

(David O. McKay, President of the Church,
CR, April, 1969, pp. 8-9.)

Parents Should Set A Proper Example For Their Children

My remarks will be to parents as well as to children. I will commence by saying that if each and every one of us who are parents will reflect upon the responsibilities devolving upon us we shall come to the conclusion that we should never permit ourselves to do anything that we are not willing to see our children do. We should set them an example that we wish them to imitate. Do we realize this? How often we see parents demand obedience, good behavior, kind words, pleasant looks, a sweet voice and a bright eye from a child or children when they themselves are full of bitterness and scolding! How inconsistent and unreasonable this is! If we wish our children to look pleasant we should look pleasant at them; and if we wish them to speak kind words to each other, let us speak kind words to them. We need not go into detail, but we should carry out this principle from year to year in our whole lives, and do as we wish our children to do. I say this with regard to our morals and our faith in our religion.

> (*Brigham Young*, President of the Church,
> *JD*, 1871, 14:192.)

Parent And Child Responsibilities

To the young people of the Church, particularly, I should like to say first that a happy home begins not at the marriage altar, but during the brilliant, fiery days of youth. The first contributing factor to a happy home is the sublime virtue of loyalty, one of the noblest attributes of the human soul. Loyalty means being faithful and true. It means fidelity to parents, fidelity to duty, fidelity to a cause or principle, fidelity to love. Disloyalty to parents during teen age is often a source of sorrow and sometimes tragedy in married life.

I have received several letters this last month from young folk—two of them in their teens—irked because of what they consider interference of parents. Young people in all the Church and all the nation should understand that both the Church and the state hold parents responsible for the conduct and protection of their children. The Church, you will recall, is very explicit in that. "...inasmuch as parents have children in Zion, or in any of her stakes which are organized, that teach them not to understand the doctrine of repentance, faith in Christ the Son of the Living God, and of baptism and the gift of the Holy Ghost by the laying on of the hands, when eight years old, the sin be upon the heads of the parents.

"For this shall be a law unto the inhabitants of Zion, or in any of her stakes which are organized." *(D&C 68:25-26)*

That is explicit, and parents, that is your responsibility.

Some of you would be surprised to know that the statute of the state requires explicitly that not only parents, but also any guardian who has charge of a child eighteen or under is held responsible for the protection of that child and for his moral teachings. Any guardian or parent that will do anything to injure the morals of the child is guilty of a misdemeanor and subject to imprisonment of not more, if I remember rightly, than six months, and a fine of not less than three hundred dollars, or both.

So, girls and boys, your parents, not only because of their love, but also by command of the Lord and by legislative enactment of the state, are compelled to watch over you and guide you. And parents, once again, that is your responsibility.

(*David O. McKay*, President of the Church,
CR, April, 1956, pp. 6-7.)

Children Should Be Given Responsibilities

[Comments on this subject were made by *Spencer W. Kimball*, President of the Church, in the *Church News* of February 23, 1974, p. 16.]

Children Should Never Neglect Parents

Children, ... do not add to [your parents] burdens by neglect, by extravagance or by misconduct. Rather suffer that your right hand be cut off, or your eye plucked out than that you would bring sorrow or anguish to your parents because of your neglect of filial affection to them. So, children, remember your parents. After they have nurtured you through the tender years of your infancy and childhood, after they have fed and clothed and educated you, after having given you a bed to rest upon and done all in their power for your good, don't you neglect them when they become feeble and are bowed down with the weight of their years. Don't you leave them, but settle down near them, and do all in your power to minister to their comfort and well-being.

(*Joseph F. Smith*, President of the Church,
IE, December, 1917, p. 105.)

Correct Children Through Kindness

I will here say to parents, that kind words and loving actions towards children, will subdue their uneducated natures a great deal better than the rod, or, in other words, than physical punishment. Although it is written that, "The rod and reproof give wisdom; but a child left to himself bringeth his mother to shame,"

and, "he that spareth his rod hateth his son; but he that loveth
him chasteneth him betimes;" these quotations refer to wise and
prudent corrections. Children who have lived in the sunbeams of
parental kindness and affection, when made aware of a parent's
displeasure, and receive a kind reproof from parental lips, are more
thoroughly chastened, than by any physical punishment that could
be applied to their persons. It is written, that the Lord "shall smite
the earth with the rod of his mouth." And again it is written, "a
whip for the horse, a bridle for the ass, and a rod for the fool's
back." The rod of a parent's mouth, when used in correction of a
beloved child, is more potent in its effects, than the rod which is
used on the fool's back. When children are reared under the rod,
which is for the fool's back, it not unfrequently occurs, that they
become so stupified and lost to every high-toned feeling and sentiment, that though you bray them in a mortar among wheat with
a pestle, yet will not their foolishness depart from them. Kind
looks, kind actions, kind words, and a lovely, holy deportment
towards them, will bind our children to us with bands that cannot
easily be broken; while abuse and unkindness will drive them from
us, and break asunder every holy tie, that should bind them to us,
and to the everlasting covenant in which we are all embraced. If
my family; and my brethren and sisters, will not be obedient to
me on the basis of kindness, and a commendable life before all
men, and before the heavens, then farewell to all influence. Earthly
kings and potentates obtain influence and power by terrorism, and
maintain it by the same means. Had I to obtain power and influence
in that way, I should never possess it in this world nor in the next.
(Brigham Young, President of the Church,
JD, 1864, 10:360-361.)

Discipline Children Through Example, Persuasion, And Love

Don't let us be fooled or misled by the claim extant in the
world today that restraints and conventions are damaging to the
psyche of a child. In promoting a permissive and unrestricted society, they would have a child undisciplined for misbehavior. This
is a false premise, and we are better advised to heed the counsel of
the Lord when he said:

> And again, inasmuch as parents have children in Zion, or in any
> of her stakes which are organized, that teach them not to understand
> the doctrine of repentance, faith in Christ the Son of the living God, and

of baptism and the gift of the Holy Ghost by the laying on of the hands, when eight years old, the sin be upon the heads of the parents.

And they shall also teach their children to pray, and to walk uprightly before the Lord. *(D&C 68:25, 28)*

Children do not learn by themselves how to distinguish right from wrong. Parents have to determine the child's readiness to assume responsibility and his capacity to make sound decisions, to evaluate alternatives, and the results of doing so. While we are teaching them, we have the responsibility to discipline them and to see that they do what is right. If a child is besmudged with dirt, we do not let him wait until he grows up to decide whether or not he will bathe. We do not let him wait to decide whether or not he will take his medicine when sick, or go to school or to church. By example, persuasion, and love we see that he does what we know is best for him. We cannot overemphasize the importance of example. The late J. Edgar Hoover said that if fathers and mothers would take their children to Sunday School and church regularly, they could strike a felling blow against the forces that contribute to juvenile delinquency.

(*N. Eldon Tanner*, First Counselor in the First Presidency, *CR*, April, 1973, p. 58.)

Reprove Betimes With Sharpness

[Comments on this subject were made by *A. Theodore Tuttle*, Member of the First Council of the Seventy, in the October, 1974, General Conference, and can be found either in the *Conference Report* of October, 1973, p. 88, or in the *Ensign* of January, 1974, p. 68.]

What Makes A Yippie?

One of the leaders of the radical Youth International Party gives his reason for being a "Yippie" and blames it mostly on his parents.

What he says may not all be true, but even if half true, it is very significant. He blames his parents for being too obedient to their children—too permissive.

Said he, as quoted in the *Indianapolis Star* recently, pertaining to his childhood and the lack of proper training he received from his indulgent parents:

"They wanted a child so badly they would do anything for me," Rubin said of his parents. "They had just total dedication to me—I knew if I cried I'd get my way; if I insisted I'd get my way; if I screamed I'd get my way. It was really total toleration, total permissiveness—it's kind of a key as to why I could become so rebellious.

"Many of the tactics I now use I learned at home. I learned how to play one parent against the other, because my mother didn't really approve of some of father's methods (of handling him)—I'm really convinced that the whole of my recent activity in the movement has been a playing out on a massive political scale of the things I learned in the family."

Anciently, the wise man said:

"Train up a child in the way he should go and when he is old he will not depart from it."

(Editorial, *CN*, January 17, 1970, p. 16.)

CHAPTER 9

CHURCH AND STATE
*(See: Civil Laws; Civil Rights; Communism and
Socialism; Constitutional Government; Military Service;
Taxes; War; Welfare and Work)*

Church Stands For Separation Of Church And State

The Church stands for the separation of church and state.
The church has no civil political functions. As the church may not
assume the functions of the state, so the state may not assume the
functions of the church. The church is responsible for and must
carry on the work of the Lord, directing the conduct of its members, one towards the other, as followers of the lowly Christ, not
forgetting the humble, the poor and needy, and those in distress,
leading them all to righteous living and a spiritual life that shall
bring them to salvation, exaltation, and eternal progression in wisdom, knowledge, understanding, and power.

Today, more than ever before in the history of the Church,
we must bring the full force of the righteous living of our people
and the full influence of the spiritual power and responsibility of
the holy Priesthood, to combat the evil forces which Satan has let
loose among the peoples of the earth. We are in the midst of a
desperate struggle between Truth and Error, and Truth will finally
prevail.

The state is responsible for the civil control of its citizens or
subjects, for their political welfare, and for the carrying forward of
political policies, domestic and foreign, of the body politic. For
these policies, their success or failure, the state is alone responsible,
and it must carry its burdens. All these matters involve and directly
affect Church members because they are part of the body politic,
and members must give allegiance to their sovereign and render it
loyal service when called thereto. But the Church, itself, as such,
has no responsibility for these policies, as to which it has no means
of doing more than urging its members fully to render that loyalty
to their country and to free institutions which the loftiest patriotism
calls for.

Nevertheless, as a correlative of the principle of separation of
the church and the state, themselves, there is an obligation running

from every citizen or subject to the state. This obligation is voiced
in that Article of Faith which declares:

> We believe in being subject to kings, presidents, rulers, and magis-
> trates, in obeying, honoring, and sustaining the law.

For one hundred years, the Church has been guided by the
following principles:

> We believe that governments were instituted of God for the bene-
> fit of man; and that he holds men accountable for their acts in relation
> to them, both in making laws and administering them, for the good and
> safety of society.

> We believe that no government can exist in peace, except such
> laws are framed and held inviolate as will secure to each individual the
> free exercise of conscience, the right and control of property, and the
> protection of life.

> We believe that all governments necessarily require civil officers
> and magistrates to enforce the laws of the same; and that such as will
> administer the law in equity and justice should be sought for and up-
> held by the voice of the people if a republic, or the will of the sovereign.

> We believe that religion is instituted of God; and that men are
> amenable to him, and to him only, for the exercise of it, unless their
> religious opinions prompt them to infringe upon the rights and liberties
> of others; but we do not believe that human law has a right to inter-
> fere in prescribing rules of worship to bind the consciences of men,
> nor dictate forms for public or private devotion; that the civil magistrate
> should restrain crime, but never control conscience; should punish guilt,
> but never suppress the freedom of the soul.

> We believe that all men are bound to sustain and uphold the
> respective governments in which they reside, while protected in their
> inherent and inalienable rights by the laws of such governments; and
> that sedition and rebellion are unbecoming every citizen thus protected,
> and should be punished accordingly; and that all governments have a
> right to enact such laws as in their own judgments are best calculated to
> secure the public interest; at the same time, however, holding sacred
> the freedom of conscience.

> We believe that every man should be honored in his station, rulers
> and magistrates as such, being placed for the protection of the innocent
> and the punishment of the guilty; and that to the laws all men owe
> respect and deference, as without them peace and harmony would be
> supplanted by anarchy and terror; human laws being instituted for the
> express purpose of regulating our interests as individuals and nations,
> between man and man; and divine laws given of heaven, prescribing
> rules on spiritual concerns, for faith and worship, both to be answered
> by man to his Maker...

We believe ... that murder, treason, robbery, theft, and the breach of the general peace, in all respects, should be punished according to their criminality and their tendency to evil among men, by the laws of that government in which the offense is committed.... *(D&C 134:1-6,8)*

Heber J. Grant, J. Reuben Clark, Jr., David O. McKay
The First Presidency
(*CR*, April, 1942, pp. 92-93.)

CHAPTER 10

CIVIL LAWS
(See: Church and State; Civil Rights; Constitutional Government;
Equal Rights Amendment; Military Service; War)

Church Members Should Take A Positive Stand On Moral Issues

We recognize the urgent need of encouraging legislators and civic groups to use their good offices to combat the evils of drinking, gambling, immorality and other vices. While strictly political matters should properly be left in the field of politics where they rightfully belong, on moral issues the Church and its members should take a positive stand.

We urge all members of the Church to wield their influence in the matter of encouraging the introduction of proper legislation that will, when enacted into law, combat evil of the kind mentioned, and safeguard the morals of members and non-members alike. Latter-day Saints must always be alert and united in contending against any influence which tends to break down the moral and spiritual strength of the people.

David O. McKay, Hugh B. Brown, N. Eldon Tanner
The First Presidency *(CL,* January 27, 1969.)

No Church Member Can Be Accepted As In Good Standing Who Rebels Against Obedience To Law

No member of the Church can be accepted as in good standing whose way of life is one of rebellion against the established order of decency and obedience to law. We cannot be in rebellion against the law and be in harmony with the Lord, for he has commanded us to "be subject to the powers that be, until he reigns whose right it is to reign. ..." *(D&C 58:22)* And one of these days he is going to come.

(Joseph Fielding Smith, President of the Church,
CR, April, 1971, p. 48.)

Saints Should Submit Themselves To The Laws Of Their Country Unless Directed Otherwise By God

A question has many times been asked of the Church and of its individual members, to this effect: In the case of a conflict between the requirements made by the revealed word of God, and those imposed by the secular law, which of these authorities would the members of the Church be bound to obey? In answer, the words of Christ may be applied—it is the duty of the people to render unto Caesar the things that are Caesar's, and unto God the things that are God's.

At the present time the kingdom of heaven as an earthly power, with a reigning King exercising direct and personal authority in temporal matters, has not been established upon the earth. The branches of the Church as such, and the members composing the same, are subjects of the several governments within whose separate realms the Church organizations exist. In this day of comparative enlightenment and freedom there is small cause for expecting any direct interference with the rights of private worship and individual devotion; in all civilized nations the people are accorded the right to pray, and this right is assured by what may be properly called a common law of humankind. No earnest soul is cut off from communion with his God; and with such an open channel of communication, relief from burdensome laws and redress from grievances may be sought from the power that holds control of nations.

Pending the overruling by Providence in favor of religious liberty, it is the duty of the saints to submit themselves to the laws of their country. Nevertheless, they should use every proper method, as citizens or subjects of their several governments, to secure for themselves and for all men the boon of freedom in religious service. It is not required of them to suffer without protest imposition by lawless persecutors, or through the operation of unjust laws; but their protests should be offered in legal and proper order. The saints have practically demonstrated their acceptance of the doctrine that it is better to suffer evil than to do wrong by purely human opposition to unjust authority. And if by thus submitting themselves to the laws of the land, in the event of such laws being unjust and subversive of human freedom, the people be prevented from doing the work appointed them of God, they are not to be held accountable for the failure to act under the higher law.

(James E. Talmage,
Articles of Faith, pp. 422-423.)

CHAPTER 11

CIVIL RIGHTS
(See: Negroes and the Church)

The Church Is For Full Civil Rights

During recent months, both in Salt Lake City and across the nation, considerable interest has been expressed in the position of the Church of Jesus Christ of Latter-day Saints on the matter of civil rights. We would like it to be known that there is in this Church no doctrine, belief, or practice that is intended to deny the enjoyment of full civil rights by any person regardless of race, color, or creed.

We say again, as we have said many times before, that we believe that all men are the children of the same God, and that it is a moral evil for any person or group of persons to deny any human being the right to gainful employment, to full educational opportunity, and to every privilege of citizenship, just as it is a moral evil to deny him the right to worship according to the dictates of his own conscience.

We have consistently and persistently upheld the Constitution of the United States, and as far as we are concerned this means upholding the constitutional rights of every citizen of the United States.

We call upon men everywhere, both within and outside the Church, to commit themselves to the establishment of full civil equality for all of God's children. Anything less than this defeats our high ideal of the brotherhood of man.

(Hugh B. Brown, First Counselor in the First Presidency, representing the First Presidency, *CR*, October, 1963, p. 91.)

Negroes Should Receive All Rights and Privileges Declared In The Declaration of Independence

No church or other organization is more insistent than The Church of Jesus Christ of Latter-day Saints, that the Negroes should receive all the rights and privileges that can possibly be given to any other in the true sense of equality as declared in the Declaration of Independence. They should be equal to "life, liberty and the pursuit of happiness." They should be equal in the matter of education. They should not be barred from obtaining knowledge and becoming proficient in any field of science, art or mechanical occupation. They should be free to choose any kind of employment, to go into business in any field they may choose and to make their lives as happy as it is possible without interference from white men, labor unions or from any other source. In their defense of these privileges the members of the Church will stand.

(Joseph Fielding Smith, President of the Council of the Twelve Apostles, Answers to Gospel Questions, 1958, 2:185.)

The Influence Of Communists In The Civil Rights Movement

Now there is nothing wrong with civil rights; it is what's being done in the name of civil rights that is alarming.

There is no doubt that the so-called civil rights movement as it exists today is used as a Communist program for revolution in America just as agrarian reform was used by the Communists to take over China and Cuba.

This shocking statement can be confirmed by an objective study of Communist literature and activities and by knowledgeable Negroes and others who have worked within the Communist movement....

As far back as 1928, the Communists declared that the cultural, economic, and social differences between the races in America could be exploited by them to create the animosity, fear, and hatred between large segments of our people that would be necessary beginning ingredients for their revolution....

Briefly, the three broad objectives were and are as follows:

1. Create hatred
2. Trigger violence
3. Overthrow established government

First, create hatred. Use any means to agitate blacks into hating whites and whites into hating blacks. Work both sides of the split. Play up and exaggerate real grievances. If necessary, don't hesitate to manufacture false stories and rumors about injustices and brutality. Create martyrs for both sides. Play upon mass emotions until they smolder with resentment and hatred.

Second, trigger violence. Put the emotional masses into the streets in the form of large mobs, the larger the better. It makes no difference if the mob is told to demonstrate "peacefully" so long as it is brought into direct confrontation with the antagonist. Merely bringing the two emotionally charged groups together is like mixing oxygen and hydrogen. All that is needed is one tiny spark. If the spark is not forthcoming from purely spontaneous causes, create it.

Third, overthrow established government. Once mob violence becomes widespread and commonplace, condition those who are emotionally involved to accept violence as the only way to "settle the score" once and for all. Provide leadership and training for guerilla warfare. Institute discipline and terrorism to insure at least passive support from the larger, inactive segment of the population. Train and battle-harden leadership through sporadic riots and battles with police. Finally, at the appointed time, launch an all-out simultaneous offensive in every major city....

The Communist program for revolution in America has been in progress for many years and is far advanced. While it can be thwarted in a fairly short period of time merely by sufficient exposure, the evil effects of what has already been accomplished cannot be removed overnight. The animosities, the hatred, the extension of government control into our daily lives—all this will take time to repair. The already-inflicted wounds will be slow in healing. But they can be healed; that is the important point....

We must not place the blame upon Negroes. They are merely the unfortunate group that has been selected by professional Communist agitators to be used as the primary source of cannon fodder. Not one in a thousand Americans—black or white—really understands the full implications of today's civil rights agitation. The planning, direction, and leadership come from the Communists, and most of those are white men who fully intend to destroy America by spilling Negro blood, rather than their own....

We must not participate in any so-called "blacklash" activity which might tend to further intensify inter-racial friction. Anti-Negro vigilante action, or mob action, of any kind fits perfectly into the Communist plan. This is one of the best ways to force the decent Negro into cooperating with militant Negro groups. The Communists are just as anxious to spearhead such anti-Negro actions as they are to organize demonstrations that are calculated to irritate white people....

We need a vast awakening of the American people as to the true nature of the Communist blueprint for revolution. ... Each of us must be willing to discuss the problem openly with our friends—especially those of the Negro race. The success or failure of Americans of all races to meet this challenge may well determine the fate of our country. If we fail, we will all lose our civil rights, black man and white man together, for we will live under perfect Communist equality—the equality of slaves.

(Ezra Taft Benson, an Apostle, *CR,* October, 1967, pp. 35-39.)

CHAPTER 12

COLA DRINKS
(See: Word of Wisdom)

**The Church Advises Against The Use Of Any Drink
Containing Harmful Habit-Forming Drugs**

The Word of Wisdom, section 89 of the Doctrine and Covenants, remains as to terms and specifications as found in that
section. There has been no official interpretation of that Word of
Wisdom except that which was given by the Brethren in the very
early days of the Church when it was declared that "hot drinks"
meant tea and coffee.

With reference to cola drinks, the Church has never officially
taken a position on this matter, but the leaders of the Church have
advised, and we do now specifically advise, against the use of any
drink containing harmful habit-forming drugs under circumstances
that would result in acquiring the habit. Any beverage that contains
ingredients harmful to the body should be avoided.

(PB, February, 1972.)

Leave Coca-Cola Alone

The head of the health department, Dr. Beatty, has requested
me to say to the Latter-day Saints that there are more injurious
ingredients in coca-cola than there are in coffee, and particularly
when some of the good people say: "Give me a double shot." I
say to the Latter-day Saints, and it is my right to say it—because
you have sung, since this conference started (whether you meant it
or not, I am not saying) --
"We thank Thee, O God, for a prophet,
    To guide us in these latter days;
We thank Thee for sending the gospel
    To lighten our minds with its rays;
We thank Thee for every blessing
    Bestowed by Thy bounteous hand;
We feel it a pleasure to serve Thee,
    And love to obey Thy command."
Now, if you mean it--I am not going to give any command,
but I will ask it as a personal, individual favor to me, to let coca-cola

alone. There are plenty of other things you can get at the soda fountains without drinking that which is injurious. The Lord does not want you to use any drug that creates an appetite for itself.

(*Heber J. Grant*, President of the Church,
CR, April, 1922, p. 165.)

Does The Church Own Stock In The Coca-Cola Company?

Does the Church own stock in the Coca-Cola Company? For some reason this question has come to me on several occasions from certain sections of the country, but I have never been able to trace it to its source. The Church of Jesus Christ of Latter-day Saints and its leading authorities are in no way associated with nor have stock in the Coca-Cola Company. Perhaps some person for some ulterior purpose circulated this report, evidently endeavoring to attack the doctrine of the Church and the teachings of the authorities in relation to the Word of Wisdom.

Personally, I have no knowledge as to the contents of cola drinks and therefore cannot give expert advice as to their contents. However, I have the statement on the examination of a capable chemist that cola drinks contain caffeine, the element that is so prevalent in coffee and other stimulants. There is one thing that I do know, however: this stimulating drink is not served in my home, and no matter where I am I personally avoid it.

If members of the Church would take the time to read carefully what the Lord has said to them in the Word of Wisdom, Section 89, in the Doctrine and Covenants, and then would heed these sayings, they would be greatly benefited. This revelation was given as a warning to the Latter-day Saints. In it tea and coffee are not mentioned, but evidently these stimulants were meant among others. In a revelation to the Prophet Joseph Smith it was made known in his day that these two stimulants were included but that the revelation was not confined in this counsel just to these two beverages. Today many other drinks and beverages have come into general use. Some of these are just as harmful--perhaps more so—than are tea and coffee. Nevertheless, members of the Church should seek for wisdom, and if they will follow the teachings that have come to us through revelation, they will learn to avoid many other things that today are offered to an unsuspecting public. The fact is beyond successful dispute or contradiction that some stimulants are being offered to the public that are detrimental to health.

(*Joseph Fielding Smith*, President of the Council
of the Twelve Apostles, IE, September, 1966, pp. 766-767.)

A Warning Against Cola Drinks

A U.S. Senate committee recently conducted hearings on malnutrition in the United States, on which severe attacks were made upon cola as an ingredient in soft drinks.

It was said that cola drinks are "non-foods," that they contain the harmful ingredient contained in coffee—caffeine—but they have no vitamins and no protein. Yet these drinks are used extensively.

One mother wrote to the American Medical Association and said that her son drinks 16 bottles of cola beverages a day, and asked if this was harmful. How naive can we be?

In this hearing Sen. Jacob Javits of New York said that the widespread consumption of cola some day may be classed as a disease, for such drinks, he added, "contain no proteins, no vitamins, but do add caffeine," although the Federal Drug Administration does not require the manufacturers to so announce it on their labels.

"Better Nutrition" magazine commenting on these hearings said that "these beverages are unhealthful for many reasons. Their load of sugar is unbuffered by any protein, the caffeine is damaging to adults, let alone to children; such drinks replace in children's diets nutritious foods like milk and fruit juices; their empty calories promote obesity and over-weight, and eventually make addicts of many people who find they cannot get through the day without their cola drinks which give them false energy."

The Church has never included soft drinks in the letter of the Word of Wisdom. But it does expect that members of the Church will have sufficient wisdom to avoid narcotics and stimulants of all kinds.

Except for medicinal purposes, drugs are very dangerous, especially when administered by untrained and unskilled persons.

This is at the basis of the present epidemic of drug consumption, even by little children. They are ignorant of the drug and its effects. They take it because "every one does it," and as a result some use the so-called heavy drugs which destroy brain cells and even cause death among hundreds of users across the nation.

Caffeine is a drug. It is classed as a narcotic. Constant use of caffeine, whether in coffee, tea or soft drinks, can have only a dangerous effect upon the human system.

Studies even now are showing that coffee may be attacked as vigorously as tobacco now is when the scientists studying it assemble all their data.

In the meantime, the Word of Wisdom is offered us by a loving God. Everyone of us should follow it and be both wise and well.

(Editorial, *CN*, April 25, 1970, p. 16.)

The Amount of Caffeine In Cola Drinks

We've been asked to publish the latest figures of the amount of caffeine in the several cola drinks. The information, furnished by each company from its own tests, per eight ounce glass, are, Dr. Pepper, 40 mg; Coca Cola, 37 mg; Royal Crown, 28 mg; and Pepsi, 24 mg. This compares to the 110 to 150 mgs in an eight ounce cup of coffee, and the 100 to 120 mgs in a like amount of tea.

(Church Editor's Report, *CN*, January 20, 1968, p. 5.)

CHAPTER 13

COMMUNISM AND SOCIALISM
(See: Political Elections and Voting Responsibilities)

Communism Is Hostile To Loyal American Citizenship And Incompatible With True Church Membership

With great regret we learn from credible sources, governmental and others, that a few Church members are joining, directly or indirectly, the Communists and are taking part in their activities.

The Church does not interfere, and has no intention of trying to interfere, with the fullest and freest exercise of the political franchise of its members, under and within our Constitution, which the Lord declared, "...I established ... by the hands of wise men whom I raised up unto this very purpose..." *(D&C 101:80)*, and which, as to the principles thereof, the Prophet, dedicating the Kirtland Temple, prayed should be "established forever." (See *D&C 109:54)*

But Communism is not a political party nor a political plan under the Constitution; it is a system of government that is the opposite of our Constitutional government, and it would be necessary to destroy our government before Communism could be set up in the United States.

Since Communism, established, would destroy our American Constitutional government to support Communism is treasonable to our free institutions, and no patriotic American citizen may become either a Communist or supporter of Communism.

To our Church members we say: Communism is not the United Order, and bears only the most superficial resemblance thereto; Communism is based upon intolerance and force, the United Order upon love and freedom of conscience and action; Communism involves forceful despoliation and confiscation, the United Order voluntary consecration and sacrifice.

Communists cannot establish the United Order, nor will Communism bring it about. The United Order will be established by the Lord in his own due time and in accordance with the regular prescribed order of the Church.

Furthermore, it is charged by universal report, which is not successfully contradicted or disproved, that Communism undertakes to control, if not indeed to prescribe, the religious life of the people living within its jurisdiction, and that it even reaches its hand into the sanctity of the family circle itself, disrupting the normal relationship of parent and child, all in a manner unknown and unsanctioned under the Constitutional guarantees under which we in America live. Such interference would be contrary to the fundamental precepts of the gospel and to the teachings and order of the Church.

Communism being thus hostile to loyal American citizenship and incompatible with true Church membership, of necessity no loyal American citizen and no faithful Church member can be a Communist.

We call upon all Church members completely to eschew Communism. The safety of our divinely inspired Constitutional government and the welfare of our Church imperatively demand that Communism shall have no place in America.

(J. Reuben Clark Jr., First Counselor in the First Presidency,
representing the First Presidency,
Deseret News, July 3, 1936, pp. 1-2.)

False Political "Isms"

We again warn our people in America of the constantly increasing threat against our inspired Constitution and our free institutions set up under it. The same political tenets and philosophies that have brought war and terror in other parts of the world are at work amongst us in America. The proponents thereof are seeking to undermine our own form of government and to set up instead one of the forms of dictatorships now flourishing in other lands. These revolutionists are using a technique that is as old as the human race,—a fervid but false solicitude for the unfortunate over whom they thus gain mastery, and then enslave them.

They suit their approaches to the particular group they seek to deceive. Among the Latter-day Saints they speak of their philosophy and their plans under it, as an ushering in of the United Order. Communism and all other similar "isms" bear no relationship whatever to the United Order. They are merely the clumsy counterfeits which Satan always devises of the gospel plan. Communism debases the individual and makes him the enslaved tool of the state to whom he must look for sustenance and religion; the United Order exalts the individual, leaves him his property, "according to his family, according to his circumstances and his wants and needs," *(D&C 51:3)* and provides a system by which he helps care for his less fortunate brethren; the United Order leaves every man free to choose his own religion as his conscience directs. Communism destroys man's God-given free agency; the United Order glorifies it. Latter-day Saints cannot be true to their faith and lend aid, encouragement, or sympathy to any of these false philosophies. They will prove snares to their feet.

Heber J. Grant, J. Reuben Clark Jr., David O. McKay,
The First Presidency, (CR, April, 1942, p. 90.)

The Deadly Challenge Of Communism

The bond of our secular covenant is the principle of constitutional government. That principle is, in itself, eternal and everlasting, despite the pretensions of temporary tyrannies. The principle of tyranny maintains that human beings are incurably selfish and therefore cannot govern themselves. This concept flies in the face of the wonderful declaration of the Prophet Joseph Smith that the people are to be taught correct principles, and then they are to govern themselves. Dictatorship, however, argues that the people should be governed by the individual or a clique who can seize power through subversion or outright bloodshed. Further, the people are declared to be without guarantees or rights, and the regime is claimed to exist beholden only to the plans and whims of the ruling tyrant.

Our founding fathers, despite some natural fears, clearly regarded the promulgation of the Constitution of the United States as their greatest triumph.

On June 12, 1955, Sir Percy Spender, Australian Ambassador to the United States, delivered a speech at the Union University at Schenectady, New York, at the time they conferred an honorary degree of Doctor of Civil Laws upon him. I agree with what he said in that speech, relating to present-day efforts, and I quote part of it as follows:

"Today, freedom—political, economic, and individual freedom—lies destroyed or is in the course of being destroyed over great areas of the globe. And it has been destroyed and is being destroyed in the name of freedom. A vast struggle for the mind of man is now being waged—a struggle in which I hope each of you with all your heart will take part. In this struggle truth is distorted by those who have not the slightest regard for truth. All the words which mean so much to us—like Liberty, Freedom, Democracy—are being despoiled and prostituted by the enemies of Liberty, Freedom, and Democracy. A ruthless dialectical battle is being waged against the Christian way of life, against political liberty, against individual freedom, and it is being waged in the name of Freedom. Black becomes White; Tyranny becomes Freedom; The Forced Labor Camp stands for Liberty; The Slave State is represented as Democracy. This is the deadly challenge of Communism. And in this challenge those who put their emphasis upon man as an economic being—and there are plenty in every so-called free country in the world today who do just that—those who explain man in terms of scientific and chemical facts and the accident of circumstance, those who treat human beings as so many 'bodies,' those who deny man's spiritual and individual existence—each of them aids and hastens the destruction of the political institutions on which our free society rests, and whether he knows it or not, supports the dialectics and the aims of International Communism...."

(David O. McKay, President of the Church,
CR, October, 1962, p. 6-7.)

A Comment On Socialism

We heard Brother Taylor's exposition of what is called Socialism this morning. What can they do? Live on each other and beg. It is a poor, unwise and very imbecile people who cannot take care of themselves.

(Brigham Young, President of the Church,
JD, 1870, 14:21.)

Communism And Socialism Cannot Live With Christianity

The plain and simple issue now facing us in America is freedom or slavery.... Our real enemies are communism and its running mate, socialism.... Nor forget that while enslavement to an individual may on occasion be eased by the human instincts of mercy and love, yet these feelings are unknown to a soulless state....

Unfortunately, one thing seems sure, we shall not get out of our present difficulties without trouble, serious trouble. Indeed, it may well be that our government and its free institutions will not be preserved except at the price of life and blood. That is the record of freedom's contest with communism and socialism in other lands....

The paths we are following, if we move forward thereon, will inevitably lead us to socialism or communism, and these two are as like as two peas in a pod in their ultimate effect upon our liberties....

We may first observe that communism and socialism—which we shall hereafter group together and dub Statism—cannot live with Christianity, nor with any religion that postulates a Creator such as the Declaration of Independence recognizes. The slaves of Statism must know no power, no authority, no source of blessing, no God, but the State. The State must be supreme in everything....

This country faces ahead enough trouble to bring us to our knees in humble, honest prayer to God for the help which he alone can give, to save us....

And do not think that all these usurpations, intimidations, and impositions are being done to us through inadvertance or mistake; the whole course is deliberately planned and carried out; its purpose is to destroy the Constitution and our constitutional government; then to bring chaos, out of which the new Statism, with its slavery, is to arise, with a cruel, relentless, selfish, ambitious crew in the saddle, riding hard with whip and spur, a red-shrouded band of night riders for despotism....

If we do not vigorously fight for our liberties, we shall go clear through to the end of the road and become another Russia, or worse....

The story is told that in the late afternoon at the battle of Marengo, Desaix reached the field after a forced march. The desperate situation was explained to him. Napolean asked him what he thought of it. His reply was: "This battle is completely lost; but it is only four o'clock; we have still time to gain one today." Bonaparte ordered him to join in an advance on their right wing. The advance was made; the new battle was won. Desaix died that day, shot through the heart.

We have largely lost the conflict so far waged. But there is time to win the final victory, if we sense our danger, and fight. Let us too, advance on the right wing.

God give us strength to preserve our liberties....

(J. Reuben Clark Jr., First Counselor in the First Presidency,
CN, September 25, 1949, pp. 2, 15.)

False Prophets and Christs In Government

False prophets and christs, as foretold by the Savior, may come to deceive us not alone in the name of religion, but if we can believe the history of Italy and Germany and Russia, they may come under the label of politicians or of social planners or so-called economists, deceitful in their offerings of a king of salvation which may come under such guise.

(Harold B. Lee, an Apostle,
CR, October, 1950, p. 131.)

The Threat Of Revolutionists

When we fail to put the love of God first, we are easily deceived by crafty men who profess a great love of humanity, while advocating programs that are not of the Lord.

In 1942 Presidents Heber J. Grant, J. Reuben Clark, Jr., and David O. McKay warned us about the increasing threat to our constitution caused by revolutionists whom the First Presidency said were "using a technique that is as old as the human race—a fervid but false solicitude for the unfortunate over whom they thus gain mastery, and then enslave them. They suit their approaches to the particular group they seek to deceive." (*The Improvement Era,* May 1942, p. 343.)

That timely counsel about "a fervid but false solicitude for the unfortunate" could have saved China and Cuba if enough people knew what the Communist masters of deceit really had in mind when they promised agrarian reform.

(*Ezra Taft Benson,* an Apostle,
CR, October, 1967, p. 35.)

CHAPTER 14

CONSTITUTIONAL GOVERNMENT
(See: Church and State; Civil Laws;
Civil Rights; Military Service; War)

Every Government Not Ordained Of God Will Crumble

Every government not ordained of God, as we have just been
hearing, will, in its time, crumble to the dust and be lost in the fog
of forgetfulness, and will leave no history of its doings.

(*Brigham Young*, President of the Church,
JD, 1871, 14:91.)

The Constitution Is Founded In The Wisdom Of God

...the Constitution of the United States is a glorious standard;
it is founded in the wisdom of God. It is a heavenly banner; it is to
all those who are privileged with the sweets of its liberty, like
the cooling shades and refreshing waters of a great rock in a thirsty
and weary land. It is like a great tree under whose branches men
from every clime can be shielded from the burning rays of the sun.

(*Joseph Smith*, President of the Church,
Documentary History of the Church, 3:304.)

Pray That Government Leaders May
Administer In Righteousness

But there is a principle here that I wish to speak about. God
dictates in a great measure the affairs of the nations of the earth,
their kingdoms and governments and rulers and those that hold
dominion. He sets up one and pulls down another, according to his
will. That is an old doctrine, but it is true today. Have we governors?
Have we a president of the United States? Have we men in authority? Yes. Is it right to traduce their characters? No, it is not. Is it
right for us to oppose them? No, it is not. Is it right for them to
traduce us? No, it is not. Is it right for them to oppress us in any
way? No, it is not. We ought to pray for these people, for those
that are in authority, that they may be led in the right way, that
they may be preserved from evil, that they may administer the
government in righteousness, and that they may pursue a course

that will receive the approbation of heaven. Well, what else? Then we ought to pray for ourselves that when any plans or contrivances or opposition to the law of God, to the Church and kingdom of God, or to his people, are introduced, and whenever we are sought to be made the victims of tyranny and oppression, that the hand of God may be over us and over them to paralyze their acts and protect us.

(*John Taylor*, President of the Quorum
of the Twelve Apostles and acting President of the Church,
JD, 1880, 21:68.)

Although Inspired, The Constitution Is Not Perfect

The signers of the Declaration of Independence and the framers of the Constitution were inspired from on high to do that work. But was that which was given to them perfect, not admitting of any addition whatever? No; for if men know anything, they must know that the Almighty has never yet found a man in mortality that was capable at the first intimation, at the impulse, to receive anything in a state of entire perfection. They laid the foundation, and it was for after generations to rear the superstructure upon it. It is a progressive—a gradual work.

(*Brigham Young*, President of the Church,
JD, 1854, 7:14.)

The Constitution Was Written By Men Who Accepted Christ

The Constitution of this government was written by men who accepted Jesus Christ as the Savior of mankind. Let men and women in the United States then continue to keep their eyes centered upon him who ever shines as a Light to all the world. Men and women who live in America, "the land of Zion," have a responsibility greater than that yet born by any other people. Theirs is the duty, the obligation to preserve not only the Constitution of the land but also the Christian principles from which sprang the immortal document.

(*David O. McKay*, an Apostle, *CR*, October, 1942, p. 70.)

The Government of The United States Began
Under The Direction of God

When our Father in heaven inspired men to write the Constitution and gave unto us the great charter that vouchsafed to us the liberty we enjoy, he did it in order that men might develop and be free, as the gospel of Jesus Christ intends that all men shall be. So the government of the United States was begun under the direction of our Father in heaven, as declared by his own word, to be an example unto the nations of the earth; and the liberties that we enjoy are pointed out in a most forceful way to the children of men.

The fact that we were a free people, that we were not a military nation, brought upon us the contempt and ridicule of some of the great armed powers, because they thought we were helpless. They did not understand that underlying this apparent peacefulness, in this great land, there was a fixed determination that men should be free; that God himself had written it, as it were, by his own finger, in the Constitution of our great government.

(*George Albert Smith*, an Apostle, *JH*, September 15, 1918.)

Our Allegiance To The Constitution

God provided that in this land of liberty, our political allegiance shall run not to individuals, that is, to government officials, no matter how great or how small they may be. Under His plan our allegiance and the only allegiance we owe as citizens or denizens of the United States, runs to our inspired Constitution which God Himself set up. So runs the oath of office of those who participate in government. A certain loyalty we do owe to the office which a man holds, but even here we owe, just by reason of our citizenship, no loyalty to the man himself. In other countries it is to the individual that allegiance runs. This principle of allegiance to the Constitution is basic to our freedom. It is one of the great principles that distinguishes this "land of liberty" from other countries.

(*J. Reuben Clark, Jr.*, First Counselor in the First Presidency, *IE*, 1940, 43:444.)

CHAPTER 15

CREMATION

Cremation Is Discouraged

Although cremation is discouraged the decision is left with the family. Local laws must be observed. If bodies are to be cremated, funeral services may be held in the usual way, but the disposition of the ashes usually makes unnecessary the offering of graveside or dedicatory prayers.

(*GHI*, 1968, p. 161.)

The Church Today Counsels Its Members Not To Cremate Their Dead

Cremation of the dead is no part of the gospel; it is a practice which has been avoided by the saints in all ages. The Church today counsels its members not to cremate their dead. Such a procedure would find gospel acceptance only under the most extraordinary and unusual circumstances. Wherever possible the dead should be consigned to the earth, and nothing should be done that is destructive of the body; that should be left to nature, "for dust thou art, and unto dust shalt thou return." *(Gen. 3:19)*

(*Bruce R. McConkie*, Member of the First Council of the Seventy, *Mormon Doctrine*, 1966, p. 172.)

Cremation Does Not Nullify Resurrection

The Church of Jesus Christ of Latter-day Saints has never taken a definite stand on this [cremation] question. Presumably no edict in relation to it will ever be taken. The matter of burial of the dead, as far as the Church is concerned, is an individual or a family matter. If any member of the Church should state in his will, or make any general statement, that he wished to be cremated, the Church authorities would not step in and interfere but would consider it something with which they had no official concern.

From the beginning of time it has been the custom to bury the dead, and in no sense whatever can I, or would I, speak in a manner to have my thoughts considered as a doctrine of the Church. I can express only my personal view, which is that when the time comes for me to die, I desire to have my body laid away in the place selected by the side of my loved ones. This custom is in keeping with historical tradition.

It is true that the mortal body in due time returns to the earth as the Lord predicted that it should. Much of the cremated body is carried off into the air and only a small portion of ash remains. However it is impossible to destroy a body. It makes no difference whether a body is consumed by fire, buried in the depths of the sea, or placed in the tomb, the time will come when every essential particle will be called back again to its own place, and the individual whose body was laid away or scattered to the winds, will be reassembled with every essential part restored. It was to bring to pass this restoration that Jesus died upon the cross, and it is by his command that the individual elements will be called back to their own place. Jesus said to the Jews:

> Verily, verily, I say unto you, The hour is coming and now is, when the dead shall hear the voice of the Son of God: and they that hear shall live:
>
> For as the Father hath life in himself; so hath he given to the Son to have life in himself;
>
> And hath given him authority to execute judgment also, because he is the Son of man.
>
> Marvel not at this: for the hour is coming in the which all that are in their graves shall hear his voice.
>
> And shall come forth; they that have done good, unto the resurrection of life; and they that have done evil, unto the resurrection of damnation *(John 5:25-26)....*

One reason for cremation, presumably, is that the world today, even much of the so-called Christian world, is denying that there is to be any resurrection. Therefore the mortal body returns to dust never to rise again. However, the resurrection is literally a coming forth from the dead of the mortal body, with every part that is an essential part intact and immortalized that the body will not die again. It is true that the immortal body will be purified, and gross material that is not an essential part will be eliminated. It makes no difference whatever as to the disposal of the body, every essential part will be restored to its proper frame. Resurrected persons will appear just as they did in mortal life, only with bodies that are celestial, bodies that are terrestrial, bodies telestial, and other bodies that receive no glory whatever.

But each will maintain its individual identity and will be so recognized after the resurrection.

(*Joseph Fielding Smith*, President of the Council of the Twelve Apostles, *Answers To Gospel Questions*, 1957, Vol. 2, pp. 99-102.)

CHAPTER 16

CRIME
(See: Capital Punishment)

Criminal Conviction Justifies Church Excommunication

When a member is convicted in courts of the land of a crime involving moral turpitude ... such as burglary, dishonesty, theft, or murder ... such is prima facie evidence justifying excommunication by a Church court.

(GHI, 1968, pp. 122-124.)

Every Man Should Frown Down Iniquity

Let every man in this Territory be a vigilant officer, and, when a thief is found in the act of stealing, take him, dead or alive. There is one trait in our officers that I delight in, and that is, they will not stand to be shot down by a set of scoundrels. Let every man be vigilant to frown down iniquity wherever it shows itself, and suffer it not to gain a foothold in our country.

(Brigham Young, President of the Church,
JD, 1862, 9:157.)

Teach Children Integrity and Honesty

[Comments on this subject were made by *Spencer W. Kimball*, President of the Church, in the October, 1974, General Conference: *Ensign*, November, 1974, p. 5, and in the April, 1975 General Conference: *Ensign*, May, 1975, p. 6.]

Excessive Concern For The Guilty May Lead To Problems

[Comments on this subject were made by *Spencer W. Kimball*, President of the Church, in the October, 1974, General Conference, and can be found in the *Ensign*, November, 1974, p. 7.]

Shoplifting Is A Disgrace

[Comments on this subject were made by *Spencer W. Kimball*, President of the Church, in the April, 1974, General Conference, and can be found in the *Ensign*, May, 1974, p. 89.]

The Administration Of Law Has Become A Science
For Protecting The Criminal From Just Punishment

I shall only take time to note here one factor that ... represents a great contributing cause of the growth and increase of lawlessness in our country. It arises from the uncertainty in the execution of the law. Perhaps in the foundation of our government, in establishing the constitution of our country and our state constitutions, the people of that generation had been under the iron heel of oppressive governments so long, that they became extremely anxious to protect the individual against encroachments of tyrannical administration of law, and therefore over-emphasized the rights of the individual and the protection of those rights, and had less concern for the larger rights and the protection of society from criminals. In this spirit the legislation has run in our states and in our nation, viz: to safeguard and to provide every possible means for the protection of the rights of those who are accused of crimes. And these laws, favoring so strongly the criminal, have been so used by skillful attorneys for the defense, that the administration of law has become a science for protecting the criminal from the just judgment and punishment of his crimes.

(*Brigham H. Roberts*, Member of the First Council
of the Seventy, *CR*, October, 1927, p. 23.)

CHAPTER 17

DANCING
(See: Music)

Church Dance Standards

Dancing that is suggestive or sensual in any way is incompatible with church standards. Avoid all grotesque contortions of the body such as shoulder or hip shaking or body jerking. As members of the Church, youth should use wisdom and judgment by adhering to acceptable church-dance standards so that good taste in dance is always exemplified. All dances should be evaluated in terms of approved dance standards.

(PB, December, 1965.)

Proper Standards At Church Dances

There is need for priesthood leaders to help youth leaders maintain proper standards at Church-sponsored dances and activities. Dress, grooming, lighting, dance style, lyrics, and music should contribute to an atmosphere in which the Spirit of the Lord may be present. Care should be taken to see that bands or musical groups performing at Church functions avoid immodest dress, over-amplified music, unworthy lyrics, and unusual lighting effects. Firm prior agreement with musical groups should be arranged to ensure proper standards at Church-sponsored activities. Final responsibility for maintaining acceptable standards remains with bishops and stake presidents.

(PB, First Quarter, 1974, p. 2.)

The Value Of Dancing

But I pause here, and for this reason—I want it distinctly understood, that fiddling and dancing are no part of our worship. The question may be asked, What are they for, then? I answer, that my body may keep pace with my mind. My mind labors like a man logging, all the time; and this is the reason why I am fond of these pastimes—they give me a privilege to throw everything off, and shake myself, that my body may exercise, and my mind rest.

What for? To get strength, and be renewed and quickened, and enlivened, and animated, so that my mind may not wear out.

(Brigham Young, President of the Church,
JD, 1852, 1:43.)

Young People: Change Partners When Dancing

My fourth suggestion concerns itself with this problem of dancing all evening with the same girl and of going steady so young. Sometimes we can use young people to help us help other young people. Let me give an illustration:

Down at the Institute of Religion in Tuscon, Arizona, 20 years ago, we had 40 boys and 45 girls who came to Mutual. The boys were prone to dance after Mutual with the same girls each night. Four or five girls sat on the side lines.

One day I said to a returned missionary, who was professing his great faith in the Gospel of Jesus Christ, "Do you love your fellow men?"

He said, "I do."

"Does that include your fellow sisters, too?"

He said, "Of course."

I said, "I doubt that. Every Tuesday night you find a little girl here and dance with her for a half hour. You are not concerned with what other girls are doing. Why don't you find another returned missionary and you two see to it that every girl here has at least two dances every Tuesday night?"

He said, "I will. I had never thought of applying the Gospel to my social life before."

Well, these two young men soon had those girls happy and everybody dancing. It worked beautifully.

I believe you should speak to a group of the finest, most popular young leaders of your wards, of your MIA groups, about this problem of dancing all night with the same girl. They do not like to do it. They do it because it is the socially acceptable thing to do. They are afraid, as individuals, to break down the custom. If you put the problem to them, brethren, and suggest that a few of them trade partners and then remind them of it once a month and watch it, I believe it would work.

(Lowell L. Bennion, CR, April, 1958, p. 86.)

[Compiler's Note: Although Brother Bennion was not a General Authority, President David O. McKay presented him to the conference as follows: "We shall now hear from Elder Lowell L. Bennion, head of the Institute at the University of Utah. He will speak and give a special message by request of the First Presidency on a question which is of vital importance, a condition of very vital importance for our young people throughout the entire Church.''']

CHAPTER 18

DEBT
(See: Welfare and Work)

Keep Out Of Debt If You Can

If there is anyone here who is in debt I would advise that when he goes home, and when I go home, too, that we will begin with a determination that we will pay our debts and meet all of our obligations just as quickly as the Lord will enable us to do it. If there is anyone here intending to go into debt for speculation, and especially if he is intending to borrow money to buy mining stock and other scaly or uncertain things, I would advise him to hesitate, pray over it, and carefully consider it before he obligates himself by borrowing money and going into debt. In other words, keep out of debt if you can. Pay your debts as soon as you can. That means me as well as anyone else.

(Joseph F. Smith, President of the Church,
CR, October, 1911, pp. 128-129.)

Get Out Of Debt When Everything Is Booming

I believe that the burdens that are upon the Latter-day Saints would be very light indeed had the people listened to the advice of our late beloved President Joseph F. Smith, to get out of debt, when everything was blooming, when they could sell all of their sheep and their cattle and nearly everything they had for about two or three times its cost instead of running, as they did, further in debt, increasing their mortgages on homes and live-stock, believing that every dollar they could borrow meant increased wealth to them. President Joseph F. Smith's warning sank into my heart. If I have had one opportunity, being in debt, to go in deeper, I have had scores offered to me, but I remembered the teaching of President Smith and I went to work that day to get out of debt and not to speculate one single solitary dollar until I did get out of debt; and, with the exception of some small loans on my life insurance policies, -I have saved by investing in a building society every month enough to pay these loans- I do not today personally owe a dollar. If I had not listened to and taken the inspired advice of Pres. Smith, I think I should be everlastingly "busted," because of the very many good things that have been offered to me since for financial investments. Pres. Smith's inspired words found echo in my heart, and I went on from then until his death, singing, "We thank Thee, O God, for a prophet to guide us," instead of adding, "providing he does not guide us to keep out of debt," as a good many people should be singing today.

(Heber J. Grant, President of the Church,
CR, April, 1923, pp. 8-9.)

Own Your Own Home

[Comments on this subject were made by *Spencer W. Kimball*, President of the Church, in the October, 1974, General Conference, and can be found in the *Ensign*, November 1974, pp. 6-7.]

Live Within Your Means

May I add again an admonition: Live within your means. Get out of debt. Keep out of debt. Lay by for a rainy day which has always come and will come again. Practice and increase your habits of thrift, industry, economy, frugality. Remember that the parable of the ten virgins, the five that were wise and the five that were foolish, can be just as applicable to matters of the temporal world as those of the spiritual.

(J. Reuben Clark Jr., First Counselor in the First Presidency,
CR, October, 1937, p. 107.)

When Bankruptcy Is Justified

There is a law called into existence for the relief of men who are oppressed because of their creditors, and through taking bankruptcy men may be released from their obligations. I have many times been asked the question, who is justified in taking bankruptcy to avoid an obligation? My answer has been—and I would like to make it here, and if I am wrong I stand to be corrected—that no Latter-day Saint, so long as his creditors give him the chance, the faintest chance, to work out and meet his obligations, ought to resort to accepting the law of bankruptcy. It is only for those who are oppressed, those who have no chance, no hope, and nothing but oppression following them. They may be justified, but surely no one who can possibly work out his problems with his creditors, ought to resort to this means of relieving himself of his obligations.

(Melvin J. Ballard, an Apostle,
CR, October, 1929, p. 52.)

Government Debt Spending May Bring Bondage To All

I fear this, that under existing conditions we are gradually drifting toward a paternal government, a government which will so intrench itself that the people will become powerless to disrupt it, in which the lives and liberties of the people at large may be jeopardized. They are pouring millions of dollars in this time of need into sources for the benefit of the people and it is a great benefit and perhaps salvation but it is going to result in this—I am going to make this statement—that if the present policy is continued it will not be long until the government will be in the banking business, it will be in the farming business, it will be in the cattle and sheep business, for many of these debts will never be paid. That will mean the appointment of innumerable agencies. The government now is overloaded with commissions and agencies, some of them administering the very laws that Congress itself has enacted. Someone else should be administering those laws. If you want to save yourself from the bondage of debt and political influences which are not of your own choosing, I ask you to think of what I have said.

(*Anthony W. Ivins*, First Counselor in the First Presidency, *CR*, October, 1932, pp. 111-112.)

Pay All Your Debts, Even If It Takes A Full Lifetime To Do So

This is a day of easy credit, and private as well as public debt is rising tremendously.

The temptation is ever present to go deeper and deeper into further obligations with too little thought being given to the day of reckoning.

It seems easy to live beyond our means when all we have to say is "charge it, please."

But each individual, nevertheless, must keep an accounting of his own affairs and make certain that he can—and does—pay every debt for which he obligates himself.

He knows his own financial strength, or he should. With the simplest of arithmetic he can add up the amounts of his payments and determine whether he can afford them.

It is not only the installment payments he must check, however. There are also the daily expenses which must be met by every family, and surely some reserve should be provided for that almost certain rainy day.

But beyond that, every individual should plan for savings which may help him eventually to live on a strictly cash basis. That will give him an economic freedom which he can have in no other way.

But whether we deal in cash or credit, we must pay our bills.

It is a dishonest act to obtain goods without paying for them, whether we acquire them by purchase or by shoplifting or by any other means.

Even in cases of bankruptcy a person should endeavor to pay all of his debts, despite the fact that under the law he may feel that he is free of them.

No court action can change the morality of a transaction. If we owe, we owe. It is that simple, and we should return to every creditor whatever is honestly due him, even if it takes us a full lifetime to do so.

We are interested in the salvation of our souls. Honesty is basic in the gospel.

If no unclean person can enter the presence of God, can a dishonest one do so?

(Editorial, *CN*, March 3, 1973, p. 16.)

CHAPTER 19

DIVORCE
(See: Marriage)

The Church Frowns Upon Divorce

The increasing divorce rate in the United States today is a threatening menace to this nation's greatness. The increase throughout the United States, and in our own state, in the percentage of divorces is alarming.

In the light of scripture, ancient and modern, we are justified in concluding that Christ's ideal pertaining to marriage is the unbroken home, and conditions that cause divorce are violations of his divine teachings. Except in cases of infidelity or other extreme conditions, the Church frowns upon divorce, and authorities look with apprehension upon the increasing number of divorces among members of the Church.

A man who has entered into sacred covenants in the house of the Lord to remain true to the marriage vow is a traitor to that covenant if he separates himself from his wife and family just because he has permitted himself to become infatuated with a pretty face and comely form of some young girl who flattered him with a smile. Even though a loose interpretation of the law of the land would grant such a man a bill of divorcement, I think he is unworthy of a recommend to have his second marriage solemnized in the temple. And any woman who will break up her home because of some selfish desire, or who has been untrue to her husband, is also untrue to the covenants she has made in the house of the Lord. When we refer to the breaking of the marriage tie, we touch upon one of the saddest experiences of life. For a couple who have basked in the sunshine of each other's love to stand by and see the clouds of misunderstanding and discord obscure the love-light of their lives is tragedy indeed. In the darkness that follows, the love sparkle in each other's eyes is obscured, and to try to restore it is fruitless....

The number of broken marriages can be reduced if couples realize even before they approach the altar that marriage is a state of mutual service, a state of giving as well as of receiving, and that each must give of himself or herself to the utmost. Harriet Beecher Stowe wisely writes: "No man or woman can create a true home who is not willing in the outset to embrace life heroically, to encounter labor and sacrifice. Only to such can this divinest power be given to create on earth that which is the nearest image of heaven."

(*David O. McKay*, President of the Church,
CR, April, 1969, pp. 8-9.)

Most Divorces Come Of Weakness And Selfishness

[Comments on this subject were made by *Spencer W. Kimball*, President of the Church, in the April, 1974, General Conference, and can be found in the *Ensign*, May, 1974, pp. 6-7.]

No Other Success Can Compensate For Failure In The Home

Another threat to our society is the increasing number of divorces and the tendency to look upon marriage as a mere contract that may be severed at the first difficulty or misunderstanding that may arise.

One of our most precious possessions is our families. The domestic relations precede, and, in our present existence, are worth more than all other social ties. They give the first throb to the heart and unseal the deep fountains of its love. Home is the chief school of human virtues. Its responsibilities, joys, sorrows, smiles, tears, hopes, and solicitudes form the chief interests of human life.

"To make a happy fireside clime
    To weans and wife,
 That's the true pathos and sublime
    O' human life."—Robert Burns

When one puts business or pleasure above his home, he that moment starts on the downgrade to soul-weakness. When the club becomes more attractive to any man than his home, it is time for him to confess in bitter shame that he has failed to measure up to the supreme opportunity of his life and flunked in the final test of true manhood. No other success can compensate for failure in the home. The poorest shack in which love prevails over a united family is of greater value to God and future humanity than any other riches. In such a home God can work miracles and will work miracles.

Pure hearts in a pure home are always in whispering distance of heaven.

In the light of scripture, ancient and modern we are justified in concluding that Christ's ideal pertaining to marriage is the unbroken home, and conditions that cause divorce are violations of his divine teaching.

Some of those conditions I name as unfaithfulness on the part of either the husband or wife, or both—habitual drunkenness, physical violence, long imprisonment that disgraces the wife and family, the union of an innocent girl to a reprobate. In these and perhaps other cases there may be circumstances which make the continuance of the marriage state a greater evil than divorce. But these are extreme cases—they are the mistakes, the calamities in the realm of marriage. If we could remove them, I would say there never should be a divorce. It is Christ's ideal that home and marriage should be perpetual--eternal.

Marriage is a sacred relationship entered into for purposes that are well recognized—primarily for the rearing of a family.

I know of no other place where happiness abides more securely than in the home. It is possible to make home a bit of heaven. Indeed, I picture heaven as a continuation of the ideal home. Some man has said: "Home filled with contentment is one of the highest hopes of this life."

An ever-decreasing birthrate, and an increasing divorce rate are ominous signs threatening the stability of the home and the perpetuity of any nation.

(*David O. McKay*, President of the Church,
CR, April, 1964, p. 5.)

Don't Expect Heaven On Earth

One more question remains in my mind, if President Smith will allow me to take two or three minutes more. In those early days we had practically no divorces, no marital upsets, no family troubles such as we have today. Today the divorce evil in America is becoming a national scandal, nothing short of it. The question is often asked, How did it happen that we had family integrity, peace, and harmony in those early days? The Church has never said that divorce should be forbidden, not be given nor taken. There may be conditions, under our frail mortal conditions, that justify divorce; but the Church has always looked askance upon it and always with sorrow.

The day journal of Brigham Young records that one day a sister came to him and said: "My husband is not good to me. I want a divorce." The journal goes on further to say that President Young talked with her about an hour, from ten to eleven in the morning. The journal gives the exact time. Then, when they had finished, he turned to the woman, and he said: "Sister, I have heard your story. I am not going to give you a divorce." As you know, Brigham Young was a friend to the cause of women. He felt that they had the first right of choice. "I will not give you a divorce," he said. "Go home and be good to your husband, and don't expect heaven on earth."

There is a tremendous lesson in that last phrase: "Don't expect heaven on earth."

A man marries a girl and expects her to be a perfect woman; she expects him to be a perfect man; both are imperfect. Their business in life is to help each other to move more nearly towards a state of perfection.

(John A. Widtsoe, an Apostle,
CR, October, 1947, pp. 152-153.)

An Insurance Against Divorce

New York legislators and feminists are promoting the idea of divorce insurance.

It would be used, according to news dispatches, "to ensure adequate child support in the event of divorce, but could also be used by childless divorced couples, and should the marriage be a lasting one, be converted to other uses."

There is no doubt about the increasing effect of divorce on the nation as the rate of separations continues to soar. And certainly there is no doubt about its adverse influence upon children in every case of separation.

But would not insurance encourage divorce and make it seem easier to bear, and therefore more attractive?

How much more important it would be to provide a type of insurance which would prevent divorce in the first place, rather than to serve as a palliative afterward?

And what is such insurance? The Lord gave it to us in the form of the Golden Rule: "All things whatsoever ye would that men should do to you, do ye even so to them."

And He gave it too, in modern revelation as He said: "Thou shalt love thy wife with all thy heart and shalt cleave unto her and none else." *(D&C 42:22)*

If couples would overcome their selfishness, and bring the gospel into their homes, there would be no need for divorce.

(Editorial, *CN,* February 3, 1973, p. 16.)

CHAPTER 20

DRESS STANDARDS
(See: Sexual Morality and Immorality)

Modesty Is A Quality Of Mind And Heart

From the beginning the Lord has directed his children to clothe their bodies. Modesty in dress is a quality of mind and heart, born of respect for oneself, one's fellowmen, and the Creator of us all. Modesty reflects an attitude of humility, decency, and propriety. Consistent with these principles and guided by the Holy Spirit, let parents, teachers, and youth consider the particulars of dress, grooming, and personal appearance, and with free agency accept responsibility and choose the right.

(PB, September, 1970.)

Maintain Modest Standards Which Will Not Embarrass Associates

The Church has not attempted to indicate just how long women's or girls' dresses should be nor whether they should wear pant suits or other types of clothing. We have always counseled our members to be modest in their dress, maintaining such standards in connection therewith as would not be embarrassing to themselves and to their relatives, friends and associates.

We have advised our people that when going to the temple they should not wear slacks or mini-skirts, or otherwise dress immodestly. We have not, however, felt it wise or necessary to give instructions on this subject relative to attendance at our Church meetings, although we do feel that on such occasions they should have in mind that they are in the house of the Lord and should conduct themselves accordingly.

Joseph Fielding Smith, Harold B. Lee, N. Eldon Tanner
The First Presidency
(CL, April 12, 1971.)

Dress Should Avoid Symbolizing Rebellion
Against Modesty

The following are the newly announced grooming standards at Church schools, as approved by the General Authorities. They

would seem to have significance for youth Churchwide, regardless
of whether you attend a Church school or not.

Within Church colleges and schools, honor has traditionally been
understood as voluntarily living in accordance with the principles and
standards of The Church of Jesus Christ of Latter-day Saints. This is the
code and rule of expectation for all students in the Church Educational
System.

Acceptance of admission at any Church college or school, therefore, is a voluntary commitment to uphold Church principles and
standards, whether on or off campus, during all periods of enrollment.

Evolving directly and immediately from this commitment is the
responsibility for each student to familiarize himself beforehand concerning the principles and standards to which he will be committing
himself.

Grooming should be in keeping with these guidelines, emphasizing
cleanliness and avoidance of dress or manner which calls attention to
itself and symbolizes either rebellion or nonconformity to the values of
modesty, humility, decency and propriety.

Students at Brigham Young University, Church College of Hawaii,
Ricks College, and LDS Business College are expected to support and
abide by the following standards of dress and appearance. Continuing
registration constitutes an affirmative consent to abide thereby.

GENERAL

The attire and grooming of both men and women should always
be neat and clean.

Shoes are to be worn in public campus areas.

Shorts are acceptable wear only in the living and athletic areas.

So-called 'grubby attire' may be worn only in the immediate living
areas of residence halls and at informal outdoor activities, but not in
dining areas.

Acceptable attire will be designated for each studentbody dance.

MEN

Slacks, polished cottons, or Levi's with sweaters, sport shirts,
ties, sport coats, and blazers all are acceptable men's wear for attendance
at classes.

Beards are not acceptable. Mustaches are not encouraged, but if
worn should be trimmed above the corners of the mouth. Long or
bushy sideburns are not acceptable. Hair must be styled so as not to
cover the ears and must be above the collar in the back.

WOMEN

Dresses, sweaters, blouses with skirts, culottes, slacks or modest
pant suits, not to include Levi's, are the only acceptable women's wear
for attendance at classes.

Women's hemlines (dresses, skirts, culottes) are to be of modest
length.

Formal wear may be either a long or short formal. It does not
include low-cut necklines or strapless gowns.

(*NE*, September, 1971, p. 18.)

Modesty Reflects An Attitude Of Humility, Decency, And Propriety

Dear Valarie,

This will acknowledge your very sweet letter. It shows me that you want to do what is right.

You ask about the proper dress for school. The Church has taken the position that whether youth are at school, attending a sacrament or other Church meeting, at a dance or an athletic or sports-camp activity, at home or away, Church standards require young men and women to be appropriately dressed. Modesty is a protection for the youth of the Church and is one of the Lord's ways to help them live clean, wholesome lives.

Girls should try always to enhance their natural beauty and femininity. They should dress appropriately for any occasion. It would seem proper to wear slacks or pants when playing kickball or the other outdoor games that you mention.

Modesty in dress is a quality of mind and heart, born of respect for oneself, one's fellowmen, and the Creator of us all. Modesty reflects an attitude of humility, decency, and propriety. Consistent with these principles and guided by the Holy Spirit, let parents, teachers, and youth discuss the particulars of dress, grooming, and personal appearance, and with free agency accept responsibility and choose the right. You should honor your parents, who love you dearly, and follow their advice or instruction after discussing your problems with them.

May the Lord bless you and give you the desire and strength to do right always. By doing this you will be happy, loved, and respected.

(*N. Eldon Tanner*, Second Counselor in the First Presidency,
F, June, 1971, p. 3.)

Men And Women Should Preserve Their God-Given Identity

The woman who is too scantily dressed, or immodestly dressed, ofttimes is the portrayal of one who is thus trying to draw the attention of the opposite sex when her natural adornments do not, in her opinion, suffice. Heaven help any woman so minded for drawing such attention. For a woman to adopt the mode of a man's dress, it is said, is to encourage the wave of sexual perversion, when men adopt women's tendencies and women become mannish in their desires.

If a woman will preserve and properly maintain her God-given identity, she can captivate and hold the true love of her husband and the admiration of those who admire natural, pure, lovely womanhood.

(*Harold B. Lee*, First Counselor in the First Presidency, *E*, February, 1972, p. 48.)

Women's Modesty And Skirt Styles

Many Latter-day Saint women have hesitated to respond to the appeal of the Church for modesty, and have yielded rather to the increasing pressure of fashion, particularly with regard to the length of their skirts.

But now the decrees of Dame Fashion are changing, and she gives the women of the world a wide choice. As for skirts, they may be mini, or maxi, or midi. It is now up to the women themselves. The choice has been returned to them!

And since this is so, have we not now reached the time when Latter-day Saint women may return to modesty and accept the styles that are now available? If the world which controls the thinking (?) in these matters—is willing that Mormon girls and women now wear skirts of modest length, should we not return to the teachings of our religion and protect our virtue with modesty.

The peculiar thing about the midi styles is that very few women want them. One young woman, on being told that hem lines were coming down, simply replied: "Not mine."

And why? Why this unwillingness to properly cover one's person? Why this fervid desire to expose the human anatomy?

The psychology of the times is in the direction of exposure. The reason for this is that such exposure is but a part of a world movement to destroy moral standards.

The sex revolution has taken over in every nation. And what has it thrust upon us. Let us list a few of its by-products:

The new morality, which is destruction of virtue in the philosophy that "anything goes," and the social disease which always follow in its wake.

Infidelity, which is being winked at now everywhere.

Free abortion, such as provided by the new law recently passed in the New York Legislature.

Short skirts. Tight skirts and tight pants regardless of the avoirdupois.

Plunging necklines.

Pornography of every description.

Filthy movies.

Filthy jokes, so-called.

Filthy stage plays, so corrupt that even the sophisticated newspaper critics begin to cringe.

And worst of all, a disregard for religion and an acceptance of the teaching that there is no God.

Can our Latter-day Saint women deliberately choose to become a part of such a world revolution as that?

Now is the time when we can return—with style—to the modest dress that befits our religion.

Now is the time when women should stop embarrassing clean-minded men by flaunting their femininity before unwilling eyes. And now is the time for them to stop displaying themselves before the hungry eyes of perverts who live on such exhibitions.

Do young girls realize what temptations they place before their boyfriends when they expose themselves virtually up to the hips when they sit down; or at times, even when they walk?

The thinking of Latter-day Saints must be re-oriented, this time away from worldliness. Our religion should be so important to us that we should willingly avoid the temptations and decrees of modern fashion and entertainment, and of all similar factors which determine what is popular and what is not. The Gospel is more important than any fashion or any type of entertainment, and Latter-day Saints should so regard it.

We should take great pride in being different from the world—in God's way—and we should not be ashamed of the Gospel teachings, even those referring to modesty and virtue. What is there to be ashamed of? Goodness?

We talk in terms of testimony. Where is our testimony of the truth of Christ's sayings if we turn our backs upon them?

Did not the Savior tell us to eschew the world and have an eye single to Him and His glory?

Did He not tell us that we cannot serve two masters? Did He not instruct us to avoid being of the world even though we live in the world?

Let us remind ourselves that only those who are valiant in the testimony of Jesus will see celestial glory, and that the manner by which we maintain or lower our standards of decency and virtue will be weighed in the balance with us on judgment day.

(Editorial, *CN*, June 27, 1970, p. 16.)

CHAPTER 21

DRUGS
(See: Word of Wisdom)

The Church Opposes Drugs Or Substances Which Result In Addiction

[Comments on this subject were made by *Spencer W. Kimball*, President of the Church, in the April, 1974, General Conference, and can be found in the *Ensign*, May, 1974, p. 7.]

Eliminate From Your Lives All Kinds Of Drugs So Far As Is Possible

[Comments on this subject were made by *Spencer W. Kimball*, President of the Church, in the October, 1974, General Conference, and can be found in the *Ensign*, November, 1974, p. 6.]

The Slavery Of Drugs

[Comments on this subject were made by *Spencer W. Kimball*, acting President of the Council of the Twelve Apostles, in the *Church News*, March 6, 1971, p. 12.]

Drug Environment Dulls Moral Sense

"Man has two creators," says William George Jordan, "his God and himself. The first Creator furnishes him the raw materials of his life—the laws and conformity with which he can make that life what he will. The second creator—himself—has marvelous powers he rarely realizes. It is what a man makes of himself that counts."

We need not shut our eyes to the fact that too many of our young folk respond to the call of the physical, because it seems the easy and natural thing to do. Too many are vainly seeking short-cuts to happiness. It should always be kept in mind that that which is most worthwhile in life requires strenuous effort. When a man seeks something for nothing and shuns effort, he is in no position to resist temptation....

In their yearning for a good time, young people are often tempted to indulge in the things that appeal only to the baser side of humanity, five of the most common of which are: (1) vulgarity and obscenity; (2) drinking and the using of narcotics and now the vicious LSD drug, especially among the young; (3) unchastity; (4) disloyalty; and (5) irreverence.

It is right, indeed, essential, to the happiness of our young people that they meet in social parties, but it is an indication of low morals when for entertainment they must resort to physical stimulation and debasement....

Drinking, using narcotics, and lewd parties form an environment in which the moral sense becomes dulled, and unbridled passion holds sway. It then becomes easy to take the final step downward in moral disgrace.

(*David O. McKay*, President of the Church,
CR, April, 1967, p. 7.)

Drugs Defile Body And Spirit

The use of a habit-forming drug of any kind violates the spirit of the Word of Wisdom and defiles both body and spirit.
(*Marion G. Romney*, Second Counselor in the
First Presidency, CR-E, May, 1974, p. 82.)

Drug Approaches Are Of The Evil One

[Comments on this subject were made by *Marvin J. Ashton*, an Assistant to the Council of the Twelve Apostles, in the April, 1971, General Conference, and can be found either in the *Conference Report* of April, 1971, p. 12, or in the *Ensign*, June, 1971, pp. 30-31.]

Focus On The Cause Rather Than The Symptom

[Comments on this subject were made by *Marvin J. Ashton*, an Assistant to the Council of the Twelve Apostles, in the April, 1971, General Conference, and can be found either in the *Conference Report* of April, 1971, pp. 12-13, or in the *Ensign*, June, 1971, pp. 30-31.]

Replace Drugs With Stability In The Home

[Comments on this subject were made by *Marvin J. Ashton*, an Assistant to the Council of the Twelve Apostles, in the April,

1971, General Conference, and can be found either in the *Confer-ence Report* of April, 1971, pp. 12-13, or in the *Ensign*, June, 1971, pp. 30-31.]

Bad Habits Reduces One's Freedom To Slavery

Improper parental example in the home is a leading cause of the wandering of youth from the principles as taught in the gospel of Jesus Christ. The use of alcohol and tobacco in the home gives license to their children to do the same, and to indulge in other drugs and narcotics, which result too often in their leaving home and wandering as hitchhikers with packs on their backs, with no purpose, no particular destination, except away from the straight and narrow path of truth and righteousness. They are really no longer free, but while claiming that they are seeking freedom, they become slaves of their own bad habits, and it is most difficult for them to come out of the wilderness and back into the light and the love which they need so badly.

(*N. Eldon Tanner*, First Counselor in the
First Presidency, *CR-E*, November, 1974, p. 85.)

"Turn On" To Inspiration, Not Hallucinations

One of today's greatest "turner oners," as the youngsters put it, is the use of drugs. And what do they do, help you or hurt you?

They can send you insane! This they have done to thousands of young Americans.

In one state mental hospital admissions of individuals for emotional problems resulting from the use of drugs has gone up in a ratio of one to 47 in a two year period. Another large hospital reports that within a year there has been an increase of 400 per cent in the number of youngsters aged 18 to 20 admitted with serious mental problems resulting from the use of drugs.

Presumptions on the part of some young people, sometimes encouraged by certain ones who claim some medical knowledge, that marijuana is no more harmful than tobacco, are proving to be completely false.

Marijuana like tobacco is habit-forming, but it is also destructive of mental health, and can destroy the entire future of young people who indulge.

The more powerful drugs, beyond any question, are causing mental problems of such seriousness that some of the patients may never recover.

In one typical community, as reported by the Associated Press recently, where 3,000 babies are born annually, one in every five will require mental health service because of the stimulants taken by the mothers, and at least 240 of those 3,000 will become patients in mental hospitals. All because their mothers wanted something to "turn them on."

Is this the kind of "turning on" that Latter-day Saints want?

What is the principal objective of our lives, and how shall we plan for it? Is it a noble aim to drug one's self into a stupor, thus becoming irresponsible, weak, a prey to every predatory person?

Is a "trip" taken mentally by use of a drug so desirable that one would risk his sanity for the rest of his life to "enjoy" it? Is there anything desirable in hallucination anyway? Or is it the clear cool mind that assures success and true happiness?

And what can give us this clarity of mind?

Clean living. Good health. Spirituality, and freedom from stimulants of all kinds, including alcohol.

Inspiration from heaven is available to everyone of us under proper conditions. The constant guidance of the Holy Spirit is promised to us if we live as we know we should.

Which is to be preferred—divine inspiration or hallucinations?

Which encourages success in school or at work—inspiration or a drug-induced stupor?

Which will help to preserve chastity—divine guidance or addiction to demoralizing narcotics?

Which will give us proper standing in the world—a clear mind or a clouded one?

So what is it that really "turns us on?" Only one thing: The Spirit of God, which comes to all who sincerely live the Gospel, and every faithful believer in Christ is entitled to its ministrations.

(Editorial, *CN*, February 15, 1969, p. 16.)

CHAPTER 22

ECUMENICAL MOVEMENT

Concerning The "Ecumenical Movement"

There are those who speak of an ecumenical movement, where theoretically, it is supposed, all churches would be brought together into a universal organization. In essence it probably would contemplate that they would give up their basic principles and be united in a nebulous organization which would not necessarily be founded on the principles as have traditionally been the doctrines of the Church of Jesus Christ from the beginning.

When the revelations of the Lord are clearly understood, there is set forth the only basis of a united and universal church. It could not be accomplished as set forth by a man-made formula; it could only be accomplished when the fulness of the principles of the gospel of Jesus Christ are taught and practiced, as declared by the apostle Paul to the Ephesians, who said that the church is "built upon the foundation of the apostles and prophets, Jesus Christ himself being the chief corner stone." *(Eph. 2:20)*

(*Harold B. Lee*, President of the Church,
CR, April, 1973, p. 8.)

Councils Alone Will Not Bring Unity
Among Different Churches

[Comments on this subject were made by *Boyd K. Packer*, an Assistant to the Council of the Twelve Apostles, in the *Church News* edition of October 28, 1967, p. 16.]

Christianity Will Never Be Reunited As One Church
Through The Uninspired Wisdom Of Men

In many respects the Christian world has made great progress in overcoming its internal differences.

In a few instances some denominations have resolved the conflicts which in the first place separated them. Any approach toward true unity in Christ is progress.

How sad it is that divisions ever arose among the followers of Jesus. But they began even while He ministered in mortality. No one can read the sixth chapter of John and fail to regret the disaffection which came among His followers even that early in the ministry.

And then later Peter denied Him and Thomas doubted Him. Jairus accepted His healing blessing but there is no record that He ever joined the Church. And Nicodemas? Just where did he stand? It is certainly to his credit that he assisted in the Lord's burial.

Human nature continued to assert itself among the early Church members, even as it does among us. And so there were divisions in the Church—denominations to use modern terminology—some were Paul-ites, some were Cephas-ites, others were Appollos-ites and some called themselves after Christ. *(1 Corinthians 1:12-13)*

Already there had been such Jewish denominations as Pharisees Sadducees, Essenes, etc.

Because some hold self-expression above self-discipline, and independence above conformance, splinter groups developed and have continued to do so even until now. This in spite of the Savior's plea for oneness—"even as my Father and I are one," and in violation of Paul's declaration to the Corinthians that Christ is not divided.

He had told the Roman saints to be of one mind, a thing he also taught both the Ephesians and the Corinthians.

He knew there was only one faith or religion or creed—one true Gospel. And he taught there was but one baptism.

How then can Christians preach many creeds and several kinds of baptism—and some no baptism at all?

If Christ is not divided, are not such divisions as these evidence of a denial of His principles—an actual departure from Christ?

Most Christians now begin to see the facts and are working toward erasing their differences.

But as they give and take—as they compromise point after point to reach harmony between the contesting parties, what pains are they taking to make sure that their decisions are acceptable to Christ?

And how can they tell what is acceptable to Him? They understand the Bible so differently that little if anything can be settled by an appeal to the scripture. And they reject the idea of modern revelation, so they cannot look to that source to settle their differences. Then what can they—what will they—do?

Only one thing—they will remain divided? It is true that some will come to terms, as a few have done already, but Christianity will never be reunited as one church through the uninspired wisdom of men.

Mankind today is so confused over what Christianity is, that nothing short of a rejection of all man-made creeds and the acceptance of a new revelation from God, can ever achieve Christian unity.

God must provide a new revelation of himself—a new definition of His Gospel—to end the confusion.

And Christians must become willing to humble themselves and accept this new dispensation of the Gospel, or they cannot be saved.

The Lord in our day has provided this new revelation. He has raised up a new prophet in the person of Joseph Smith, and through him has sent word of a new Christian era to all free peoples.

What will they do with it?

Will tradition prove to be stronger than new revelation? And will mankind turn away from a new dispensation of truth in our day, preferring the "traditions of the elders and the scribes?"

This they did nearly 2,000 years ago! Are we of today any wiser than they?

(Editorial, *CN*, October 18, 1969, p. 16.)

CHAPTER 23

EDUCATION
*(See: Children: Needs, Responsibilities, and Discipline;
Evolution; Husbands and Fathers; Sex Education;
Womenhood and Motherhood)*

The Church Encourages Educational Or Vocational Training

The Church has long encouraged its members, and especially its youth, either to obtain a college education or to become well trained in some vocation in a trade school. In our fast growing industrial society, this becomes almost a necessity, for unless our young people are well educated, or well trained, they will not be able to obtain proper jobs or positions in the future. The jobs that require no education or training are decreasing from year to year and soon will be practically non-existent.

We therefore strongly suggest that you urge all young people under your supervision to engage in formal study of some kind beyond high school. Of equal importance is the selection of an educational program that takes into account each individual's interests, talents, and goals....

> *David O. McKay, Hugh B. Brown, N. Eldon Tanner,*
> *Joseph Fielding Smith,* The First Presidency
> (*CL*, April 1, 1966.)

Seek Truth Wherever It Can Be Found

The very purpose of the Church organization is to promulgate Truth among men. Members of the Church are admonished to acquire learning by study, by faith and prayer, and to seek after everything that is virtuous, lovely or of good report, or praiseworthy. In this seeking after Truth, they are not confined to narrow limits of dogma, or creed, but are free to launch into the realm of the infinite for they know that "truth is truth wherever it is found, whether on Christian or on heathen ground."

Indeed, one of the fundamental teachings of the Church is that salvation itself depends upon knowledge, for it is impossible for a man to be saved in ignorance.

...If a person gains more knowledge and intelligence in this life through his diligence and obedience than another, he will have so much the advantage in the world to come. *(D&C 130:19)*

But gaining knowledge is one thing, and applying it is another. Wisdom is the right application of knowledge to the development of a noble and Godlike character. A man may possess a profound knowledge of history and of mathematics; he may be an authority in physiology, biology, or astronomy. He may know all about whatever has been discovered pertaining to general and natural science, but if he has not, with this knowledge, that nobility of soul which prompts him to deal justly with his fellow men, to practice virtue and honesty in personal life, he is not a truly educated man.

Character is the aim of true education; and science, history, and literature are but means used to accomplish this desired end. Character is not the result of chance, but of continuous right thinking and right acting. True education seeks to make men and women not only good mathematicians, proficient linguists, profound scientists, or brilliant literary lights, but also, honest men, with virtue, temperance, and brotherly love. It seeks to make men and women who prize truth, justice, wisdom, benevolence, and self-control as the choicest acquisitions of a successful life.

It is regrettable that modern education so little emphasizes these fundamental elements of true character. The principal aim of many of our schools and colleges seems to be to give the students purely intellectual attainment and means of gaining a livelihood, and to give but passing attention to the nobler and more necessary development along moral lines. This is particularly noticeable along the lines of self-control. Notwithstanding the study of hygiene in our public schools and the hundreds of books written in condemnation, for example, of the use of tobacco and alcoholic beverages, too many of our school children are ignorantly sapping their intellectual strength and blunting their moral sensibilities by the promiscuous use of the cigaret and other forms of tobacco. The small percentage of those who reach college add to the tobacco and drinking habit sexual indulgence, which leaves them stranded as moral wrecks when they are scarcely launched on their life's journey.

Boys and girls of the present generation, unfortunately, begin early to date steadily. They become too free with one another. Being young, they lack perspective and the ability to distinguish between momentary thrills and long-range happiness; and thus, because they are lacking in the virtue of self-control, the happiness of a lifetime is sometimes sacrificed for pleasure which, "like poppies spread, you seize the flower, its bloom is shed."[1] The man who wrote that line knew how momentary those pleasures are.

What, then, is true education? It is awakening a love for truth, a just sense of duty, opening the eyes of the soul to the great purpose and end of life. It is not teaching the individual to love the good for personal sake; it is to teach him to love the good for the sake of the good itself; to be virtuous in action because he is so in heart; to love and serve God supremely, not from fear, but from delight in His perfect character.

Upon the teacher rests much of the responsibility of lifting society to this high level. Ralph Waldo Emerson, reputedly the wisest American, said, "Character is higher than intellect. A great soul will be fit to live as well as to think."

Students, choose the paramount purpose of true education, and let it be yours as you seek your education! Teachers, yours is the responsibility to teach not only by precept, but by example!

(*David O. McKay*, President of the Church,
I, August, 1961, pp. 253-254.)

Studies Should Provide Spiritual Growth

Courses required of all students in our public schools should include the important areas of study that directly or indirectly provide the student with opportunities for spiritual growth and religious inspiration. From such study it is reasonable to expect that our students will better understand how vital has been the role of religion at critical moments in history; how important spiritual insights in religious faith can be in the lives of men and women; how closely related are human greatness and such qualities as honesty, integrity, humility, generosity, and compassion.

We may expect in our students more idealism and less cynicism, more wholesome courage and faith in the future, and less pessimism and foreboding fear. We may hope for increased tolerance of racial and religious differences, increased respect for those of opposite political views or for those of lower social and economic levels; increased awareness of the basic and inviolable dignity of the individual man or woman. We may contribute to the development

---

[1] From Robert Burns' "Tam O' Shanter."

of a more sensitive social conscience—a greater sense of responsibility for the less fortunate in our society. We may even, perhaps, without knowing it, bring a boy or girl closer to God.

(*David O. McKay*, President of the Church,
IE, June, 1968, p. 33.)

The Real Purpose Of School Is To Develop Character

There are four fundamental institutions that contribute to our success and happiness: first, the home; second, the Church; third, the school; fourth, the government.

In the home we give our children their physical life, but we should also give them their spiritual enlightenment. That home training should be supplemented by the Church; and besides that supplementary teaching, the Church should instill faith in the hearts of the children who come from those homes. That is the duty of the Church. That is why you built these edifices—the only reason. In blessing those children, you give glory to God. That is the only way you can honor him. Oh, I know you can kneel down and, in words, praise the Lord, but His work and His glory is to bring to pass the immortality and eternal life of man. This Church is built to help Him.

The third factor is the school, the duty of which is to instill patriotism and loyalty to the government and society. I think the real purpose of the school is to develop character! Educators say it is to teach the three "R's," science, social science, etc. That is why schools are maintained, but the main purpose (and I wish it were instilled in the heart of every teacher throughout this great country), is to develop character, loyalty to God, to the government, loyalty to the home, and loyalty to the individual himself. "Character is higher than intellect; a great soul will be fit to live, as well as to think."

Fourth is the government, the duty of which is to protect these other three in the fulfillment of their mission, not to dictate, but to protect and guide; and ... to give freedom to these other institutions and to the individual.

(*David O. McKay*, President of the Church,
CN, August 24, 1963, p. 13.)

Obtain The Understanding Which Flows From God

I am pleased to know that President Young made arrangements before his death for the endowment of a college in this neighborhood [Logan], and the brethren acting as trustees in the matter are feeling interested, and are taking steps for the accomplishment of that object. And that object is, as I understand it, to afford our own children greater facilities to become learned, and that they also have the privilege to learn trades, and agriculture, and horticulture, and become progressive, intellectual and informed in regard to all these things, and that they may comprehend the earth on which we stand, the materials of which it is composed, and the elements with which we are surrounded. And then, by having faith in God, we might stand as far above the nations in regard to the arts and sciences, politics, and every species of intelligence, as we now do in regard to religious matters. This is what we are aiming at; and if there is anything good and praiseworthy in morals, religion, science, or anything calculated to exalt and ennoble man, we are after it. But with all our getting, we want to get understanding, and that understanding which flows from God.

(*John Taylor*, President of the Council of the Twelve Apostles and acting President of the Church, *JD*, 1878, 20:48.)

Elimination Of Prayer From The Public Schools By The Supreme Court Is A Misinterpretation Of The First Amendment

For a hundred years boys and girls born in America, and they who later obtained citizenship in this great country, have felt that they are "endowed by their Creator, with certain Unalienable Rights, that among these are Life, Liberty and the pursuit of Happiness," and that these rights are endowed by our Creator.

Recent rulings of the Supreme Court would have all reference to a Creator eliminated from our public schools and public offices.

It is a sad day when the Supreme Court of the United States would discourage all reference in our schools to the influence of the phrase "divine providence" as used by our founders of the Declaration of Independence.

Evidently the Supreme Court misinterprets the true meaning of the First Amendment, and are now leading a Christian nation down the road to atheism.

(*David O. McKay*, President of the Church, *CN*, June 22, 1963, p. 2. For further views on the above see: *David O. McKay, RSM*, 1962, 49:877-878.)

Youth Should Avoid Intemperate Conduct Against Law And Order On School Campuses

We believe it is essential that our young people gain sufficient education to care for themselves in this highly specialized age, and also to serve their fellowmen, and we have in the past and shall continue in the future to support education at all levels.

We have little sympathy, however, with the spirit of disruption and dissidence that is sometimes found on the campuses of the land. We urge our youth to avoid these displays of intemperate conduct and rather to be found on the side of law and order and circumspect action.

It is our hope and prayer that in all nations men may live in peace, respecting each other's beliefs and forms of worship, and that the spirit of unity and brotherhood may abound on every side.

We know there are many people who seek to live upright lives and who desire to maintain substantially the same standards to which we adhere. We welcome their encouragement and hope they will feel to accept the hand of Christian fellowship from us, as all of us seek those great goals so basic to true worship and unity.

(*Joseph Fielding Smith*, President of the Church, *CR*, April, 1970, p. 5.)

Profanity Is The Effort Of A feeble Brain Trying To Express Itself

[Comments on this subject were made by *Spencer W. Kimball*, President of the Church, in the October, 1974, General Conference, and can be found in the *Ensign*, November, 1974, p. 7.]

CHAPTER 24

ENERGY CONSERVATION

What To Do To Conserve Energy

In this holiday season we urge members of the Church everywhere to contemplate the words of the Savior:

> Inasmuch as ye have done it unto the least of these my brethren, ye have done it unto me. *(Matthew 25:40)*

There continues to be much hungering and suffering generally in the world. In the months ahead there could be more.

We therefore suggest that you be even more mindful of the needy in your area as well as throughout the world. Specifically we suggest that you and your family observe more diligently these teachings of the Church: ...

Conserve energy. We reaffirm our suggestion to Church members a year ago to join car pools, observe prescribed speed limits, lower thermostats where feasible, and eliminate unnecessary consumption of electricity or fuel....

These are times to remember, perhaps more than ever before, that inner strength, happiness, and peace come through keeping the commandments of Him whom we honor at Christmas time.

Spencer W. Kimball, N. Eldon Tanner, Marion G. Romney
The First Presidency
(*CL*, December 16, 1974.)

CHAPTER 25

ENVIRONMENTAL CLEANLINESS

Church Members Urged To Let Their Light
Shine Through Cleanliness And Beauty

We earnestly call upon members of the Church everywhere to clean up and beautify their homes, surroundings, farms, and places of business.

Our homes and our buildings are showcases of what we believe. They should be attractive and give every indication of cleanliness, orderliness, and self-esteem.

'Let all things be done in order,' the Lord has counseled us. *(D&C 58:55)* His words spoken in the Sermon on the Mount have important meaning today:

> Let your light so shine before men, that they may see your good works, and glorify your Father which is in heaven. *(Matt. 5:16)*

We suggest that priesthood quorums, Young Adult, and other Church groups organize themselves to assist the elderly, the fatherless, and the needy in improving the appearance of their homes and surroundings and in properly maintaining them.

Parents and Sunday School and Primary teachers are asked to instruct class members in orderliness, in respecting buildings and property generally, in taking care of their belongings, and in keeping them in their proper places.

We urge that this improvement begin immediately and that procedures be established for maintaining our homes, buildings, and surroundings so that they always bespeak the high standards of the Church which we embrace.

Spencer W. Kimball, N. Eldon Tanner, Marion G. Romney
The First Presidency
(E, November, 1974, p. 125.)

Keep Your Property In A Beautiful State Of Appearance

[Comments on this subject were made by *Spencer W. Kimball*, President of the Church, in the October, 1974, General Conference: *Ensign*, November, 1974, p. 4, and in the April, 1975, General Conference: *Ensign*, May, 1975, p. 5.]

CHAPTER 26

EQUAL RIGHTS AMENDMENT

The "Equal Rights Amendment" Is Dangerous

On April 28, 1842, the Prophet Joseph Smith, following organization of the Relief Society, declared: "I now turn the key in your (women's) behalf in the name of the Lord ... And this society shall rejoice, and knowledge and intelligence shall flow down (upon women) from this time henceforth."

With this declaration, when women's organizations were almost nonexistent, the Prophet placed the Church in the fore-front of those who have taught the dignified and exalted place of women. To this end Church leaders from those early times have advocated programs to enhance the status of women as daughters of God. They have also actively given encouragement and support to legislative measures designed to safeguard the welfare of women, the home and the family.

Over a period of many decades, women have been accorded special protection and the status properly due them. More recently, these include equality of opportunity in political, civil and economic spheres.

But now there are many who feel that the way to take care of inequities that may have existed in the past, or may presently exist, is to ratify the Equal Rights Amendment to the Constitution. Legislators in a number of states will be faced with decisions on this question in the next few weeks.

Both Mrs. Belle S. Spafford, recently retired president of the nearly one-million-member, world-wide Relief Society of the Church, and her successor, Mrs. Barbara B. Smith, have spoken forthrightly on this question, the former in a widely published interview with George W. Cornell, religion editor of the Associated Press; the latter in a recent talk before the University of Utah Institute of Religion. Among their statements were these:

"It appears that the Equal Rights Amendment is not only imperfect, but dangerous."

"The blanket approach of the Equal Rights Amendment is a confused step backward in time, instead of a clear stride into the future."

The Equal Rights Amendment is not the way. It ... will not fulfill their hopes, but rather would work to the disadvantage of both women and men.

It "is so broad that it is inadequate, inflexible, and vague; so all-encompassing that it is nondefinitive."

Legislative hearings and debate will doubtless produce millions of words uttered on both sides with much emotion. But all of this will not change the fact that men and women are different, made so by a Divine Creator. Each has his or her role. One is incomplete without the other.

Out of innate wisdom and the experience of centuries, law-makers have enacted measures for the benefit and protection of each of the sexes, but more particularly of women. In this country they have already provided statutory equality of opportunity in political, civil and economic affairs. If this has not always been extended it has usually been the result of no enforcement rather than absence of law.

The writer of the lead story in the January 1975 issue of the prestigious "Nation's Business" summarizes a thorough presentation of the case with these words concerning the Equal Rights Amendment:

"The amendment is unnecessary.

"The amendment is uncertain.

"The amendment is undesirable."

He concludes by saying, "It seems to me highly doubtful that the people desire any such thing as 'unisex' in their law. But if five more states ratify the pending amendment, that is what the people will get."

(Editorial, *CN*, January 11, 1975, p. 16.)

CHAPTER 27

EVOLUTION

The Origin Of Man

Inquiries arise from time to time respecting the attitude of the Church of Jesus Christ of Latter-day Saints upon questions which, though not vital from a doctrinal standpoint, are closely connected with the fundamental principles of salvation. The latest inquiry of this kind that has reached us is in relation to the origin of man. It is believed that a statement of the position held by the Church upon this important subject will be timely and productive of good.

In presenting the statement that follows we are not conscious of putting forth anything essentially new; neither is it our desire so to do. Truth is what we wish to present, and truth--eternal truth—is fundamentally old. A restatement of the original attitude of the Church relative to this matter is all that will be attempted here. To tell the truth as God has revealed it, and commend it to the acceptance of those who need to conform their opinions thereto, is the sole purpose of this presentation.

"God created man in his own image, in the image of God created he him; male and female created he them." In these plain and pointed words the inspired author of the book of Genesis made known to the world the truth concerning the origin of the human family. Moses, the prophet-historian, "learned," as we are told, "in all the wisdom of the Egyptians," when making this important announcement, was not voicing a mere opinion, a theory derived from his researches into the occult lore of that ancient people. He was speaking as the mouthpiece of God, and his solemn declaration was for all time and for all people. No subsequent revelator of the truth has contradicted the great leader and law-giver of Israel. All who have since spoken by divine authority upon this theme have confirmed his simple and sublime proclamation. Nor could it be otherwise. Truth has but one source, and all revelations from heaven are harmonious with each other. The omnipotent Creator, the maker of heaven and earth—had shown Moses everything pertaining to this planet, including the facts relating to man's origin, and the authoritative pronouncement of that mighty prophet and seer to the house of Israel, and through Israel to the whole world, is couched in the simple clause:

> God created man in his own image. *(Genesis 1:27; Pearl of Great Price—Book of Moses, 1:27-41)*

The creation was two-fold—firstly spiritual, secondly temporal. This truth, also, Moses plainly taught—much more plainly than it has come down to us in the imperfect translations of the Bible that are now in use. Therein the fact of a spiritual creation, ante-dating the temporal creation, is strongly implied, but the proof of it is not so clear and conclusive as in other records held by the Latter-day Saints to be of equal authority with the Jewish scriptures. The partial obscurity of the latter upon the point in question is owing, no doubt, to the loss of those "plain and precious" parts of sacred writ, which, as the Book of Mormon informs us, have been taken away from the Bible during its passage down the centuries *(I Nephi 13:24-29)*. Some of these missing parts the Prophet Joseph Smith undertook to restore when he revised those scriptures by the spirit of revelation, the result being that more complete account of the creation which is found in the book of Moses, previously cited. Note the following passages:

> And now, behold I say unto you, that these are the generations of the heaven and the earth, when they were created in the day that I, the Lord God, made the heaven and the earth,
>
> And every plant of the field before it was in the earth, and every herb of the field before it grew.
>
> For I, the Lord God, created all things of which I have spoken, spiritually, before they were naturally upon the face of the earth. For I, the Lord God, had not caused it to rain upon the face of the earth.
>
> And I, the Lord God, had created all the children of men, and not yet a man to till the ground; for in heaven created I them, and there was not yet flesh upon the earth, neither in the water, neither in the air.
>
> But I, the Lord God, spake, and there went up a mist from the earth, and watered the whole face of the ground.
>
> And I, the Lord God, formed man from the dust of the ground, and breathed into his nostrils the breath of life; and man became a living soul, the first flesh upon the earth, the first man also.
>
> Nevertheless, all things were before created, but spiritually were they created and made, according to my word *(Pearl of Great Price—Book of Moses, 3:4-7. See also chapters 1 and 2, and compare with Genesis 1 and 2)*.

These two points being established, namely, the creation of man in the image of God, and the two-fold character of the creation, let us now inquire: What was the form of man, in the spirit and in the body, as originally created? In a general way the answer is given in the words chosen as the test of this treatise. "God created man in his own image." It is more explicitly rendered in the Book of Mormon thus: "All men were created in the beginning after mine own image" *(Ether, 3:15)*. It is the Father who is speaking. If, therefore, we can ascertain the form of the "Father of spirits," "The God of the spirits of all flesh," we shall be able to discover the form of the original man.

Jesus Christ, the Son of God, is "the express image" of His Father's person *(Hebrews 1:3)*. He walked the earth as a human being, as a perfect man, and said, in answer to a question put to Him: "He that hath seen me hath seen the Father" *(John 14:9)*. This alone ought to solve the problem to the satisfaction of every thoughtful, reverent mind. The conclusion is irresistible, that if the Son of God be the express image (that is, likeness) of His Father's person, then His Father is in the form of man; for that was the form of the Son of God, not only during His mortal life, but before His mortal birth, and after His resurrection. It was in this form that the Father and the Son, as two personages, appeared to Joseph Smith, when, as a boy of fourteen years, he received his first vision. Then if God made man—the first man—in His own image and likeness, he must have made him like unto Christ, and consequently like unto men of Christ's time and of the present day. That man was made in the image of Christ, is positively stated in the Book of Moses:

> And I, God, said unto mine Only Begotten, which was with me from the beginning, Let us make man in our image, after our likeness; and it was so. * * * * And I, God, created man in mine own image, in the image of mine Only Begotten created I him, male and female created I them" *(2:26, 27)*.

The Father of Jesus is our Father also. Jesus Himself taught this truth, when He instructed His disciples how to pray: "Our Father which art in heaven," etc. Jesus, however, is the firstborn among all the sons of God—the first begotten in the spirit, and the only begotten in the flesh. He is our elder brother, and we, like Him, are in the image of God. All men and women are in the similitude of the universal Father and Mother, and are literally the sons and daughters of Deity.

"God created man in His own image." This is just as true of the spirit as it is of the body, which is only the clothing of the spirit, its complement; the two together constituting the soul. The

spirit of man is in the form of man, and the spirits of all creatures
are in the likeness of their bodies. This was plainly taught by the
Prophet Joseph Smith *(D&C 77:2)*.

Here is further evidence of the fact. More than seven hundred
years before Moses was shown the things pertaining to this earth,
another great prophet, known to us as the brother of Jared, was
similarly favored by the Lord. He was even permitted to behold the
spirit-body of the foreordained Savior, prior to His incarnation; and
so like the body of a man was His spirit in form and appearance,
that the prophet thought he was gazing upon a being of flesh and
blood. He first saw the finger and then the entire body of the
Lord—all in the spirit. The Book of Mormon says of this wonderful
manifestation:

> And it came to pass that when the brother of Jared had said these
> words, behold, the Lord stretched forth His hand and touched the
> stones one by one with His finger; and the veil was taken from off the
> eyes of the brother of Jared, and he saw the finger of the Lord; and it
> was as the finger of a man, like unto flesh and blood; and the brother of
> Jared fell down before the Lord, for he was struck with fear.
>
> And the Lord saw that the brother of Jared had fallen to the
> earth; and the Lord said unto him, Arise, why hast thou fallen?
>
> And he saith unto the Lord, I saw the finger of the Lord, and
> feared lest he should smite me, for I knew not that the Lord had flesh
> and blood.
>
> And the Lord said unto him, Because of thy faith thou hast seen
> that I shall take upon me flesh and blood; and never has man come
> before me with such exceeding faith as thou hast; for were it not so, ye
> could not have seen my finger. Sawest thou more than this?
>
> And he answered, Nay, Lord, show thyself unto me.
>
> And the Lord said unto him, Believest thou the words which I
> shall speak?
>
> And he answered, Yea, Lord, I know that thou speakest the
> truth, for thou art a God of truth and canst not lie.
>
> And when he had said these words, behold, the Lord showed
> himself unto him, and said, Because thou knowest these things ye are
> redeemed from the fall; therefore ye are brought back into my presence;
> therefore I show myself unto you.
>
> Behold, I am He who was prepared from the foundation of the
> world to redeem my people. Behold, I am Jesus Christ, I am the Father
> and the Son. In me shall all mankind have light, and that eternally, even
> they who shall believe on my name; and they shall become my sons and
> my daughters.
>
> And never have I shewed myself unto man whom I have created,
> for never hath man believed in me as thou hast. Seest thou that ye are
> created after mine own image? Yea, even all men were created in the
> beginning after mine own image.

> Behold, this body, which ye now behold, is the body of my
> spirit, and man have I created after the body of my spirit; and even as I
> appear unto thee to be in the spirit, will I appear unto my people in the
> flesh *(Ether, 3:6-16)*.

What more is needed to convince us that man, both in spirit and in body, is the image and likeness of God, and that God Himself is in the form of man?

When the divine Being whose spirit-body the brother of Jared beheld, took upon Him flesh and blood, He appeared as a man, having "body, parts and passions," like other men, though vastly superior to all others, because He was God, even the Son of God, the Word made flesh: in Him "dwelt the fulness of the Godhead bodily." And why should He not appear as a man? That was the form of His spirit, and it must needs have an appropriate covering, a suitable tabernacle. He came into the world as He had promised to come *(III Nephi, 1:13)*, taking an infant tabernacle, and developing it gradually to the fulness of His spirit stature. He came as man had been coming for ages, and as man has continued to come ever since. Jesus, however, as shown, was the only begotten of God in the flesh.

Adam, our great progenitor, "the first man," was, like Christ, a pre-existent spirit, and like Christ he took upon him an appropriate body, the body of a man, and so became a "living soul." The doctrine of the pre-existence,—revealed so plainly, particularly in latter days, pours a wonderful flood of light upon the otherwise mysterious problem of man's origin. It shows that man, as a spirit, was begotten and born of heavenly parents, and reared to maturity in the eternal mansions of the Father, prior to coming upon the earth in a temporal body to undergo an experience in mortality. It teaches that all men existed in the spirit before any man existed in the flesh, and that all who have inhabited the earth since Adam have taken bodies and become souls in like manner.

It is held by some that Adam was not the first man upon this earth, and that the original human being was a development from lower orders of the animal creation. These, however, are the theories of men. The word of the Lord declares that Adam was "the first man of all men" *(Moses 1:34)*, and we are therefore in duty bound to regard him as the primal parent of our race. It was shown to the brother of Jared that all men were created in the beginning after the image of God; and whether we take this to mean the spirit or the body, or both, it commits us to the same conclusion: Man began life as a human being, in the likeness of our heavenly Father.

True it is that the body of man enters upon its career as a tiny germ or embryo, which becomes an infant, quickened at a certain stage by the spirit whose tabernacle it is, and the child, after being born, develops into a man. There is nothing in this, however, to indicate that the original man, the first of our race, began life as anything less than a man, or less than the human germ or embryo that becomes a man.

Man, by searching, cannot find out God. Never, unaided, will he discover the truth about the beginning of human life. The Lord must reveal Himself, or remain unrevealed; and the same is true of the facts relating to the origin of Adam's race—God alone can reveal them. Some of these facts, however, are already known, and what has been made known it is our duty to receive and retain.

The Church of Jesus Christ of Latter-day Saints, basing its belief on divine revelation, ancient and modern, proclaims man to be the direct and lineal offspring of Deity. God Himself is an exalted man, perfected, enthroned, and supreme. By His almighty power He organized the earth, and all that it contains, from spirit and element, which exist co-eternally with Himself. He formed every plant that grows, and every animal that breathes, each after its own kind, spiritually and temporally—"that which is spiritual being in the likeness of that which is temporal, and that which is temporal in the likeness of that which is spiritual." He made the tadpole and the ape, the lion and the elephant; but He did not make them in His own image, nor endow them with Godlike reason and intelligence. Nevertheless, the whole animal creation will be perfected and perpetuated in the Hereafter, each class in its "distinct order or sphere," and will enjoy "eternal felicity." That fact has been made plain in this dispensation (D&C 77:3).

Man is the child of God, formed in the divine image and endowed with divine attributes, and even as the infant son of an earthly father and mother is capable in due time of becoming a man, so the undeveloped offspring of celestial parentage is capable, by experience through ages and aeons, of evolving into a God.

Joseph F. Smith, John R. Winder, Anthon H. Lund,
The First Presidency
(IE, November, 1909, pp. 75-81.)

Theory Of Evolution Offers Perplexing Problems

Youth need religion to comply properly with the purposes of creation. There is a purposeful design permeating all nature, the crowning event of which is man. Here, on this thought, science again leads the student up to a certain point, and sometimes leaves him with his soul unanchored. For example, evolution's theory of the creation of the world offers many perplexing problems to the inquiring mind. Inevitably, a teacher who denies divine agency in creation, who insists that there is no intelligent purpose in it, undoubtedly impresses the student with the thought that all may be chance.

I say that no youth should be left without a counterbalancing thought. Even the skeptical teacher should be fair enough to say that Charles Darwin himself, when he faced the great questions of eventual annihilation, if creation is dominated only by chance, wrote: "It is an intolerable thought that man and all other sentient things are doomed to complete annihilation, after such long-continued, slow progress."

(David O. McKay, President of the Church,
IE, June, 1968, p. 32.)

Concerning The Biblical Creation Story

In these respects we differ from the Christian world, for our religion will not clash with or contradict the facts of science in any particular. You may take geology, for instance, and it is a true science; not that I would say for a moment that all the conclusions and deductions of its professors are true, but its leading principles are; they are facts—they are eternal; and to assert that the Lord made this earth out of nothing is preposterous and impossible. God never made something out of nothing; it is not in the economy or law by which the worlds were, are, or will exist. There is an eternity before us, and it is full of matter; and if we but understand enough of the Lord and his ways, we would say that he took of this matter and organized this earth from it. How long it has been organized it is not for me to say, and I do not care anything about it. As for the Bible account of the creation we may say that the Lord gave it to Moses, or rather Moses obtained the history and traditions of the fathers, and from these picked out what he considered necessary, and that account has been handed down from age to age, and we have got it, no matter whether it is correct or not, and whether the Lord found the earth empty and void, whether he made it out of nothing or out of the 'rude elements;' or whether he made it in six days or in as many millions of years, is and will remain a matter of speculation in the minds of men unless he gives revelation on the subject. If we understood the process of creation there would be no mystery about it, it would be all reasonable and plain, for there is no mystery except to the ignorant.

(*Brigham Young*, President of the Church,
JD, 1871, 14:116.)

This Earth Was Formed Out Of Other Planets

The world and earth are not synonymous terms. The world is the human family. This earth was organized or formed out of other planets which were broken up and remodeled and made into the one on which we live. The elements are eternal.... In the translation "without form and void," it should read, "empty and desolate." The word "created" should be "formed or organized."

(*Joseph Smith*, President of the Church, January 5, 1841;
A Compendium of the Doctrines of the Gospel, 1898 edition, p. 287.)

The Earth Prior To Man's Habitation

Now we have been in the habit of thinking that the various kinds of animals that have lived, according to geologists, were the first flesh on the earth, and we go away back millions of ages to see that these lower formations of life existed before man. But the Lord gives us different information from this. He shows us that among all the animated creatures of flesh, man was the first that was ever placed upon the earth in this temporal condition, contradicting the theories of geologists—that is, so far as placing man on the earth in this present probation is concerned. What may have taken place millions of ages before the world was organized temporally for man to inhabit is not revealed; but, so far as this present chance is concerned, that took place about six thousand years ago, man was the first being that came upon the earth and inhabited a body of flesh and bones. Afterwards, on the seventh day, out of the ground the Lord God created the beasts of the field. Go back to the first chapter of Genesis, and you will find that the beasts, etc., were formed on the sixth day or period, and that on the seventh there was no flesh on the earth. God then created, out of the ground, the beasts of the field.

(*Orson Pratt*, an Apostle,
JD, 1879, 21:201.)

The Earth Could Have Been Reorganized Millions Of Times

As the elements of all worlds were not created, but are eternal, and as they have always been the tabernacle or dwelling place of God, they must have eternally been acted upon by His Spirit; consequently must have passed through an endless series of operations without beginning. Instead of seeking to trace out evidences of a beginning to the elements, we shall at once pronounce them eternal...

How many thousands of millions of times the elements of our globe have been organized and disorganized; or how many millions of shapes or forms the elements have been thrown into in their successive organizations and disorganizations; or how widely the particles have been diffused through boundless space; or of how many different worlds the particles have, at one time and another, formed component parts; or how long they have been parts of the solar system; or how long that system itself has formed a branch of our stellar heavens—is unknown to us mortals.

(Orson Pratt, an Apostle,
The Seer, 1854, pp. 248-249.)

CHAPTER 28

FASTING

A Proper Fast Is Refraining From Eating Two Meals On Fast Day

In order that there may be no misunderstanding as to the attitude of the Church regarding the proper observance of the fast, we are pleased to quote the following statement by the First Presidency as recently approved by us:

"There is nothing in the revelations indicating the duration of the fast, the accepted meaning of the fast being to abstain from eating and drinking. It has normally been considered that a proper fast consists of refraining from eating two meals on fast day, and in practice the fast is usually broken after the fast meeting. President Joseph F. Smith, in discussing this subject as contained in *Gospel Doctrine* made this statement: 'It is more important to obtain the true spirit of love for God and man, 'purity of heart and simplicity of intention,' than it is to carry out the cold letter of the law. The Lord has instituted the fast on a reasonable and intelligent basis, and none of his works are vain or unwise.... but let it be remembered that the observance of the fast day by abstaining twenty-four hours from food and drink is not an absolute rule, it is no iron-clad law to us, but it is left with the people as a matter of conscience, to exercise wisdom and discretion."

Sincerely yours,
David O. McKay, Hugh B. Brown,
N. Eldon Tanner, Joseph Fielding Smith, The First Presidency
(CL, April 8, 1966.)

The Proper Fast Day Observance

A proper fast day observance consists of abstaining from food and drink for two consecutive meals, attending the fast and testimony meeting, and making a generous offering to the bishop for the care of those in need.

(GHI, 1968, p. 40.)

The Fast Meeting

The first Sunday of each month is usually designated as a day of fasting and prayer on which a special testimony meeting is held. Adequate time should be allowed for testimony bearing. Preachments, travelogues, long drawnout narrations of experiences and routine repetitious statements should be discouraged. Every encouragement should be given to the bearing of brief, heartfelt testimonies and the relating of faith-promoting experiences.

(*GHI*, 1968, p. 40.)

Individual Circumstances And The Principle Of Fasting

Now, while the law requires the saints in all the world to fast from "even to even" and to abstain both from food and drink, it can easily be seen from the scriptures and especially from the words of Jesus that it is more important to obtain the true spirit of love for God and man, "purity of heart and simplicity of intention," than it is to carry out the cold letter of the law. The Lord has instituted the fast on a reasonable and intelligent basis, and none of his works are vain or unwise. His law is perfect in this as in other things. Hence, those who can are required to comply thereto; it is a duty from which they cannot escape. But let it be remembered that the observance of the fast day by abstaining twenty-four hours from food and drink is not an absolute rule; it is no iron-clad law to us, but it is left with the people as a matter of conscience to exercise wisdom and discretion. Many are subject to weakness, others are delicate in health, and others have nursing babies; of such it should not be required to fast. Neither should parents compel their little children to fast. I have known children to cry for something to eat on fast day. In such cases, going without food will do them no good. Instead, they dread the day to come and in place of hailing it, dislike it, while the compulsion engenders a spirit of rebellion in them, rather than a love for the Lord and their fellows. Better teach them the principle and let them observe it when they are old enough to choose intelligently than to so compel them.

But those should fast who can, and all classes among us should be taught to save the meals which they would eat or their equivalent for the poor. None are exempt from this; it is required of the saints, old and young, in every part of the Church. It is no excuse that in some places there are no poor. In such cases the fast donation should be forwarded to the proper authorities for transmission to such stakes of Zion as may stand in need.

So shall we gain favor in the sight of God and learn the acceptable fast before him.

(*Joseph F. Smith*, President of the Church,
IE, December, 1903, p. 146.)

Prayer, Meditation, And A Minimum Of Physical
Work Should Be Exercised When Fasting

A certain kind of devil goes not out except by fasting and prayer, the scripture tells us. *(See Matt. 17:21)* Periodic fasting can help clear up the mind and strengthen the body and the spirit. The usual fast, the one we are asked to participate in for fast Sunday, is for 24 hours without food or drink. Some people, feeling the need, have gone on longer fasts of abstaining from food but have taken the needed liquids. Wisdom should be used, and the fast should be broken with light eating. To make a fast most fruitful, it should be coupled with prayer and meditation; physical work should be held to a minimum, and it's a blessing if one can ponder on the scriptures and the reason for the fast.

(Ezra Taft Benson, President of the Council of the Twelve Apostles, *CR-E*, November, 1974, pp. 66-67.)

CHAPTER 29

FOOD STORAGE

Prepare For The Day Of Scarcity

We renew the counsel given to the Saints from the days of Brigham Young until now,—be honest, truthful, industrious, frugal, thrifty. In the day of plenty, prepare for the day of scarcity. The principle of the fat and lean kine, is as applicable today as it was in the days when, on the banks of the Nile, Joseph interpreted Pharaoh's dream. Officials now warn us, and warn again, that scant days are coming.

We renew our counsel, and repeat our instructions. Let every Latter-day Saint that has land produce some valuable, essential foodstuff thereon and then preserve it; or if he cannot produce an essential foodstuff, let him produce some other kind and exchange it for an essential foodstuff; let them who have no land of their own, and who have knowledge of farming and gardening, try to rent some, either by themselves or with others, and produce food-stuff thereon, and preserve it. Let those who have land produce enough extra to help their less fortunate brethren.

The Welfare plan should be carried forward with redoubled energy that we may care for the worthy, needy poor and unfortunate, and many of us may hereafter enter that class who now feel we are secure from want.

As the Church has always urged since we came to the Valleys, so now we urge every Church householder to have a year's supply of essential foodstuffs ahead. This should, so far as possible, be produced by each householder and preserved by him. This course will not only relieve from any impending distress those households who so provide themselves, but will release just that much food to the general national stores of foodstuffs from which the public at large must be fed.

The utmost care should be taken to see that foodstuffs so produced and preserved by the householder, do not spoil, for that would be waste, and the Lord looks with disfavor upon waste. He has blessed His people with abundant crops; the promise for this year is most hopeful. The Lord is doing His part; He expects us to do ours.

Heber J. Grant, J. Reuben Clark, Jr., David O. McKay
The First Presidency, (*CR*, April, 1942, pp. 89-90.)

Maintain A Year's Supply Of Food
For Your Family

...Maintain a year's supply of food for your family. Use prudence and seek reliable information on what and how to store, and observe local laws and ordinances in storage procedures....

Spencer W. Kimball, N. Eldon Tanner, Marion G. Romney
The First Presidency, (*CL*, December 16, 1974.)

Keep Up Your Year's Supply Of Commodities

[Comments on this subject were made by *Spencer W. Kimball*, President of the Church, in the October, 1974, General Conference, and can be found in the *Ensign*, November, 1974, p. 6.]

Food Storage Essentials

For over 100 years we have been admonished to store up grain. "Remember the counsel that is given," said Elder Orson Hyde, " '...Store up all your grain,' and take care of it! ... And I tell you it is almost as necessary to have bread to sustain the body as it is to have food for the spirit; for the one is as necessary as the other to enable us to carry on the work of God upon the earth." *(Journal of Discourses, Vol. 5, p. 17.)* And he also said: "There is more salvation and security in wheat, than in all the political schemes of the world...." *(JD, Vol. 2, p. 207.)*

As to the foodstuffs which should be stored, the Church has left that decision primarily to the individual members. Some excellent suggestions are available from the Church Welfare Committee. "All grain is good for the food of man..." *(D&C 89:16)* the Lord states, but he particularly singles out wheat. Dry, whole, hard grains, when stored properly, can last indefinitely, and their nutritional value can be enhanced through sprouting, if desired.

It would be well if every family have on hand grain for at least a year. And may I remind you that it generally takes several times as much land to produce a given amount of food when grains are fed to livestock and we consume the meat. Let us be careful not to overdo beef cattle and other livestock projects on our welfare farms.

From the standpoint of food production, storage, handling, and the Lord's counsel, wheat should have high priority. Water, of course, is essential. Other basics could include honey or sugar, legumes, milk products or substitutes, and salt or its equivalent.

The revelation to store food may be as essential to our temporal salvation today as boarding the ark was to the people in the days of Noah.

President Harold B. Lee has wisely counseled that "Perhaps if we think not in terms of a year's supply of what we ordinarily would use, and think more in terms of what it would take to keep us alive in case we didn't have anything else to eat, that last would be very easy to put in storage for a year ... just enough to keep us alive if we didn't have anything else to eat. We wouldn't get fat on it, but we would live; and if you think in terms of that kind of annual storage rather than a whole year's supply of everything that you are accustomed to eat which, in most cases, is utterly impossible for the average family, I think we will come nearer to what President Clark advised us way back in 1937." (Welfare Conference Address, Oct. 1, 1966.)

(*Ezra Taft Benson*, an Apostle,
CR, October, 1973, pp. 90-91.)

If We Are Obedient, Our Families Will Never Lack

Some members of the Church have said to me, "Why should we keep a store of food on hand? If a real emergency came in this lawless world, a neighbor would simply come with his gun and take it from us. What would you do if a person came and demanded your food?" I replied that I would share whatever I had with him, and he wouldn't have to use a gun to obtain that assistance either.

"I wouldn't," replied one man. "I have a gun, and I wouldn't hesitate to use it to defend my family. Anyone would have to kill me first in order to get food away from me! After all, they bring their own misery on themselves by not being prepared!"

Well, one way to solve this problem is to convert your neighbors to become obedient Latter-day Saints with their own supply of food. If every family were provided for, our stores would be safe for the use of our families. But not all people have sufficient faith to share with others as did the widow who shared with Elijah. I remember the words of another prophet who loved the poor and the unfortunate. He said:

And also, ye yourselves will succor those that stand in need of your succor; ye will administer of your substance unto him that standeth in need; and ye will not suffer that the beggar putteth up his petition to you in vain, and turn him out to perish.

Perhaps thou shalt say: The man has brought upon himself his misery; therefore I will stay my hand, and will not give unto him of my food, nor impart unto him of my substance that he may not suffer, for his punishments are just—

But I say unto you, O man, whosoever doeth this the same hath great cause to repent; and except he repenteth of that which he hath done he perisheth forever, and hath no interest in the kingdom of God.

For behold, are we not all beggars? Do we not all depend upon the same Being, even God, for all the substance which we have, for both food and raiment, and for gold, and for silver, and for all the riches which we have of every kind?" *(Mosiah 4:16-19)*

I sincerely believe if we do everything in our power to be obedient to the will of God, we and our families will never lack. If we are obedient as true followers of Christ and share what we have with those less fortunate than we, the Lord will keep his promise to watch over us and care for us. I will then be glad that I have stores of food on hand so I can be of assistance to others. Perhaps like the widow who fed Elijah, the meal will then never fail in our barrels nor the oil ever fail in our cruses until prosperity comes again.

(Theodore M. Burton, an Assistant to the Council
of the Twelve Apostles,
CR-E, May, 1974, p.62.)

CHAPTER 30

GAMBLING
(See: Card Playing)

The Church Is Opposed To Gambling In Any Form

The Church has been and now is unalterably opposed to gambling in any form whatever. It is opposed to any game of chance, occupation, or so-called business, which takes money from the person who may be possessed of it without giving value received in return. It is opposed to all practices the tendency of which is to encourage the spirit of reckless speculation, and particularly to that which tends to degrade or weaken the high moral standard which the members of the Church, and our community at large, have always maintained.

We therefore advise and urge all members of the Church to refrain from participation in any activity which is contrary to the view herein set forth.

Heber J. Grant, A. W. Ivins, Charles W. Nibley, The First Presidency *(IE,* September, 1929, 30:1100. *Spencer W. Kimball,* President of the Church, repeated this theme in the April, 1975, General Conference. See the *Ensign,* May, 1975, p. 6.)

Concerning Raffling And Games Of Chance

These are highly objectionable and must not be sponsored or permitted in connection with any Church function. The selling of chances in any form, however disguised, is not to be permitted.
(GHI, 1968, p. 60.)

Games Of Chance Are Not Approved Entertainment For Church Organizations

Among the vices of the present age gambling is very generally condemned. Gambling under its true name is forbidden by law, and is discountenanced by the self-respecting elements of society. Nevertheless, in numerous guises the demon of chance is welcomed in the home, in fashionable clubs, and at entertainments for worthy charities, even within the precincts of sacred edifices. Devices for raising money by appealing to the gambling instinct are common accessories at church socials, ward fairs, and the like.

Whatever may be the condition elsewhere, this custom is not to be sanctioned within this Church; and any organization allowing such is in opposition to the counsel and instruction of the Church.

Without attempting to specify or particularize the many objectionable forms given to this evil practice amongst us, we say again to the people that no kind of chance game, guessing contest, or raffling device can be approved in any entertainment under the auspices of our Church organizations.

The desire to get something of value for little or nothing is pernicious; and any proceeding that strengthens that desire is an effective aid to the gambling spirit, which has proved a veritable demon of destruction to thousands. Risking a dime in the hope of winning a dollar in any game of chance is a species of gambling.

Let it not be thought that raffling articles of value, offering prizes to the winners in guessing-contests, the use of machines of chance, or any other device of the kind is to be allowed or excused because the money so obtained is to be used for a good purpose. The Church is not to be supported in any degree by means obtained through gambling.

Let the attention of stake and ward officers, and those in charge of auxiliary organizations of the Church be directed to what has been written on this subject and to this present reminder. An article over the signature of the President of the Church was published in the *Juvenile Instructor*, October 1, 1920 (Volume 37, p. 592), in which were given citations from earlier instruction and advice to the people on this subject. For convenience, part of that article is repeated here. In reply to a question as to whether raffling and games of chance are justifiable when the purposes to be accomplished are good, this was said: "We say emphatically, No. Raffle is only a modified name of gamble."

President Young once said to Sister Eliza R. Snow: "Tell the sisters not to raffle. If the mothers raffle, the children will gamble. Raffling is gambling." Then it is added: "Some say, What shall we do? We have quilts on hand-we cannot sell them, and we need means to supply our treasury, which we can obtain by raffling for the benefit of the poor. Rather let the quilts rot on the shelves than adopt the old adage, 'The end will sanctify the means.' As Latter-day Saints, we cannot afford to sacrifice moral principle to finanacial gain."

As was further stated in the article cited, the General Board of the Deseret Sunday School Union has passed resolutions expressing its unqualified disapproval of raffling and of all games of chance, for the purpose of raising funds for the aid of the Sunday School. And the general authorities of the Church have said, as they now say, to the people: Let no raffling, guessing-contests, or other means of raising money, by appealing to the spirit of winning by chance, be tolerated in any organization of the Church.

Joseph F. Smith, John R. Winder, Anthon H. Lund,
The First Presidency
(IE, December, 1908, p. 143-145.)

Saints Should Not Work Or Participate In Gambling Casinos

Inquiry has been received from the presidency of one of the stakes in Las Vegas regarding the attitude that the Church should assume in the matter of appointing to administrative positions or issuing temple recommends to employees in gambling casinos, more specifically employees who are dealers, pit bosses, cashiers in tellers windows, change girls, bartenders, cocktail waitresses and cigar and cigarette girls.

This question came before the Council of the First Presidency and Quorum of the Twelve for consideration some months ago, and it was the sentiment of the Council at that time that we do not want any of our members participating in these gambling dens. President McKay indicated that while he did not want to rule arbitrarily on this matter that we cannot handle whiskey and gambling without being scarred by it, and that our people should stay away from such places. The President further said that we had better not temporize with these things.

In a subsequent consideration of the matter it was decided to convey this information to stake presidents who are concerned with this problem and advise that we should not appoint to administrative positions nor issue temple recommends to people in these gambling places whose employment requires them to meet the public and participate in the manner indicated. We hope that our brethren and sisters can find employment in a more desirable environment.

Sincerely yours,
David O. McKay, Hugh B. Brown, N. Eldon Tanner,
Joseph Fielding Smith, The First Presidency
(CL, August 30, 1966.)

Do Not Sacrifice Moral Principles For Financial Gain

Is it proper to raffle property for the benefit of missionaries? No; raffling is a game of chance, and hence leads to gambling; for that reason, if for no other, it should not be encouraged among the young men of the Church. President Young declared raffling to be a modified name of gambling; said that "as Latter-day Saints we cannot afford to sacrifice moral principles to financial gain," and advised the sisters through the *Woman's Exponent* not to raffle. President Lorenzo Snow endorsed and approved of these sentiments; and I have often expressed my unqualified disapproval of raffling; the General Sunday School Board have declared against it; and finally the state law makes it unlawful to raffle with dice; and if it is unlawful with dice, in principle, is it not just as injurious with any other device? With all these objections, should it not be clear to anyone that raffling horses, quilts, bicycles and other property is not sanctioned by the moral law nor approved by the general Church authorities? But it continues just the same, and if you do not believe in it, you should refuse to patronize it, so helping the cause. Now, how shall we aid the missionary who wishes to sell a horse, or what not? Let everybody give a dollar, and let the donors decide by vote to what worthy man, not of their number, the horse shall be given. No chance about that—it is pure decision, and it helps the people who wish to buy chances solely for the benefit of the missionary to discourage the gambling propensities of their natures. However, here is an additional thought: The element of chance enters very largely into everything we undertake, and it should be remembered that the spirit in which we do things decides very largely whether we are gambling or are entering into legitimate business enterprises.

(*Joseph F. Smith*, President of the Church, *IE*, February, 1903, p. 308.)

The Hell-Holes Of Satan

President Harold B. Lee said, "Today you are witnessing the fulfillment (of a prophecy concerning Satan's dominion). Today is the day when the devil has power over his own dominion." (*Harold B. Lee, Decisions for Successful Living, Deseret Book Co., 1973, p. 221.*) That is a prophetic statement from a prophet of God. He also said, "(Satan) is the master of deceit, adulteration and counterfeit. There is hardly a human appetite that he has not prostituted to his own evil designs; virtue he betrays into vice; and things invented and designed as benefactors to mankind he diverts to his own ends. No palace of art or temple of music was ever more glamorously decorated," the prophet continued, "than the hell-holes of Satan that are labeled saloons, bars, road houses and gambling clubs. With blazing neon signs and lighted 'white ways' the cheap and the tawdry are dressed in tinseled garb, and with sensuous music from the nether regions issuing forth from such places, the passerby are enticed to partake." *(Decisions for Successful Living, p. 155.)*

(Bernard P. Brockbank, an Assistant to the Council of the Twelve Apostles, *CR-E,* May, 1974, p. 113.)

CHAPTER 31

HOME AND FAMILY LIFE
(See: Children: Needs, Responsibilities, and Discipline;
Divorce; Husbands and Fathers; Marriage;
Womenhood and Motherhood)

Home: The Strength Of A Nation

An essential, fundamental element in the building and in the perpetuity of a great people is the home. The strength of a nation, especially of a republican nation, is in the intelligent and well-ordered homes of the people. In the well-ordered home we may experience on earth a taste of heaven. It is there that the babe in a mother's caress first experiences a sense of security, finds in the mother's kiss the first realization of affection, discovers in mother's sympathy and tenderness the first assurance that there is love in the world.

(*David O. McKay*, President of the Church,
CR, April, 1969, p. 5.)

Let Love Abound In The Home

Homes are more permanent through love. Oh, then, let love abound! Though you fall short in some material matters, study and work and pray to hold your children's love. Establish and maintain your family hours always. Stay close to your children. Pray, play, work, and worship together. This is the counsel of the Church. Would you have a strong and virile nation?—then keep your homes pure. Would you reduce delinquency and crime?—then lessen the number of broken homes. It is time that civilized peoples realized that the home largely determines whether children shall be of high or low character. Home-building, therefore, should be the paramount purpose of parents and of the nation.

(*David O. McKay*, President of the Church,
CR, April, 1967, p. 135.)

Strengthen The Home

Our youth are in danger. Keep your home ties strong, brethren. See to it, as we have all tried to say, and as I have repeated it many times and some have quoted it in this conference, that "the greatest of the Lord's work you brethren will ever do as fathers will be within the walls of your own home." Don't neglect your wives, you brethren. Don't neglect your children. Take time for family home evening. Draw your children around about you. Teach them, guide them, and guard them. There was never a time when we needed so much the strength and the solidarity of the home. If we will do this, this church will grow by leaps and bounds in strength and influence throughout the world.

(*Harold B. Lee*, President of the Church,
CR, April, 1973, p. 130.)

Make Your Home An Anchor In This Day Of Turmoil

Now as we return to our homes from this conference, let me ask you a question. What are you members of the Church going to do about all that which you have seen and heard? The all-important thing is not that we remember all that has been said, but the important thing is how you have been made to feel by what has been said and done here. If we can begin to see the strengthening of the bonds of fellowship and love in each branch of the Church in these stakes and missions where you live, if you will now resolve that you will have a new sense of responsibility in furthering the work of the Lord, and if you will strengthen your family ties and be mindful of your children, then this conference will have been a complete success. Be sure that the home is made the strong place to which children can come for the anchor they need in this day of trouble and turmoil. Then love will abound and your joy will be increased.

So, my beloved brothers and sisters, continuing these thoughts, will you husbands be kind to your wives; and you wives, will you try to understand your husbands even if they are sometimes stubborn and thoughtless, as they might be on occasion. Love them and have faith in them, even when they don't have faith in themselves.

(*Harold B. Lee*, President of the Church,
CR, Munich Conference, August, 1973, p. 112.)

The Importance Of Spirituality In The Home

Every home has both body and spirit. You may have a beautiful house with all the decorations that modern art can give or wealth bestow. You may have all the outward forms that will please the eye and yet not have a home. It is not home without love. It may be a hovel, a log hut, a tent, a wickiup, if you have the right spirit within, the true love of Christ, and love for one another—fathers and mothers for the children, children for parents, husband and wife for each other—you have the true life of the home that Latter-day Saints build and which they are striving to establish.

No matter what they may be without, are your homes pure within? Are morning prayers offered there regularly? Or do the things of this world take you away from your homes and make you deprive yourself of morning prayers with the children? "Woe to that home where the mother abandons her holy mission or neglects the divine instruction, influence, and example—while she bows, a devotee at the shrine of social pleasure; or neglects the essential duties in her own household, in her enthusiasm to promote public reform."

We must consider the home; it is the spring of life, if you please, of our social conditions today. It is no wonder, when we think of some home pictures that are shown to us, that millions and billions of dollars are spent trying to purify streams made impure by the unholy fountains of home life in the world.

From such homes as these come the men who are trespassing upon the rights of others, come women who are degraded, and who are dragging their virtue and that of others in the mud. It is such homes from which springs much of the evil in society today. I wish the money now spent in police and detective work could be used in purifying those homes. What the world needs today is good parents. Where parents are incapable of rearing their children properly, the state should assist by means of guardians of the young who should be required to do individual work.

(*David O. McKay*, an Apostle,
CR, October, 1907, p. 63.)

Five Points For True Home Building

President McKay gave five points for true home building as follows:

1—Let us substitute the present tendency toward a low view of marriage with the lofty view which God gives it.

Yesterday I stood at the altar of the temple, as I have stood many a time, and saw two hearts—two souls—slipping into one. As two dew drops on the stem of a rose when the sun comes out in the morning, one slipping into the other, the two becoming one. That high view of marriage in the mind of that young bridegroom and the appreciation of the sacredness of marriage by the bride, I think is one of the sublimest things in all the world.

They had the high view of marriage, not a low view of it as a means of gratifying passion. Let us look upon marriage as a sacred obligation and a covenant.

2—Teach the young of both sexes the responsibilities and ideals of marriage so that they may realize that marriage involves obligation and is not an arrangement to be terminated at pleasure.

In this regard it is the duty of parents to set an example in the home that children may see and absorb, as it were, the sacredness of family life and the responsibility associated therewith.

3—Instruct young girls in the fundamental arts of housekeeping, so that when responsibilities of wifehood come, they may be free from the difficulties and perplexities which arise from ignorance and inexperience.

4—Marriages should be solemnized as far as possible in the house of God. This will minimize the evils that follow run-away marriages.

5—To give young people the right start in life, we must discuss with our children and friends questions of motive and subjects like birth, love, marriage, death, and destiny.

The president also added:

Teach the young that the foundations of a happy home are laid before even the bride and bridegroom kneel at the marriage altar.

And again he said:

Go into the homes of true Latter-day Saints and there see if the most substantial part of the nation—the home—is not the best that can be found. The family tie is an eternal one; it is not one of experiment; it is not one of satisfying passion; it is an eternal union between husband and wife, between parents and children. That eternal bond is one that must be held sacred by the man as well as by the woman. The safety of our nation depends upon the purity and strength of the home.

(Editorial, *CN*, June 10, 1970, p. 16.)

CHAPTER 32

HOMOSEXUALITY
(See: Sexual Morality and Immorality)

Homosexuality Is A Sin In The Same Degree As Adultery

A homosexual relationship is viewed by The Church of Jesus Christ of Latter-day Saints as sin in the same degree as adultery and fornication.

In summarizing the intended destiny of man, the Lord has declared: "For behold, this is my work and my glory—to bring to pass the immortality and eternal life of man." *(Moses 1:39.)* Eternal life means returning to the Lord's exalted presence and enjoying the privilege of eternal increase. According to his revealed word, the only acceptable sexual relationship occurs within the family between a husband and a wife.

Homosexuality in men and women runs counter to these divine objectives and, therefore, is to be avoided and forsaken. Church members involved to any degree must repent. "By this ye may know if a man repenteth of his sins—behold, he will confess them and forsake them." *(D&C 58:43.)* Failure to work closely with one's bishop or stake president in cases involving homosexual behavior will require prompt Church court action.

(PB, February, 1973.)

Convince Homosexuals Through Kind Persuasion
Of Possible Forgiveness

[L.D.S.] Leaders should generally approach these unhappy [homosexual] people in the true spirit of the gospel of love and understanding rather than of condemnation. They are sons and daughters of God and made in the image of God, and intended to become like God in righteousness and honor and integrity and virtue.

They should be convinced through kind persuasion that a total continuing repentance could bring them forgiveness for the transgression. They can also be assured that in spite of all they may have heard from other sources, they can overcome and can return to total normal, happy living.

Many of these people have reached their present depressed state on a long road of gradual deterioration and cannot be expected to perfect themselves instantly. Consequently, high ideals and positive programs should be suggested to them and frequent visits will help them gain self mastery.

The inspiration of the Lord will generally bring happy solutions to these problems....

> *Joseph Fielding Smith, Harold B. Lee, N. Eldon Tanner*
> The First Presidency (*CL*, March 19, 1970.)

Every Form Of Homosexuality Is Sin

[Comments on this subject were made by *Spencer W. Kimball*, President of the Church, in the October, 1974, General Conference, and can be found in the *Ensign*, November, 1974, p. 8.]

Homosexuality And Sodom And Gomorrah

Many influences—more than ever before in my lifetime—are seeking to break down chastity with its divinely declared sanctity. The schoolroom, the press, authors, poets, artists, dramatists, musicians—all, consciously or unconsciously, are adding fuel to this flame of sexuality that is sweeping over the world....

Reports, too frequent and well-authenticated to be ignored, are that some teachers in our colleges—some near and some farther off—are teaching their unmarried students that the sex urge is like hunger and thirst and is to be satisfied at their wills. I have spoken about this on other occasions. I now repeat: He who teaches this depraved doctrine is acting as an emissary of Satan. No amount of ridicule, sarcasm, no trifling pettifoggery with scientific truths, no atheistic sophistries, can change this fundamental fact.

There are other abominations that go along with this. With genuine apologies, I will mention some by way of warning.

The person who teaches the nonsinfulness of self-pollution is in the same class with the teachers who prostitute the sex urge.

So also the person who teaches or condones the crimes for which Sodom and Gomorrah were destroyed—we have coined a softer name for them than came from old; we now speak of homosexuality, which, it is tragic to say, is found among both sexes.... Not without foundation is the contention of some that the homosexuals are today exercising great influence in shaping our art, literature, music, and drama.

I forebear to more than mention that abomination of filth
and loathsomeness of the ancients—carnal knowledge with beasts.
(*J. Reuben Clark, Jr.*, Second Counselor in the First Presidency,
RSM, December, 1952, pp. 793-795.)

CHAPTER 33

HUNTING AND TREATMENT OF ANIMALS

Animals Should Not Be Killed Except For Food

I have just a few words to say in addition to those that have already been said, in relation to shedding blood and to the destruction of life. I think that every soul should be impressed by the sentiments that have been expressed here this evening by all who have spoken, and not less with reference to the killing of our innocent little birds, natives of our country, who live upon the vermin that are indeed enemies to the farmer and to mankind. It is not only wicked to destroy them, it is abominable, in my opinion. I think that this principle should extend, not only to the bird life but to the life of all animals.

When I visited, a few years ago, the Yellowstone National Park, and saw in the streams and the beautiful lakes birds swimming quite fearless of man, allowing passersby to approach them as closely almost as tame birds, and apprehending no fear of them, and when I saw droves of beautiful deer herding along the side of the road as fearless of the presence of men as any domestic animal, it filled my heart with a degree of peace and joy that seemed to be almost a foretaste of that period hoped for when there shall be none hurt and none to molest in all the land, especially among all the inhabitants of Zion. These same birds, if they were to visit other regions, inhabited by man, would, on account of their tameness, doubtless become more easily a prey to the gunner. The same may be said of those beautiful creatures—the deer and antelope. If they should wander out of the park, beyond the protection that is established there for these animals, they would become, of course, an easy prey to those who were seeking their lives.

I never could see why a man should be imbued with a blood-thirsty desire to kill, and destroy animal life. I have known men—and they still exist among us—who enjoy what is, to them, the "sport" of hunting birds and slaying them by the hundreds, and who will come in after a day's "sport" boasting of how many harmless birds they have had the skill to slaughter, and day after day, during the season when it is lawful for men to hunt and kill (the birds having had a season of protection and not apprehending danger) go out by scores or hundreds, and you may hear their guns early in the morning on the day of the opening as if great armies had met in battle; and the terrible work of slaughtering the innocent birds goes on.

I do not believe any man should kill animals or birds unless he needs them for food, and then he should not kill innocent little birds that are not intended for food for man. I think it is wicked for men to thirst in their souls to kill almost everything which possesses animal life. It is wrong, and I have been surprised at prominent men whom I have seen whose very souls seemed to be athirst for the shedding of animal blood. They go off hunting deer, antelope, elk, anything they can find, and what for? "Just for the fun of it!" Not that they are hungry and need the flesh of their prey, but just because they love to shoot and to destroy life. I am a firm believer, with reference to these things, in the simple words of one of the poets:

"Take not away the life you cannot give,
For all things have an equal right to live."

(Joseph F. Smith, President of the Church,
JI, April, 1913, pp. 308-309.)

It Is A Grevious Sin To Neglect Animals Under Our Care

If the Latter-day Saints could look at things as they are, they would see that there is a grevious sin upon this people for neglecting their stock and letting them perish; turning their sheep on to the range for a few hours, and bringing them up and penning them twenty hours out of the twenty-four, until they become diseased and sickly. If the people could see as an angel sees, they would behold a great sin in neglecting the stock which the Lord has given them, for it is the Lord who gives us the increase of cattle and sheep, yet many of the people treat them as a thing of naught.... These are all the gifts of God; and when we treat lightly His gifts, it is a sign we desire that which we should not possess.... We should take a course to preserve our lives and the lives of the animals committed to our care.

(Brigham Young, President of the Church,
JD, May 17, 1868, 12:218.)

There Is No Religion In Abusing Animals

We have our Spanish fixings—a pair of spurs that will weigh seven pounds, ringing and gingling as though all hell was coming. Why don't you put them away? I want you to make an ox goad with a spike in the end of it, and ram that into your horse, and get this instead of spurs, and destroy a horse at once. I cannot keep a decent horse, neither can brother Brigham, or any other man; for the boys will kill them. Let them rest: they are as good as we are in their sphere of action; they honour their calling, and we do not, when we abuse them: they have the same life in them that you have, and we should not hurt them. It hurts them to whip them, as bad as it does you; and when they are drawing as though their daylights would fly out of them, you must whip, whip, whip. Is there religion in that? No; it is an abuse of God's creation that he has created for us.

(Heber C. Kimball, First Counselor in the First Presidency,
JD, August 2, 1857, 5:137.)

CHAPTER 34

HUSBANDS AND FATHERS
*(See: Birth Control; Children; Needs, Responsibilities, and
Discipline; Divorce; Home and Family Life; Marriage;
Womenhood and Motherhood.)*

The Dignity of Priesthood Leadership In The Home

There is no higher authority in matters relating to the family organization, and especially when that organization is presided over by one holding the Higher Priesthood, than that of the father. This authority is time honored, and among the people of God in all dispensations it has been highly respected and often emphasized by the teachings of the Prophets who were inspired of God. The Patriarchal order is of divine origin, and will continue throughout time and eternity. There is then a particular reason why men, women and children should understand this order and this authority in the households of the people of God, and seek to make it what God intended it to be, a qualification and preparation for the highest exaltation for His children. In the home the presiding authority is always vested in the father, and in all home affairs and family matters there is no other authority paramount.

(Joseph F. Smith, President of the Church,
JI, March 1, 1902.)

Husbands Should Treat Wives Kindly

Husbands, do you love your wives and treat them right, or do you think that you yourselves are some great moguls who have a right to crowd upon them? They are given to you as a part of yourself, and you ought to treat them with all kindness, with mercy and long suffering, and not be harsh and bitter, or in any way desirous to display your authority. Then, you wives, treat your husbands right, and try to make them happy and comfortable. Endeavor to make your home a little heaven, and try to cherish the good Spirit of God. Then let us as parents train up our children in the fear of God and teach them the laws of life. If you do, we will have peace in our bosoms, peace in our families, and peace in our surroundings.

(John Taylor, President of the Council of the Twelve Apostles
and acting President of the Church,
JD, 1879, 21:118-119.)

The Priesthood Gives No Man The Right To Abuse His Wife

I would like to emphasize tonight something that has been referred to before and that is that men, who have been married to women and have agreed before witnesses that they will keep the commandments of God and live as they should, sometimes are so selfish, so willful, that they forget that their wives have some rights. I want to say that the priesthood does not give any man a right to abuse his wife. The priesthood does give him a right to be kind, to be faithful, to be honorable, to teach the truth and to teach his children the truth, and when he does that he will not fall away into sin. There never has been a time in the history of the world when we have needed divine guidance more than now.

(George Albert Smith, President of the Church, *CR*, April, 1949, p. 189.)

Husbands Should Be True To Their Vows

Husbands...God expects you to be true to your vows, to be true to yourselves, and to be true to your wives and children. If you become covenant-breakers, you will be dealt with according to the laws of God. And the men presiding over you have no other alternative than to bring the covenant-breaker to judgment. If they fail to do their duty, we shall be under the necessity of looking after them, for righteousness and purity must be maintained in our midst.

(John Taylor, President of the Church, *JD*, 1883, 24:171-172.)

Control Your Temper

I mention this now, because I think we are sometimes cruel to our wives. I have here two letters, one anonymous, another signed by a woman. They are asking "What shall we do? Our husbands are cruel to us."

Says one, "My husband has a terrible temper. He comes home and scolds the children. He is cruel to me. At first he seemed to be a good, loving husband, but when my first baby was born, then were born my troubles."

I cannot imagine a man being cruel to a woman. I cannot imagine her so conducting herself as to merit such treatment. Perhaps there are women in the world who exasperate their husbands, but no man is justified in resorting to physical force or in exploding his feelings in profanity. There are men, undoubtedly, in the world who are thus beastly, but no man who holds the priesthood of God shall so debase himself.

(David O. McKay, President of the Church, *CR,* October, 1951, p. 181.)

Fathers Should Not Neglect Their Wives

If there is any man who ought to merit the curse of Almighty God it is the man who neglects the mother of his child, the wife of his bosom, the one who has made sacrifice of her very life, over and over again, for him and his children. That is, of course, assuming that the wife is a pure and faithful mother and wife.

(Joseph F. Smith, President of the Church, *IE,* December, 1917, p. 195.)

Unchristianlike For Fathers To Assume The Role Of Dictatorship

Fathers, too, must assume their proper role and responsibility. Children need both parents. While they are at home fathers should assume with mothers the duties attendant upon the young children, the discipline and training of the older ones, and be a listening ear for those who need to discuss their problems or want guidance and counseling. Through love establish a good relationship and line of communication with your children.

I would urge all husbands, fathers, sons, and brothers to show our great respect and love and try to be worthy of the women who are our wives, mothers, daughters, sisters, and sweethearts. There is no surer way for a man to show his lack of character, good breeding, and quality than for him to show lack of respect for woman or to do anything that would discredit or degrade her. It is unchristianlike, unfair, and displeasing to God for any husband or father to assume the role of dictatorship and adopt the attitude that he is superior in any way to his wife.

At the Area Conference in Munich, Germany, President Lee said: "If you husbands remember that the most important of the Lord's work you will ever do will be within the walls of your own home, you can maintain close family ties....If you will strengthen your family ties and be mindful of your children, be sure that home is made a strong place in which children can come for the anchor they need in this day of trouble and turmoil, then love will abound and your joy will be increased.

(N. Eldon Tanner, First Counselor in the First Presidency, *CR,* October, 1973, pp. 127-128.)

How Husbands Can Make Home A Happy Place

Now, to those of us who are husbands and children, let us help our mothers and wives be happy in our homes. Let us love them, honor them, respect them, revere them. Let us help them fulfill their call from the Lord. Let us be sure we do our part to make our homes pleasant. Let us help them have time for mental improvement, for educational growth, for cultural pursuits, and for developing talents. A home will be blessed and enriched when a mother is encouraged in these paths.

I know a young mother who has a great talent in music. She sings beautifully and plays the piano with great feeling and ability. Every week she gives a lesson to each of her four little children. Every day she spends a few minutes alone with each child, sometimes sharing with them her love for art or music. Besides blessing her children and her husband with great talents, she leads a choir and gives joy to many with her singing. When women develop their talents, it is a blessing to themselves and their families.

Remember too, brethren, a cheery "please," "thank you," or "I'm sorry, dear" will go a long way to heal the wounds of a sometimes frustrating day. It's amazing what a two-minute phone call to your wife at midday can do for her spirits. You sons and daughters and husbands, it is important for our exaltation that our wives and mothers enjoy and learn their profession well. Let us do our part to help them.

(H. Burke Peterson,
First Counselor in the Presiding Bishopric,
CR-E, May, 1974, p. 33.)

CHAPTER 35

HYPNOTISM

Warning Against Hypnosis And Mind Control Courses

Reports have been received of unfortunate results to persons engaging in group hypnosis demonstrations or in popular mind control courses of study. There are reports that some Church leaders have arranged hypnosis demonstrations as a means of entertainment. Leaders should advise members of the Church against participating in such activities. Certainly, they should not be sponsored or encouraged by leaders of the Church as has been reported.

(PB, August, 1972.)

Hypnotism Limits Free Agency

Hypnotism is a reality, and though some who claim to have this mysterious power are only tricksters, yet others do really hypnotise those who submit to them. From what I understand and have seen, I should advise you not to practise hypnotism. For my own part I could never consent to being hypnotised or allowing one of my children to be. The free agency that the Lord has given us is the choicest gift we have. As soon, however, as we permit another mind to control us, as that mind controls its own body and functions, we have completely surrendered our free agency to another; and so long as we are in the hypnotic spell—and that is as long as the hypnotist desires us to be—we give no consent in any sense whatever to any thing we do. The hypnotist might influence us to do good things, but we could receive no benefit from that, even if we remembered it after coming out of the spell, for it was not done voluntarily. The hypnotist might also influence us to do absurd and even shocking, wicked things, for his will compels us.

Hypnotism is very much like the plan that Satan desired the Father to accept before this earth was peopled. He would make them do good and save them in spite of themselves. The Savior, on the other hand, proposed to give free agency to all, and save those who would accept salvation. Our Father rejected Satan's plan, and sacrificed a third part of his children for the sake of upholding this true principle, that men have the right to act for themselves, and shall be responsible for their own actions.

(Francis M. Lyman, an Apostle, *IE,* April, 1903, p. 420.)

The Value Of Hypnotism

Reputable doctors sometimes use hypnotherapy, a limited form of hypnotism, in connection with the practice of their profession. Their sole apparent purpose is to relieve pain and aid patients in perfecting their physical well-being. It is claimed that there are many people who have been benefited materially by this practice and that the ills normally attending hypnotical practices have not resulted. This medical practice of hypnotism obviously does not carry the same opprobrium that attaches to hypnotism in general.

(Bruce R. McConkie,
Member of the First Council of the Seventy,
Mormon Doctrine, 1966, p. 371.)

CHAPTER 36

MARRIAGE
*(See: Birth Control; Home and Family Life;
Husbands and Fathers; Negroes and the Priesthood;
Womanhood and Motherhood)*

Maintain A Lofty View Of Marriage

To look upon marriage as a mere contract that may be entered into at pleasure in response to a romantic whim, or selfish purposes, and severed at the first difficulty or misunderstanding that may arise, is an evil meriting severe condemnation, especially in cases wherein children are made to suffer because of such separation. Marriage is a sacred relationship entered into for purposes that are well recognized—primarily for the rearing of a family. A flippant attitude toward marriage, the ill-advised suggestion of "companionate marriage," the base, diabolical theory of "free sex experiment," and the ready-made divorce courts are dangerous reefs upon which many a family bark is wrecked.

In order to lessen the breaking up of homes, the present tendency toward a low view of marriage should be subsitituted by the lofty view of marriage that Jesus the Christ gives it. Let us look upon marriage as a sacred obligation and a covenant that is eternal, or that may be made eternal.

(David O. McKay, President of the Church,
CR, April, 1969, p. 9.)

Parents Should Make Home A Heaven On Earth

To all the families in Israel we say: The Family is the most important organization in time or in eternity. Our purpose in life is to create for ourselves eternal family units. There is nothing that will ever come into your family life that is as important as the sealing blessings of the temple and then keeping the covenants made in connection with this order of celestial marriage.

To parents in the Church we say: Love each other with all your hearts. Keep the moral law and live the gospel. Bring up your children in light and truth; teach them the saving truths of the gospel; and make your home a heaven on earth, a place where the Spirit of the Lord may dwell and where righteousness may be enthroned in the heart of each member.

(Joseph Fielding Smith, President of the Church, *CR,* April, 1972, p. 13.)

All Normal People Should Marry

[Comments on this subject were made by *Spencer W. Kimball,* President of the Church, in the October, 1974, General Conference, and can be found in the *Ensign,* November, 1974, p. 8.]

Warning Against Postponing Or Forbidding Marriage

[Comments on this subject were made by *Spencer W. Kimball,* President of the Church, in the April, 1974, General Conference, and can be found in the *Ensign,* May, 1974, p. 6.]

Priesthood Holders Have The Responsibility To Marry

I think that is enough to give you the other side of the story from the girls who are frustrated. All women have a desire for companionship. They want to be wives: they want to be mothers: and when men refuse to assume their responsibility of marriage, for no good reason, they are unable to consummate marriage. Brethren, we are not doing our duty as holders of the priesthood when we go beyond the marriageable age and withhold ourselves from an honorable marriage to these lovely women, who are seeking the fulfillment of a women's greatest desire to have a husband, a family, and a home.

Now don't misunderstand me. I am not trying to urge you younger men to marry too early. I think therein is one of the hazards of today's living. We don't want a young man to think of marriage until he is able to take care of a family, to have an institution of his own, to be independent. He must make sure that he has found the girl of his choice, they have gone together long enough that they know each other, and that they know each other's faults and they still love each other. I have said to the mission presidents (some of whom have been reported to us as saying to missionaries, "Now, if you are not married in six months, you are a failure as a missionary"). "Don't you ever say that to one of your missionaries. Maybe in six months they will not have found a wife: and if they take you seriously, they may rush into a marriage that will be wrong for them."

Please don't misunderstand what we are saying, but, brethren, think more seriously about the obligations of marriage for those who bear the holy priesthood at a time when marriage should be the expectation of every man who understands the responsibility: for remember, brethren, that only those who enter into the new and everlasting covenant of marriage in the temple for time and eternity, only those will have the exaltation in the celestial kingdom. That is what the Lord tells us.

Now, brethren, will you think seriously about that, and take from us our counsel, and don't rush hastily into it. Take time, yes, but don't neglect your responsibility and your obligations as holders of the holy priesthood.

(Harold B. Lee, President of the Church, *CR*, October, 1973, pp. 119-120.)

Men Should Not Abuse Their Wives

...Let us instruct young people who come to us, to know that a woman should be queen of her own body. The marriage covenant does not give the man the right to enslave her or to abuse her or to use her merely for the gratification of his passion. Your marriage ceremony does not give you that right.

(David O. McKay, President of the Church, *CR*, April, 1952, pp. 86-87.)

Warning Against Polygamy Cults

[Comments on this subject were made by *Spencer W. Kimball*, President of the Church, in the October, 1974, General Conference, and can be found in the *Ensign*, November, 1974, p. 5.]

Enroaching Dangers Against Marriage As A
Divine Institution

The exalted view of marriage as held by this Church is given expressively in five words found in the 49th section of the *Doctrine and Covenants*. "Marriage is ordained of God." That revelation was given in 1831 when Joseph Smith was only twenty-five years of age. Considered in the circumstances under which it was given, we find in it another example among hundreds of others corroborative of the fact that he was inspired of the Lord. "Watchmen of Zion, I am trusting you," was a message given in song at the opening of this session. Before me are assembled thousands of watchmen in Zion. Presiding officers in stakes, wards, quorums, and auxiliaries, it is your duty and mine to uphold the lofty conception of marriage as given in this revelation and to guard against encroaching dangers that threaten to lower the standard of the ideal home....

It is said that the best and noblest lives are those which are set toward high ideals. Truly no higher ideal regarding marriage can be cherished by young people than to look upon it as a divine institution. In the minds of the young such a standard is a protection to them in courtship, an ever present influence inducing them to refrain from doing anything which may prevent their going to the Temple to have their love consummated in an enduring and eternal union. It will lead them to seek divine guidance in the selecting of their companions, upon the wise choice of whom their life's happiness here and hereafter is largely dependent. "Our home joys," says Pestalozzi, "are the most delightful earth affords, and the joy of parents in their children is the most holy joy of humanity. It makes their hearts pure and good; it lifts them up to their Father in Heaven." Such joys are within the reach of most men and women if high ideals of marriage and home be properly fostered and cherished.

And yet, if I mistake not the signs of the times, the sacredness of the marriage covenant is dangerously threatened. There are some who question whether family life is permanent as a social organization. They claim that marriage ties will be and should be but temporary, that children will be born not in families, but in the life of the state. Recently in a trip east I observed to my dismay an increasing number of "Gretna Greens," places where the marriage ceremony may be performed at any hour of the day or night without any previous arrangement. The license is issued and the ceremony performed while the couple wait; already I know of at least two couples that have been entrapped by such enticements and both cases have ended in disappointment and sorrow. In some instances these places are nothing more than opportunities for legalized immorality. Oh how far they fall below the true ideal! As far as lies within our power, we must warn young couples against secret and hasty marriages.

It is vital also to counteract the insidious influences of printed literature that speaks of the "bankruptcy of marriage," that advocates trial marriages, and that places "extra marital relations" on a par with "extra-marital friendships."

I need say little about the growing evil of divorce and the resultant broken homes. You know that it is almost as easy to get a divorce as it is to get married. Today, one out of five marriages in the United States ends in divorce or annulment. One of the peace officers in Salt Lake reported recently that eighty-six per cent of the delinquent cases come from such broken homes. America seems to be drifting toward a low level as regards to law of family and home, with the result that sin and crime are increasing to an alarming extent among the youth of our fair land.

I mention these things not in the spirit of pessimism nor as a crier of impending calamity, but with the desire to call attention to the necessity of our maintaining the high standard of marriage set forth in the revelations of the Lord.

(David O. McKay, Second Counselor in the
First Presidency, CR, April, 1935, pp. 110-111.)

Homebreaking Is Sin

[Comments on this subject were made by *Spencer W. Kimball*, an Apostle, in the October, 1962, General Conference, and can be found in the *Conference Report* of that same month and year on page 58.]

Husband And Wife Are To Be Faithful To Each Other

[Comments on this subject were made by *Spencer W. Kimball*, an Apostle, in the October, 1962, General Conference, and can be found in the *Conference Report* of that same month and year on pages 57-58.]

CHAPTER 37

MILITARY SERVICE
(See: War)

**Church Members To Come To The
Defense Of Their Country**

The members of the Church have always felt under obligation to come to the defense of their country when a call to arms was made; on occasion the Church has prepared to defend its own members.

In the days of Nauvoo, the Nauvoo Legion was formed, having in view the possible armed defense of the Saints against mob violence. Following our expulsion from Nauvoo, the Mormon Battalion was recruited by the national government for service in the war with Mexico. When Johnston's army was sent to Utah in 1857 as the result of malicious misrepresentations as to the actions and attitude of the territorial officers and the people, we prepared and used measures of force to prevent the entry of the army into the valleys. During the early years in Utah, forces were raised and used to fight the Indians. In the war with Spain, members of the Church served with the armed forces of the United States, with distinction and honor. In the World War, the Saints of America and of European countries served loyally their respective governments, on both sides of the conflict. Likewise in the present war, righteous men of the Church in both camps have died, some with great herosim, for their own country's sake. In all this our people have but served loyally the country of which they were citizens or subjects under the principles we have already stated. We have felt honored that our brethren have died nobly for their country; the Church has been benefited by their service and sacrifice.

Nevertheless, we have not forgotten that on Sinai, God commanded "Thou shalt not kill;" nor that in this dispensation the Lord has repeatedly reiterated that command. He has said:

And now, behold, I speak unto the church. Thou shalt not kill; and he that kills shall not have forgiveness in this world, nor in the world to come.

And again, I say, thou shalt not kill; but he that killeth shall die. *(D&C 42:18-19; and see 59:6)*

At another time the Lord commanded that murderers should "be delivered up and dealt with according to the laws of the land; for remember that he hath no forgiveness." *(ibid 79)* So also when land was to be obtained in Zion, the Lord said:

> Wherefore, the land of Zion shall not be obtained but by purchase or by blood, otherwise there is none inheritance for you.
>
> And if by purchase, behold you are blessed;
>
> And if by blood, as you are forbidden to shed blood, lo, your enemies are upon you, and ye shall be scourged from city to city, and from synagogue to synagogue, and but few shall stand to receive an inheritance. *(D&C 63:29-31)*

But all these commands, from Sinai down, run in very terms against individuals as members of society, as well as members of the Church, for one man must not kill another as Cain killed Abel; they also run against the Church as in the case of securing land in Zion, because Christ's Church should not make war, for the Lord is a Lord of peace. He has said to us in this dispensation:

> Therefore, renounce war and proclaim peace.... *(D&C 98:16)*

Thus the Church is and must be against war. The Church itself cannot wage war, unless and until the Lord shall issue new commands. It cannot regard war as a righteous means of settling international disputes; these should and could be settled—the nations agreeing—by peaceful negotiation and adjustment.

But the Church membership are citizens or subjects of sovereignties over which the Church has no control. The Lord Himself has told us to 'befriend that law which is the constitutional law of the land:'

> And now, verily I say unto you concerning the laws of the land, it is my will that my people should observe to do all things whatsoever I command them.
>
> And that law of the land which is constitutional, supporting that principle of freedom in maintaining rights and privileges, belongs to all mankind, and is justifiable before me.
>
> Therefore, I, the Lord, justify you, and your brethren of my church, in befriending that law which is the constitutional law of the land;
>
> And as pertaining to law of man, whatsoever is more or less than this cometh of evil. *(D&C 98:4-7)*

While by its terms this revealed word related more especially to this land of America, nevertheless the principles announced are worldwide in their application, and they are specifically addressed to "you" (Joseph Smith), "and your brethren of my church." When, therefore, constitutional law, obedient to these principles, calls the manhood of the Church into the armed service of any country to which they owe allegiance, their highest civic duty requires that they meet that call. If, harkening to that call and obeying those in command over them, they shall take the lives of those who fight against them, that will not make of them murderers, nor subject them to the penalty that God has prescribed for those who kill, beyond the principle to be mentioned shortly. For it would be a cruel God that would punish His children as moral sinners for acts done by them as the innocent instrumentalities of a sovereign whom He had told them to obey and whose will they were powerless to resist.

Heber J. Grant, J. Reuben Clark, Jr., David O. McKay
The First Presidency *(CR*, April, 1942, pp. 93-95.)

When In Military Service Live Clean Lives

To our young men who go into service, no matter whom they serve or where, we say live clean, keep the commandments of the Lord, pray to Him constantly to preserve you in truth and righteousness, live as you pray, and then whatever betides you the Lord will be with you and nothing will happen to you that will not be to the honor and glory of God and to your salvation and exaltation. There will come into your hearts from the living of the pure life you pray for, a joy that will pass your powers of expression or understanding. The Lord will be always near you; He will comfort you; you will feel His presence in the hour of your greatest tribulation; He will guard and protect you to the full extent that accords with His all-wise purpose. Then, when the conflict is over and you return to your homes, having lived the righteous life, how great will be your happiness—whether you be of the victors or of the vanquished—that you have lived as the Lord commanded. You will return so disciplined in righteousness that thereafter all Satan's wiles and stratagems will leave you untouched. Your faith and testimony will be strong beyond breaking. You will be looked up to and revered as having passed through the fiery furnace of trial and temptation and come forth unharmed. Your brethren will look to you for counsel, support, and guidance. You will be the anchors to which thereafter the youth of Zion will moor their faith in man.

Heber J. Grant, J. Reuben Clark, Jr., David O. McKay
The First Presidency *(CR*, April, 1942, p. 96.)

CHAPTER 38

MISSION RESPONSIBILITY

The Qualifications For Missionaries

It is our duty, divinely imposed, to continue urgently and militantly to carry forward our missionary work. We must continue to call missionaries and send them out to preach the gospel, which was never more needed than now, which is the only remedy for the tragic ills that now afflict the world, and which alone can bring peace and brotherly love back amongst the peoples of the earth. We must continue to call to missionary work those who seem best able to perform it in these troublous and difficult days. Our duty under divine command imperatively demands this. We shall not knowingly call anyone for the purpose of having him evade military service, nor for the purpose of interfering with or hampering that service in any way, nor of putting any impediment in the way of government. These would be unworthy motives for a missionary life. Our people have furnished and we expect them to continue to furnish their full quota for those purposes, but we see no alternative, until new rules are made by the government, but to continue to call the best and most effective men into missionary work, if they are available therefor.

Having in mind that the worldwide disaster in material and spiritual matters has brought vital and difficult problems to the nation and to the Church,--the nation because of need of manpower for the armed forces and defense works, and to the Church because of the imperative need it brings to us to employ in our missionary work the experience, testimony and faith possessed by our more mature brethren, we have instructed our bishops, presidents of branches, and presidents of missions, to confine until further notice, their recommendations of brethren for missionary service in the field, to those who on March 23, 1942, were seventies or high priests. Furthermore, in recommending these brethren, none but those who are and have been living worthily, should be chosen; and as to these, they should choose those only who have not received their notice of induction, who are not likely to receive it within a short time, and who have a real desire to do missionary work.

To preach the gospel, under ordination from the Priesthood

of God, is a great privilege, to be enjoyed by those only who are thoroughly qualified and who are and have been strictly living the commandments and attending to their Church duties. Every bishop will carefully examine everyone whom he considers for a mission, to be sure he meets these requirements. No lukewarm or unworthy person should be recommended. The bishop must not in any way play favorites, thus avoiding giving just ground among the people of his ward for that unworthy, unrighteous thought, sometimes voiced by those whose sons have gone into the service, that because their sons have gone into the army, every other parent's son should go into the army, and that none should be sent on missions. This feeling has behind it thoughts that do not comport with the teachings of our Heavenly Father. Moreover, those going on missions are amenable to selection for army service so soon as they return. A mission exempts from army service only for the term of the mission.

Heber J. Grant, J. Reuben Clark Jr., David O. McKay
The First Presidency *(CR, April, 1942, pp. 91-92.)*

Every Able And Worthy Young Man Should Fill A Mission

[Comments on this subject were made by *Spencer W. Kimball*, President of the Church, in the April, 1974, General Conference, and can be found in the *Ensign*, May, 1974, p. 87.]

Concerning Young Sisters Who Wish To Do Missionary Work

Indeed, there are more doors opened to us now than we can enter with the number of missionaries who are available. We hope to see the day when every worthy and qualified young Latter-day Saint man will have the privilege of going forth on the Lord's errand to stand as a witness of the truth in the nations of the earth....We also have and can use many young sisters in this work, although the same responsibility does not rest upon them that rests upon the brethren, and our greater concern with reference to young sisters is that they enter proper marital unions in the temples of the Lord.

(Joseph Fielding Smith, President of the Church,
CR, October, 1970, p. 7.)

When Receiving A Missionary Call Fill It Expertly

[Comments on this subject were made by *Spencer W. Kimball*, President of the Church, in the October, 1974, General Conference, and can be found in the *Ensign*, November, 1974, pp. 82-83.]

The Proper Spirit Of Missionary Service

The gospel of Jesus Christ was restored in the year 1830, after centuries of darkness had passed. When the call was given, the missionaries of the Church of Jesus Christ of Latter-day Saints went out into the world—not to criticize others, not to find fault, but to say to our Father's other children:

> Keep all the good that you have received, keep all the truth that you have learned, all that has come to you in your homes, in your institutions of learning, under your many facilities for education, keep it all; and then let us divide with you additional truths that have been revealed by our Heavenly Father in our day.

Under that ministry, beginning, as I have said, in that conference when there were only sixty-three members of the priesthood present, there have been thousands upon thousands of missionaries; more than seventy thousand have gone out into the world, and in love and kindness they have gone from door to door saying to our Father's other children:

> Let us reason with you; let us explain to you something that we are sure will make you happy as it has made us happy!

That is the history of the missionary work of the Church with which we are identified. Today we have missionaries scattered in many parts of the earth; some of them are in the armed services and rejoicing in their testimonies, they have been glad to divide the truth with those with whom they came in contact.

(George Albert Smith, President of the Church, *CR*, October, 1946, p. 5.)

Missionaries Should Have A Worthy Character

There are certain standards by which we should be guided in calling our missionaries. First, call no young man or young woman, for the purpose of saving him or her. The young man is getting wayward and you think a mission would do him good. It would. But that is not why you are sending him out. Choose the young men and young women who are worthy to represent the Church, see that they are sufficiently mature, and, above all, that they have character....

Let each one whom you interview sense the fact that he is going out as a representative. Some of the brethren have urged that each ward should have in the mission field a certain percentage of the ward membership. That is not an ideal. If you have no one who is worthy and financially able to represent the Church, do not send anybody out, but sit down with these young men and young women and say, "If you accept this call willingly, you go out as a trusted representative of the Church and of the Lord Jesus Christ." And to be trusted, young men, is a greater compliment than to be loved, and you cannot violate that trust. You are obligated to keep that trust between now and the time you go to the missionary home. Maintain the Church standards with your companions who will want to give you a farewell party. We have heard of some missionaries who have been called who have joined in with their fraternity friends in actions that reflected discredit upon themselves and upon the missionary cause.

Tell the young man, "From now on, from this very moment, you are a trusted representative of this ward, of your parents and of the Lord Jesus Christ."

(*Joseph Fielding Smith*, an Apostle,
CR, April, 1950, pp. 176-178.)

The Greatest Missionaries Have Been Humble Men

[Comments on this subject were made by *A. Theodore Tuttle*, Member of the First Council of the Seventy, in the October, 1974, General Conference, and can be found in the *Ensign*, November, 1974, p. 72]

Save Your Money For A Mission

[Comments on this subject were made by *A. Theodore Tuttle*, Member of the First Council of the Seventy, in the October, 1974, General Conference, and can be found in the *Ensign*, November, 1974, p. 72.]

Marriage Does Not Take Precedence Over Missionary Service

[Comments on this subject were made by *A. Theodore Tuttle*, Member of the First Council of the Seventy, in the October, 1974,

General Conference, and can be found in the *Ensign*, November, 1974, p. 71.]

Beware Of The Girl Who Places A Low Premium On Missionary Service

[Comments on this subject were made by *A. Theodore Tuttle*, Member of the First Council of the Seventy, in the October, 1974, General Conference, and can be found in the *Ensign*, November, 1974, p. 72.]

CHAPTER 39

MUSIC
(See: Dancing)

Seek The Guidance Of The Spirit In Selecting Music

Through music, man's ability to express himself extends beyond the limits of the spoken language in both subtlety and power. Music can be used to exalt and inspire or to carry messages of degradation and destruction. It is therefore important that as Latter-day Saints we at all times apply the principles of the Gospel and seek the guidance of the Spirit in selecting the music with which we surround ourselves.

Harold B. Lee, N. Eldon Tanner, Marion G. Romney
The First Presidency, *(PB*, August, 1973.)

The Highest Standards Of Music Performance Must Be Maintained

Music is a most important part of our religious services and our recreational activities. The highest standards in music literature and musical performance must be maintained. Musical numbers for religious services should be sung or played at such moderate tempo as to instill faith and devotion in the singers and hearers and teach the doctrines of the restored gospel.

Love songs, popular ballads, spirituals, and songs not in harmony with the doctrines of the Church are not to be used.

Singers and instrumentalists can properly select numbers from the hymnbook.

Instrumental numbers in Sacrament meetings are to be limited to organ, piano, and string instruments. Special instrumental numbers in Sacrament meetings would be more appropriate if limited to postlude and prelude....

Music in Church meetings should follow the pattern set in general conference of the Church, and any musical innovations that precede or follow the prayers in Church meetings are not approved.

The practice, common in some churches of the world, of sitting quietly after the final prayer, presumably to meditate upon what has been said, while a few bars of music are played on the piano or organ is not approved.

(GHI-IE, April, 1964, p. 309.)

Acceptable Dance Music

The kind of music that is played and sung is more responsible than anything else for proper or improper dancing. Consequently, all dance bands should be informed of church standards and are to conform thereto. Dance bands, orchestras, or records should not be used without prior approval of church leaders. This determination should never be left to a disc jockey or others who may not be familiar with LDS standards.

1. Lyrics
   Music lyrics should never be suggestive or off color but always dignified and in good taste.

2. Style of Singing
   Sensual or wild singing should be avoided. Loud shouting that works people up to a high emotional frenzy is never in good taste.

3. Musical Beat
   A definite beat is needed but should not be extreme. A loud, wild, primitive beat is to be avoided as it does not meet church standards.

4. Orchestra
   Music for dancing should be moderate. A dance band or orchestra should produce happy, bright, cheerful music to inspire a wholesome atmosphere where dancing can be enjoyed as intended by Brigham Young when he said: "If we are dancing properly, a priesthood bearer could walk off the dance floor, administer to the sick in a proper way, and feel good about it."

(PB, December, 1965.)

Disapproval of Jesus Christ Superstar
And Other Similar Productions

Leaders in the Church should not authorize or permit the use of the rock opera *Jesus Christ Superstar* in any Church-sponsored meetings. We regard it as being incompatible with the spirit and doctrine of the Church concerning the divinity of the Savior.

Church leaders should be careful that other productions of a similar nature not be permitted in any Church-sponsored gatherings.

(*PB*, August, 1971.)

Warning Against Musical Performances Aimed At Destroying Sacred Principles

Jesus Christ Superstar ... is a profane and sacreligious attack upon true Christianity....

We feel it our responsibility to warn our people against the present day wave of musical performances which are aimed at the destruction of sacred principles, which form the very foundation upon which we stand....

Jesus Christ Superstar ... strips Jesus Christ of His divine attributes. Its prevailing theme presents the falsehood that our Lord is 'just a man ... just the same as anyone I know ...' He and His apostles are portrayed in earthly roles living below Christian standards.

Joseph Fielding Smith, Harold B. Lee, N. Eldon Tanner
The First Presidency
(B.Y.U. *The Daily Universe*, October 11, 1971, p. 1.)

Concerning The Different Types Of Music

[An entire Conference talk on this subject was made by *Boyd K. Packer*, an Apostle, in the October, 1973, General Conference. His talk can be found either in the *Conference Report* of October, 1973, pp. 21-25, or in the *Ensign*, of January, 1974, pp. 25-28.]

Improve Musical Talents

I would like to say right here that it delights my heart to see our people everywhere improving their talents as good singers. Everywhere we go among our people we find sweet voices and talent for music. I believe that this is a manifestation to us of the purpose of the Lord in this direction toward our people, that they will excel in these things, as they should excel in every other good thing. I can remember, when I was a young boy, hearing my father sing. I do not know how much of a singer he was, for at that time I was not capable of judging as to the quality of his singing, but the hymns he sang became familiar to me in the days of my childhood.

When we listen to this choir, we listen to music, and music is truth. Good music is gracious praise of the Lord. It is delightsome to the ear, and it is one of our most acceptable methods of worshipping. And those who sing in the choir and in all the choirs of the Saints should sing with the Spirit and with understanding. They should not sing merely because it is a profession, or because they have a good voice; but they should sing also because they have the spirit of it, and can enter into the spirit of prayer and praise the Lord who gave them their sweet voices. My soul is always lifted up, and my spirit cheered and comforted, when I hear good music. I rejoice in it very much indeed.

(*Joseph Fielding Smith*, President of the Council of the Twelve Apostles, *CR*, October, 1969, pp. 109-110.)

CHAPTER 40

NEGROES AND THE CHURCH
(See: Civil Rights)

Conferring Of The Priesthood Must Await God's Revelation

In view of confusion that has arisen, it was decided at a meeting of the First Presidency and the Quorum of the Twelve to restate the position of the Church with regard to the Negro both in society and in the Church.

First, may we say that we know something of the sufferings of those who are discriminated against in a denial of their civil rights and Constitutional privileges. Our early history as a church is a tragic story of persecution and oppression. Our people repeatedly were denied the protection of the law. They were driven and plundered, robbed and murdered by mobs, who in many instances were aided and abetted by those sworn to uphold the law. We as a people have experienced the bitter fruits of civil discrimination and mob violence.

We believe that the Constitution of the United States was divinely inspired, that it was produced by "wise men" whom God raised up for this "very purpose," and that the principles embodied in the Constitution are so fundamental and important that, if possible, they should be extended "for the rights and protection" of all mankind.

In revelations received by the first prophet of the Church in this dispensation, Joseph Smith (1805-1844), the Lord made it clear that it is "not right that any man should be in bondage one to another." These words were spoken prior to the Civil War. From these and other revelations have sprung the Church's deep and historic concern with man's free agency and our commitment to the sacred principles of the Constitution.

It follows, therefore, that we believe the Negro, as well as those of other races, should have his full Constitutional privileges as a member of society, and we hope that members of the Church everywhere will do their part as citizens to see that these rights are held inviolate. Each citizen must have equal opportunities and protection under the law with reference to civil rights.

However, matters of faith, conscience, and theology are not within the purview of the civil law. The first amendment to the Constitution specifically provides that "Congress shall make no law respecting an establishment of religion, or prohibiting the free exercise thereof."

The position of The Church of Jesus Christ of Latter-day Saints affecting those of the Negro race who choose to join the Church falls wholly within the category of religion. It has no bearing upon matters of civil rights. In no case or degree does it deny to the Negro his full privileges as a citizen of the nation.

This position has no relevancy whatever to those who do not wish to join the Church. Those individuals, we suppose, do not believe in the divine origin and nature of the Church, nor that we have the priesthood of God. Therefore, if they feel we have no priesthood, they should have no concern with any aspect of our theology on priesthood so long as that theology does not deny any man his Constitutional privileges.

A word of explanation concerning the position of the Church:

The Church of Jesus Christ of Latter-day Saints owes its origin, its existence, and its hope for the future to the principle of continuous revelation. "We believe all that God has revealed, all that He does now reveal, and we believe that He will yet reveal many great and important things pertaining to the Kingdom of God."

From the beginning of this dispensation, Joseph Smith and all succeeding presidents of the Church have taught that Negroes, while spirit children of a common Father, and the progeny of our earthly parents Adam and Eve, were not yet to receive the priesthood, for reasons which we believe are known to God, but which He has not made fully known to man.

Our living prophet, President David O. McKay, has said, "The seeming discrimination by the Church toward the Negro is not something which originated with man; but goes back into the beginning with God....

"Revelation assures us that this plan antedates man's mortal existence, extending back to man's pre-existent state."

President McKay has also said, "Sometime in God's eternal plan, the Negro will be given the right to hold the priesthood."

Until God reveals His will in this matter, to him whom we sustain as a prophet, we are bound by that same will. Priesthood, when it is conferred on any man comes as a blessing from God, not of men.

We feel nothing but love, compassion, and the deepest appreciation for the rich talents, endowments, and the earnest strivings of our Negro brothers and sisters. We are eager to share with men of all races the blessings of the gospel. We have no racially-segregated congregations.

Were we the leaders of an enterprise created by ourselves and operated only according to our own earthly wisdom, it would be a simple thing to act according to popular will. But we believe that this work is directed by God and that the conferring of the priesthood must await His revelation. To do otherwise would be to deny the very premise on which the Church is established.

We recognize that those who do not accept the principle of modern revelation may oppose our point of view. We repeat that such would not wish for membership in the Church, and therefore the question of priesthood should hold no interest for them. Without prejudice they should grant us the privilege afforded under the Constitution to exercise our chosen form of religion just as we must grant all others a similar privilege. They must recognize that the question of bestowing or withholding priesthood in the Church is a matter of religion and not a matter of Constitutional right.

We extend the hand of friendship to men everywhere and the hand of fellowship to all who wish to join the Church and partake of the many rewarding opportunities to be found therein.

We join with those throughout the world who pray that all of the blessings of the gospel of Jesus Christ may in the due time of the Lord become available to men of faith everywhere. Until that time comes we must trust in God, in His wisdom and in His tender mercy.

Meanwhile we must strive harder to emulate His Son, the Lord Jesus Christ, whose new commandment it was that we should love one another. In developing that love and concern for one another, while awaiting revelations yet to come, let us hope that with respect to these religious differences, we may gain reinforcement for understanding and appreciation for such differences. They challenge our common similarities, as children of one Father, to enlarge the outreachings of our divine souls.

(David O. McKay,) Hugh B. Brown, N. Eldon Tanner
The First Presidency, (*CL*, December 15, 1969.)

Why The Negro May Not Now Hold The Priesthood

The attitude of the Church with reference to Negroes remains as it has always stood. It is not a matter of the declaration of a policy but of direct commandment from the Lord, on which is founded the doctrine of the Church from the days of its organization, to the effect that negroes may become members of the Church but that they are not entitled to the priesthood at the present time. The prophets of the Lord have made several state-ments as to the operation of the principle. President Brigham Young said:

> Why are so many of the inhabitants of the earth cursed with a skin of blackness? It comes in consequence of their fathers rejecting the power of the holy priesthood, and the law of God. They will go down to death. And when all the rest of the children have received their blessings in the holy priesthood, then that curse will be removed from the seed of Cain, and they will then come up and possess the priesthood, and receive all the blessings which we now are entitled to. *(JD-11:272)*

President Wilford Woodruff made the following statement: "The day will come when all that race will be redeemed and possess all the blessings which we now have."

The position of the Church regarding the Negro may be understood when another doctrine of the Church is kept in mind, namely, that the conduct of spirits in the premortal existence has some determining effect upon the conditions and circumstances under which these spirits take on mortality, and that while the details of this principle have not been made known, the principle itself indicates that the coming to this earth and taking on mortal-ity is a privilege that is given to those who maintained their first estate; and that the worth of the privilege is so great that spirits are willing to come to earth and take on bodies no matter what the handicap may be as to the kind of bodies they are to secure; and that among the handicaps, failure of the right to enjoy in mortality the blessings of the priesthood, is a handicap which spirits are willing to assume in order that they might come to earth. Under this principle there is no injustice whatsoever involved in this deprivation as to the holding of the priesthood by the Negroes.

David O. McKay, Stephen L. Richards, J. Reuben Clark, Jr.
The First Presidency
(The First Presidency, August 17, 1951. Quoted by
William E. Barrett in *Mormonism and the Negro.*)

Intermarriage With Negroes Is Contrary To Church Doctrine

[Compilers Note: In answering a letter by Dr. Lowery Nelson, once head of the Department of Sociology at Brigham

Young University, the First Presidency of the Church wrote as follows:]

We might make this initial remark: the social side of the Restored Gospel is only an incident of it; it is not the end thereof.

The basic element of your ideas and concepts seems to be that all God's children stand in equal positions before Him in all things.

Your knowledge of the Gospel will indicate to you that this is contrary to the very fundamentals of God's dealings with Israel dating from the time of His promise to Abraham regarding Abraham's seed and their position vis-a-vis God Himself. Indeed, some of God's children were assigned to superior positions before the world was formed. We are aware that some Higher Critics do not accept this, but the Church does.

Your position seems to lose sight of the revelations of the Lord touching the pre-existence of our spirits, the rebellion in heaven, and the doctrines that our birth into this life and the advantages under which we may be born, have a relationship in the life heretofore.

From the days of the Prophet Joseph even until now, it has been the doctrine of the Church, never questioned by any of the Church leaders, that the Negroes are not entitled to the full blessings of the Gospel.

Furthermore, your ideas, as we understand them, appear to contemplate the intermarriage of the Negro and White races, a concept which has heretofore been most repugnant to most normal-minded people from the ancient patriarchs till now. God's rule for Israel, His Chosen People, has been endogamous. Modern Israel has been similarly directed.

We are not unmindful of the fact that there is a growing tendency, particularly among some educators, as it manifests itself in this area, toward the breaking down of race barriers in the matter of intermarriage between whites and blacks, but it does not have the sanction of the Church and is contrary to Church doctrine.

George Albert Smith, J. Reuben Clark, Jr., David O. McKay
The First Presidency
(*Letter* written to Dr. Lowry Nelson, Provo, Utah,
by the First Presidency of the Church on July 17, 1947.
Letter on file at Brigham Young University.)

Designation, Not Discrimination

There is a difference between "designation" and "discrimination." It's the Lord's Priesthood, and he has the power to designate to whom it shall be given, and that power of designation has never been given to man. Therefore, there can be no discrimination among men dealing with a power over which they have no right to designate.

(*Henry D. Moyle*, First Counselor in the First Presidency, May 27, 1962. Quoted by John J. Stewart, *The Glory of Mormonism*. p. 154.)

CHAPTER 41

PEACE
(See: Military Service; War)

Only Through Obedience To The Gospel Of Jesus Christ Will Mankind Find Peace And Happiness

Today, many nations have lost their independence; men, defeated, have been compelled to labor for their conquerors, property has been seized without recompense, and millions of people have surrendered all guarantees of personal liberty.

Force and compulsion will never establish the ideal society. This can come only by a transformation within the individual soul—a life redeemed from sin and brought in harmony with the divine will. Instead of selfishness, men must be willing to dedicate their ability, their possessions, their lives, if necessary, their fortunes, and their sacred honor for the alleviation of the ills of mankind. Hate must be supplanted by sympathy and forbearance. Peace and true prosperity can come only by conforming our lives to the law of love, the law of the principles of the gospel of Jesus Christ. A mere appreciation of the social ethics of Jesus is not sufficient—men's hearts must be changed!

In these days of uncertainty and unrest, liberty-loving people's greatest responsibility and paramount duty is to preserve and proclaim the freedom of the individual, his relationship to Deity, and the necessity of obedience to the principles of the gospel of Jesus Christ. Only thus will mankind find peace and happiness.

(David O. McKay, President of the Church,
CR, October, 1962, pp. 7-8.)

The Mission Of The Church Is To Establish Peace

Men may yearn for peace, cry for peace, and work for peace, but there will be no peace until they follow the path pointed out by the living Christ. He is the true light of men's lives.

The mission of The Church of Jesus Christ of Latter-day Saints is to establish peace. The living Christ is its head. Under Him tens of thousands of men in the Church are divinely authorized to represent Him in variously assigned positions. It is the duty of these representatives to manifest brotherly love first toward one another, then toward all mankind; to seek unity, harmony, and peace in organizations within the Church, and then by precept and example extend these virtues throughout the world.

I pray that each day may find members of the Church truer, purer, nobler than the last; that they, with intellect and hearts united, may hasten the day when "the Lord will bless His people with peace" that they may "lift up an ensign of peace, and make a proclamation of peace unto the ends of the earth."

(David O. McKay, President of the Church,
CN, October 10, 1964, p. 4.)

How To Achieve Peace In A Negative Era

One of the most important teachings of Jesus Christ is his statement: "Blessed are all the peacemakers, for they shall be called the children of God." *(3 Ne. 12:9.)*

It is impossible to pick up a newspaper or listen to a news broadcast without learning of some new quarrel among nations, some new argument among politicians, some new expression of prejudice against a race or a people, or some new outburst against a person or an idea. When I read or hear of these continuing disputes, I am aware of their negative nature. People nowadays seem to be continually against something or somebody. We appear to live in a negative era. What could have brought all this about?

The answer appears to me to be that each person today wants to "do his own thing," to demonstrate his complete independence of everything and everyone. We forget that we are not, and cannot be, totally independent of one another either in thought or action. We are part of a total community. We are all members of one family, as Paul reminded the Greeks at Athens when he explained that God "hath made of one blood all nations of men to dwell on all the face of the earth." *(Acts 17:26.)*

It is small wonder then that people everywhere yearn for peace, even when quarreling one with another....

The reason Jesus Christ achieved perfection was that, instead of following his own desires and "doing his own thing," he followed the desires and the will of God, his perfect Father. Jesus said:

> For I have not spoken of myself; but the Father which sent me, he gave me a commandment, what I should say, and what I should speak.
> And I know that his commandment is life everlasting: whatsoever I speak therefore, even as the Father said unto me, so I speak." *(John 12:49-50.)*

That is a perfect way to achieve peace and harmony in our lives. If we would only follow the instructions of a perfect God, instead of following the instructions of men or blindly responding to our own selfish desires we would have peace.

(Theodore M. Burton, an Assistant to the Council of the Twelve Apostles, *CR-E*, November, 1974, pp. 54-55.)

The Proper Philosophy Of Peace

It is a curious commentary on human nature that men who cry for peace look upon peace as something that may be picked as an apple from a tree, something that lies about within easy reach of humanity. If I pick an apple from a tree, I have first planted the tree, cared for it, watered it, brought it to maturity. Then in due time I may have the fruit.

So with peace. It is not a thing by itself to be picked up casually; but it is the fruit of something precedent. Like the tree, something must be planted and nourished and cared for, if we are to obtain peace.

It is a marvel to thinking men that those who write on peace fail to understand that it can be obtained only by the use of a body of principles which, if obeyed, in time would give us peace. We cannot begin with peace; we must begin with the philosophy or the system which, if accepted and honored, will lead to peace. Failure to understand that seems to be the error of the nations at this time, of the organizations and conventions of nations, assembled in great meetings on this side and the other side of the Atlantic. They have so far failed to touch upon the foundations of peace, upon the issues which are the aids to peace. They clamor for the peace they want, without yielding obedience to the methods by which that peace may be obtained.

(John A. Widtsoe, an Apostle, *CR*, October, 1946, p. 12.)

Peace Cannot Be Legislated Into Existence

Peace upon earth is not to be established by Congress or Parliament, or by a group of international representatives. Peace is not a thing that can be taken on, then off again, as we do a piece of clothing. Peace is quite different from that. Peace cannot be legislated into existence. It is not the way to lasting peace upon earth. That, every man here understands....

Peace comes from within; peace is myself, if I am a truly

peaceful man. The very essence of me must be the spirit of peace. Individuals make up the community, and the nation—an old enough doctrine, which we often overlook—and the only way to build a peaceful community is to build men and women who are lovers and makers of peace. Each individual, by that doctrine of Christ and His Church, holds in his own hands the peace of the world.

That makes me responsible for the peace of the world, and makes you individually responsible for the peace of the world. The responsibility cannot be shifted to someone else. It cannot be placed upon the shoulders of Congress or Parliament, or any other organization of men with governing authority.

I wonder if the Lord did not have that in mind when he said: ..."the kingdom of God is within you," *(Luke 17:21)*, or perhaps we should re-emphasize it and say: "The kingdom of God is within you."

(*John A. Widtsoe*, an Apostle,
CR, October, 1943, p. 113.)

Love All Men, Including Your Enemies

Peacemakers are those who try to save themselves and their fellows from strife. Our Heavenly Father delights in peace, and all who seek to bring about peace shall be like God in that respect and shall be called the children of God.

Was not Christ the great peacemaker? He encouraged men to love and understand each other so that they could live together in peace.

The Lord has commanded us to love all men, including our enemies. He expects us to be peacemakers. He asks us to work out a reconciliation in a Christlike manner with those with whom we have difficulties or misunderstandings. It is his will that we should tolerate abuse rather than retaliate in a spirit of anger. It is better to turn the other cheek, to go the extra mile, to give our coat and our cloak also, than to offend.

(*O. Leslie Stone*, an Assistant to the Council of the
Twelve Apostles, *CR-E*, November, 1974, p. 31.)

CHAPTER 42

POLITICAL ELECTIONS AND VOTING RESPONSIBILITIES

Exercise Voting Franchise According To Convictions

The citizens of this great country are in the midst of a political campaign for the purpose of selecting candidates for office in local and state positions.

We reiterate the advice given by the leaders of the Church from time to time that it is the duty of every citizen to exercise the voting franchise in accordance with his or her convictions. We have not in the past, nor do we now seek to bring coercion or compulsion upon the membership of the Church as to their political actions. On the contrary, we have urged and do now urge that all citizens, men and women, vote according to their honest convictions. The voter should study this government and make up his mind as to what he wishes his government to be, and then, if he is so minded, vote for the one he believes will most nearly carry out his ideas about our government and its free institutions.

The General Authorities of the Church as such do not favor one political party over another; the Church has no candidate or candidates for political office; we do not undertake to tell people how to vote. We do, however, most earnestly urge every citizen of our beloved country to take advantage of the privilege and opportunity to participate in the local primaries where representatives of both political parties will be selected, and that they exercise their God-given franchise to make their wishes known at the election polls.

It is contrary to our counsel and advice that ward, branch or stake premises, chapels or other Church facilities be used in any way for political campaign purposes, whether it be for speech-making, distribution of literature, or class discussions. Needless to say, we are unalterably opposed to the use of our Sacrament or other Church meetings for any such purposes, and those who attempt to use the Church facilities to further their political ambitions are injuring their cause and doing the Church a disservice.

We appeal to all candidates for public office to take notice of this instruction and conduct their campaigns in such manner as strictly to comply with this requirement pertaining to the use of our Church buildings.

Again we urge every member of the Church who is qualified to vote to exercise his God-given franchise.

David O. McKay, Hugh B. Brown,
N. Eldon Tanner, Joseph Fielding Smith
The First Presidency, (*CL*, September 2, 1966.)

The Church Does Not Endorse Political Parties

The First Presidency has previously [*CN*-10/24/64] issued a statement urging you as citizens to participate in the great democratic processes of our national election in accordance with your honest political convictions.

We have urged you, above all, to try to support good and conscientious candidates of either party who are aware of the great dangers inherent in communism and who are truly dedicated to the constitution in the tradition of our fathers. We have suggested also that you should support candidates who pledge their sincere fidelity to our liberty—a liberty which aims at the preservation of both personal and property rights.

We again urge you to study the issues, analyze the candidates on these grounds and then exercise your franchise as free men and women. We urge you not to sell your birthright for a mess of pottage.

In giving this advice, we leave it to you to make your own choice, for the Church as such does not endorse either party. Recent receptions accorded by the First Presidency to leaders of the different parties do not imply any official endorsement by the Church.

David O. McKay, Hugh B. Brown, N. Eldon Tanner
The First Presidency, (*Deseret News*, November 2, 1964, p. 1.)

Support Candidates Aware Of The Dangers Of Communism

We find ourselves now immersed in a great political campaign in America for the purpose of selecting candidates for office in local, state, and national positions. We urge you as citizens to participate in this great democratic process, in accordance with your honest political convictions.

However, above all else, strive to support good and conscientious candidates, of either party, who are aware of the great dangers inherent in communism, and who are truly dedicated to the Constitution in the tradition of our Founding Fathers.

They should also pledge their sincere fealty to our way of liberty—a liberty which aims at the preservation of both personal and property rights.

Study the issues, analyze the candidates on these grounds, and then exercise your franchise as free men and women.

Sincerely yours,

David O. McKay, Hugh B. Brown, N. Eldon Tanner
The First Presidency, (*CN*, October 24, 1964, p. 2.)

Church Members Are Free To Join Anti-Communist Organizations

Members of the Church are free to join anti-communist organizations if they desire and their membership in the Church is not jeopardized by so doing. The Church is not opposing the John Birch Society or any other organization of like nature; however, it is definitely opposed to anyone's using the Church for the purpose of increasing membership for private organizations sponsoring these various ideologies.

(*David O. McKay*, President of the Church, representing the First Presidency, *CN*, March 16, 1963, p. 2.)

The Church Does Advocate Principles Of Good Government

[Comments on this subject were made by *Spencer W. Kimball*, President of the Church, in the April, 1974, General Conference, and can be found in the *Ensign*, May, 1974, p. 4.]

Elect Officials Of Unimpeachable Honor

Let us in The Church of Jesus Christ of Latter-day Saints, as citizens of this beloved land, use our influence to see that men and women of upright character, of unimpeachable honor, are elected to office....

(*David O. McKay*, President of the Church, *CR*, April, 1964, p. 6.)

Elect Men Who Sustain Principles Of Civil And Religious Liberty

Are we a political people? Yes, very political indeed. But what party do you belong to or would you vote for? I will tell you whom we will vote for: we will vote for the man who will sustain the principles of civil and religious liberty, the man who knows the most and who has the best heart and brain for a statesman; and we do not care a farthing whether he is a whig, a democrat, a barn-burner, a republican, a new light or anything else. These are our politics.

(*Brigham Young*, President of the Church,
JD, 1869, 13:149.)

It Is A Sin To Vote For Wicked Men

We engage in the election the same as in any other principle; you are to vote for good men, and if you do not do this it is a sin; to vote for wicked men, it would be sin. Choose the good and refuse the evil. Men of false principles have preyed upon us like wolves upon helpless lambs. Damn the rod of tyranny; curse it. Let every man use his liberties according to the Constitution. Don't fear man or devil; electioneer with all people, male and female, and exhort them to do the thing that is right. We want a President of the U. S., not a party President, but a President of the whole people; for a party President disfranchises the opposite party. Have a President who will maintain every man in his rights.

(*Hyrum Smith*, Patriarch to the Church, 1844,
Documentary History of the Church, 6:323.)

How To Determine Who To Vote For

All through the last political campaign they were saying, "Why doesn't the Church tell us how we should vote?" If the Church had done that, we would have a lot of Democrats or Republicans who would have wanted to apostatize. We believe in being subject to kings, presidents, rulers and magistrates. We are told to obey the laws of God and we will have no need to break the laws of the land. When they would ask me who to vote for in the coming election, I would tell them to read Mosiah 29 [in the *Book of Mormon*] and Section 134 of the *Doctrine and Covenants*, pray about that, and any Latter-day Saint could know who to vote for in any given election. It is just as simple as that.

(*Harold B. Lee*, an Apostle,
B.Y.U. Speeches Of The Year, April 19, 1961.)

CHAPTER 43

PORNOGRAPHY
(See: Sexual Morality and Immorality)

Avoid Smut In Any Of Its Insidious Forms

Pornographic filth continues to flood this country as well as other nations of the world.

There is abundant evidence of the damaging effect of obscenity on the solidarity of the family, on the moral fiber of the individual.

We, with many leaders outside the church, are deeply concerned about this growing obscenity in print, on record and tape, on television, and in motion pictures.

We therefore urge Latter-day Saint parents to teach their children to avoid smut in any of its many insidious forms. "Let virtue garnish thy thoughts unceasingly." *(D&C 121:45.)*

The Lord has also said: "Set in order your houses; keep slothfulness and uncleanness far from you." *(D&C 90:18.)*

We also encourage Latter-day Saints as citizens to exert every effort to fight the inroads of pornography in their communities. History is replete with examples of nations which have fallen in a large measure through licentiousness.

Harold B. Lee, N. Eldon Tanner, Marion G. Romney
The First Presidency, *(CN, October 7, 1972, p. 5.)*

Church Members Should Fight Pornography

The circulation of pornographic pictures, books, magazines, and films in nearly every community has now reached an alarming stage.

Its detrimental effect upon standards of morality is becoming so serious that all thoughtful people must unite to combat it.

Financially interested persons, claiming "the right to sell whatever the public will buy," merchandise their questionable wares with no regard for the consequences.

The sale of unclean printed matter, the showing of salacious films, the presentation of objectionable TV programs, and the dissemination of immoral material through other means have become so offensive that decent citizenry can no longer remain silent.

Even the sanctity of the home is invaded as direct-by-mail merchants thrust their debasing products upon boys and girls, many of tender years, whose names they subtly obtain for their nefarious purposes.

These merchants seem to have no concern for the morals of the people, nor for the well-being of the communities at large which invariably must suffer through the crime and corruption that always result from a lowering of standards of decency.

We are unalterably opposed to sexual immorality and to all manner of obscenity. We proclaim in the strongest terms possible against the evil and wicked designs of men who would betray virtuous manhood and womanhood, enticing them to thoughts and actions leading to vice, the lowering of standards of clean living, and the breaking up of the home.

We call upon the members of the Church and all other right-thinking people to join in a concerted movement to fight pornography wherever it may be found, whether in books and magazines, on the screen, or in materials sent through the post office.

We also urge legislators and civil authorities in every state and community to do all in their power to curb this pernicious evil.

Local as well as federal processes may be required to stem this tide, and yet such action will come only if an aroused electorate makes its feelings known.

It seems incredible that elected officials can be so far misled as to suppose that they are acting in the public interest when they allow this debasing condition to continue.

Minorities seeking to make financial gain at the expense of a silent majority should not be permitted to bring widespread tragedy upon others for want of a strong expression in defense of decency.

Every father and mother should be aroused to the danger, and should demand an immediate termination of this flagrant vice.

David O. McKay, Hugh B. Brown, N. Eldon Tanner,
Joseph Fielding Smith, Thorpe B. Isaacson
The First Presidency, (*CL*, February 19, 1966.)

Pornography And Its Relationship To Crime

[Comments on this subject were made by *Spencer W. Kimball*, President of the Church, in the October, 1974, General Conference, and can be found in the *Ensign*, November, 1974, p. 7.]

Shun Filth Wherever It Is

Priesthood bearers intent on magnifying their callings will shun as the plague the filth in our permissive society wherever it is—in literature, on the stage or screen, in recreational centers, or elsewhere. God will not countenance an unclean priesthood.
(*Marion G. Romney*, Second Counselor
in the First Presidency, *CR-E*, May, 1974, p. 82.)

Concerning *R* And *X* Rated Movies

All of us, by the flip of a switch, allow much highly questionable and some downright objectionable filth to occupy the center stage of our family circle. Public attitude against smut has very gradually been lulled into a state of mild resistance—so mild, in fact, that the adversary has already won a major victory whether we are ready to admit it or not....

How about taking just five minutes each week to review the TV log and then establishing a few rules that all the family agrees to concerning viewing time and on which channel.

Why not make some effort to find out something about the next movie that will engage your family's undivided attention for two and a half or three hours and will probably cost you far more than you contributed to the poor and the needy that month. It goes without saying that all X and R rated movies are automatically eliminated.

Robert L. Simpson, Assistant to the Council
of the Twelve, (*CR-E*, January, 1973, pp. 112-113.)

CHAPTER 44

RIGHT TO WORK LAWS

The Church Is Against "Closed Shops"

By the direction of the First Presidency we [*The Deseret News*] are reprinting today, as setting forth in general terms the attitude, heretofore and now, of the Church toward Unionism, an editorial appearing in *The Deseret News* on Friday, September 26, 1941, and also statements made by President Joseph F. Smith in 1903:

No one at all conversant with industrial history and practices can deny that in many places and under adverse conditions labor must have some organization in order to protect its members against exploitation. Furthermore, labor is entitled to a fair return for its work. What is a fair return is not a fixed sum, but is dependent upon the economic conditions of a given time and in a given place. It can never be an amount that does not leave some profit to the owner else the owner closes up and labor is without work.

But labor is not compelled to work. Slavery is forbidden by the Constitution. It would be monstrous to have a society where this was not true.

The opposite of this principle is equally true: Every man has a right to work. As President McKay once said: 'The right to work is a divine right.' No man and no group may destroy divine rights and escape the punishments that follow. A society where the right to work is denied is a society of anarchy and chaos.

Thus for their own sakes and for the welfare of the whole social body of which they are a vital part and in which they have a vital interest, labor must operate under certain restrictions and within certain limitations. It is unnecessary to trace out all these restrictions and limitations. But some of the more obvious and important are:

Labor may not legally, nor in wisdom for themselves, engage in sabotage. Force inevitably leads to counter force, and that spells social and economic ruin in the end.

Labor may not legally, nor in wisdom for labor, intimidate or coerce the worker. The worker must be left free to work when he will, be idle when he will, and to work for what he wishes, when he wishes, and where he wishes. Intimidation and coercion spell plain slavery which destroys free society.

Finally, there must be no 'closed shop' because this means the denial of the divine right to work. It is not necessary for the protection of labor and sets up a labor tyranny which too often falls under the direction of concepts, ideals, and pernicious practices foreign to the American way of life.

Sabotage, intimidation, coercion, the 'closed shop' are un-American, un-democratic, uneconomic, criminal and wholly contrary to the principles upon which any stable society can and must be organized.

No true patriot can foster, promote, or take part in any such activities or in any organization making use of them. No Church member can engage in any such activities thereto and yet maintain in his heart the spirit of the Master without which no one attains the righteous life. Honor and strength to those workers—men and women—who stand stoutly and persistently against these subversive influences.

The statements made by President Joseph F. Smith in August and June of 1903, are as follows:

If we are to have labor organizations among us, and there is no good reason why our young men might not be so organized, they should be formed on a sensible basis, and officered by men who have their families and all their interests around them. The spirit of goodwill and brotherhood, such as we have in the Gospel of Christ, should characterize their conduct and organizations. For be it known, the religious note is and should remain the dominant note of our character and of all our actions.

While there is no reason why workmen should not join together for their own mutual protection and benefit, there is every reason why in so doing they should regard the rights of their fellows, be jealous of the protections of property, and eliminate from their methods of warfare, boycotts, sympathetic strikes, and the walking delegate.

Labor unions will find that the same eternal law of justice applies to unions that applies to individuals, that fair dealing and rational conduct must be maintained if financial misfortunes are averted. Where there are Latter-day Saints in unions they should assume a conservative attitude and never arouse men's prejudices by inflaming their passions. There can be no objections to a firm and persistent contention for the right of labor, if the contention is maintained in the spirit of reason and fairness. Above all things, the Latter-day Saints should hold sacred the life and liberty of their fellowmen, as also their rights of property and maintain inviolate every right to which humanity is entitled.

The unions are forcing our people into an inconsistent and dangerous attitude when they compel Latter-day Saints within the union to make war upon their brethren who are without the union, and thereby denying the most sacred and God-given rights of one class of Saints that another class may gain some advantage over a third person, their employer. Such conduct is destructive of the liberty which every man is entitled to enjoy, and will lead in the end to the spirit of contention and apostasy.

It is not easy to see how the Latter-day Saints can endorse the methods of modern labor unions. As a people we have suffered too much from irrational class prejudice and class hatred to participate in violent and unjust agitation. No one denies the right of laborers to unite in demanding a just share of the prosperity of our country, provided the union is governed by the same spirit that should activate men who profess the guidance of a Christian conscience.

In the present status of capital and labor there should be mutual interests, and at the same time workmen should realize that there is a limit to the pressure which capital can endure by the demands made upon it. Competition has always given some measure of relief to the laborer by the demands of capital for human service and men should not therefore abandon themselves to the supposed power of arbitrary demands which labor unions are now making in many cases upon their employers. The contention for the recognition of unions is often a very indefinite factor, for no one seems to know just what the recognition means now, or what it is to mean in the future. If recognition means the exclusive right of any class of men to gain a livelihood by their work, then recognition should be persistently and forcefully resisted.

The Latter-day Saints, whether in the unions or out of them, know very well whether individual or united demands are arbitrary and unjust, and they will lose nothing by a manly refusal to violate their sense of justice.

Heber J. Grant, J. Reuben Clark Jr., David O. McKay
The First Presidency *(Deseret News*, November 29, 1941, p. 1.)

State Right To Work Laws Should Be Maintained

[Compilers Note: The following was a statement made by *President David O. McKay* representing the First Presidency. It declared that "the Church supports voluntary unionism through State Right To Work Laws.]

We stand for the Constitution of the United States and for all rights thereby to both sovereign states of the union and to the individual citizen.

We believe it is fundamental that the right to voluntary unionism should once again be reestablished in this nation and that state right to work laws should be maintained inviolate.

At the very basis of all our doctrines stands the right to the free agency of man. We are in favor of maintaining this free agency to the greatest extent possible. We look adversely upon any infringement thereof not essential to the proper exercise of police power of the state.

(David O. McKay, President of the Church, representing the First Presidency, *Salt Lake Tribune*, September 17, 1961.)

Saints Should Avoid Unions That Deprive Them Of Freedom Of Choice

Latter-day Saints should avoid affiliation with any committee, any group, any union that would, through coercion of force, deprive a person of the free exercise of his or her freedom of choice. It is understood, of course, that any person is free to join a union, when to do so favors his best interests; but no one should be compelled to join, or be deprived of any right as a citizen, including the right to honest labor, if he chooses not to become a member of a union or especially organized group.

(*David O. McKay*, Second Counselor in the First Presidency,
CR, April, 1940, p. 118.)

We are facing a crisis. You brethren and sisters should know the attitude of the Church regarding efforts of some so-called labor organizations toward coercing members of our Church into unions. I think we need not quibble. We have no apology to offer. It is un-American when five percent of this nation attempts to force ninety-five percent along a particular line of action. It is undemocratic. Yet that is just what is being attempted.

I sympathize with labor, too. So do you. We are in favor of paying the highest wages that the employer or the business man employing labor can afford to pay. There is nobody in this Church who wants to cut down wages, but we do resent the un-American attempt to say, for example, to one of our young boys who has given two years of his life to the Church and who has returned to work: "You can't remain on this job unless you pay the dues and join our union."

It isn't right. No matter what difficulties we may face, let us stand for what is right. I repeat, it is not a matter of reducing wages; it is just a question of having individual liberty to work as well as to "worship God according to the dictates of our own conscience." We will make no discrimination against a man who is or is not a member of a union, but request that a good day's work be given for compensation received. No man shall be discriminated against in regard to these things.

(*David O. McKay*, Second Counselor in the First Presidency,
IE, August, 1973, p. 496.)

CHAPTER 45

SABBATH DAY OBSERVANCE

Sabbath Observance Is The Order Of The Church

Sabbath observance is the order of the Church and is one of the basic commandments of the Lord. Hiking and camping trips on Sunday are not approved. Youth groups or others should not travel to or return from camps on Sunday, and when they are in camp on this day, all activities should conform to the teachings and spirit of the gospel. Such activities should be planned so that the Aaronic Priesthood and others are back in the ward or branch on Sunday to perform their regular assignments. When this is not possible and Church services are planned to be held out of the wards, a member of the bishopric should be present to conduct the service where possible: otherwise, he should delegate someone qualified to do so.

(GHI, 1968, p. 38.)

Proper And Improper Activities For The Sabbath Day

The Lord's day is a holy day—not a holiday. It has been set apart as a day of rest and worship. A sacred Sabbath begets reverence for God. It is not pleasing in His sight that the day be given over to pleasure seeking in places of amusement or elsewhere.

Sunday Schools and meetings have been so arranged as to meet the convenience of the people and leave a considerable portion of the Sabbath day without Church appointments. We earnestly appeal to the people to keep their meeting appointments faithfully and to utilize that portion of Sunday not appointed for meetings in promoting family association in the home, with the purpose of stimulating and establishing greater home fealty, a closer companionship among parents and children, and more intimate relations among kindred.

We believe it is unnecessary for families to go beyond their own homes or those of their kindred for the relaxation and association which are proper for the Sabbath day, and we therefore discourage more traveling than is necessary for this purpose and attendance upon appointed meetings.

Let all unnecessary labor be suspended and let no encouragement be given by the attendance of members of the Church at places of amusement and recreation on the Sabbath day. If Sunday is spent in our meetings and in our homes, great blessings will come to our families and communities.

Heber J. Grant, Anthony W. Ivins, Charles W. Nibley
The First Presidency
(CL, September 1, 1928.)

What We Should And Should Not Do On The Sabbath Day

To observe the Sabbath day properly is the plain duty of every Latter-day Saint—and that includes the young men and young women and the boys and girls. It may seem strange that it should be necessary to repeat this often asserted fact. But there appear to be some people, and sometimes whole communities, who neglect this duty and therefore stand in need of this admonition.

What are we required to do on the Sabbath day? The revelations of the Lord to the Prophet Joseph are very plain on this subject and these should govern us, for they are in strict harmony with the teachings of the Savior. Here are some of the simple requirements:

The Sabbath is appointed unto you to rest from your labors.

The Sabbath is a special day for you to worship, to pray, and to show zeal and ardor in your religious faith and duty—to pay devotions to the Most High.

The Sabbath is a day when you are required to offer your time and attention in worship of the Lord, whether in meeting, in the home, or wherever you may be—that is the thought that should occupy your mind.

The Sabbath is a day when, with your brethren and sisters, you should attend the meetings of the saints, prepared to partake of the sacrament of the Lord's supper; having first confessed your sins before the Lord and your brethren and sisters and forgiven your fellows as you expect the Lord to forgive you.

On the Sabbath day you are to do no other thing than to prepare your food with singleness of heart that your fasting may be full. This is what the Lord calls fasting and prayer.

The reason for this required course upon the Sabbath day is also plainly stated in the revelations. It is that one may more fully keep himself unspotted from the world, and to this end, also, the saints are required to go to the house of prayer and offer up their sacraments on the Sabbath day.

Now, what is the promise to the saints who observe the Sabbath? The Lord declares that inasmuch as they do this with cheer-

ful hearts and countenances, the fulness of the earth is theirs:
"the beasts of the field and the fowls of the air, and that which
climbeth upon the trees and walketh upon the earth; Yea, and the
herb, and the good things which come of the earth, whether for
food or for rainment, or for houses, or for barns, or for orchards,
or for gardens, or for vineyards." (D&C 59.)

These are all made for the benefit and use of man to please
the eye and to gladden the heart, to strengthen the body and to
enliven the soul. All are promised to those who keep the commandments and this important one, to observe properly the Sabbath day.

The Lord is not pleased with people who know these things
and do them not.

Men are not resting from their labors when they plow and
plant and haul and dig. They are not resting when they linger a-
round the home all day on Sunday, doing odd jobs that they
have been too busy to do on other days.

Men are not showing zeal and ardor in their religious faith
and duty when they hustle off early Sunday morning on the cars,
automobiles, to the canyons, the resorts, and to visit friends or
places of amusement with their wives and children. They are not
paying their devotions in this way to the Most High.

Not in seeking pleasure and recreation do they offer their
time and attention in the worship of the Lord, nor can they thus
rejoice in the spirit of forgiveness and worship that comes with
partaking of the holy sacrament.

Boys and young men are not fasting with singleness of heart
that their joy may be full when they spend the Sabbath day
loafing around the village ice-cream stand or restaurant, playing
games, or in buggy riding, fishing, shooting, or engaged in physical
sports, excursions, and outings. Such is not the course that will
keep them unspotted from the world, but rather one that will
deprive them of the rich promises of the Lord, giving them sorrow
instead of joy, and unrest and anxiety instead of the peace that
comes with works of righteousness.

Let us play and take recreation to our hearts' content during
other days, but on the Sabbath let us rest, worship, go to the house
of prayer, partake of the sacrament, eat our food with singleness
of heart, and pay our devotions to God that the fulness of the
earth may be ours and that we may have peace in this world and
eternal life in the world to come.

"But," says one, "In our settlement we have no other day
for amusement and sports, excursions and outings, ball games and
races."

Then demand one.

Is it possible that parents in the face of the promises of the Lord will deny a day in the week when their children may have recreation, and so force them to spend the Sabbath in sports!

One prominent man in one of the northern stakes where ball games and other sports are said to be the rule on Sunday asked what could be done to remedy the evil. He was told to try a half holiday on one of the week days.

"Then," he replied, "we can have no change nor remedy. Here are hundreds of acres of hay and ripening fields crying for workmen, and we cannot spare our boys for play."

The best reply to such an argument is the question: Which is best—to let the hay go to ruin, or the boy?...Let the hay go; save the boy. He is worth more than all your material possessions. Save him in the spirit of the gospel—protect him from Sabbath breaking—by offering a little temporal sacrifice, and the Lord will keep his promise to you. Get together in your ward, unitedly select a day for play and recreation; and like faithful saints demand that the Sabbath day as far as you and yours are concerned shall be devoted to the Lord, our God.

> (*Joseph F. Smith*, President of the Church,
> *IE*, July, 1910, pp. 842-844.)

A good modern eighth commandment might read something like this: Do not so overwork and fret on Saturday as to deprive the Sabbath of the devotions and worship that belong to it as a day of rest.

In the home, Saturday is the day set apart for house cleaning, for extra cooking, for mending and all sorts of repairs that the Sabbath is thought to require. In business, Saturday is a day for picking up all loose ends, for closing up all the unfinished details of a week's work.

The consequences of our modern treatment of the last day of the week are too often manifested in an indolence and supine indifference that make our feelings and a total lack of energy almost incompatible with the spirit of worship. No worn-out man or woman, by the excessive toil of an early Saturday morning and a late Saturday night, can properly worship God in spirit and in truth.

> (*Joseph F. Smith*,
> President of the Church
> *JI*, July, 1909, p. 295.)

Make No Sunday Purchases

[Comments on this subject were made by *Spencer W. Kimball,* President of the Church, in the October, 1974, General Conference, and can be found in the *Ensign,* November, 1974, p. 6.]

How To Keep The Sabbath Holy

I plead with you, my brethren and sisters, to observe the Sabbath day and keep it holy. This is one of the great Ten Commandments the Lord has given, and do not get the idea that this commandment was a part of the law of Moses which was done away in Christ. The Decalogue was older than Moses, it continued after Moses passed away. The Lord has reiterated these commandments, he has renewed them and commanded us in our day to observe them and keep them sacredly and holy, and therefore I plead with you.

We ought not to be playing baseball on the Sabbath day. We ought not to be going to the resorts, we ought to keep away from these picture houses on the Sabbath day. It was my privilege some years ago to go through the East Central States Mission. In the city of Goldsborough, on the Sabbath day, we were granted the use of the leading show house, the best one in the city, in which to hold our meetings, three of them, morning, afternoon and night, without any charge. It was free for us to hold religious services and closed against the amusements which were in that house all other days of the week. The people were quiet, there were no great gatherings on the streets, in the parks, or shouting at baseball games or other sports. The people were quietly engaged in prayer and going to their churches. I thought, Why can't we have that among our own people in the West? I felt somewhat ashamed. We cannot do anything, it seems, today in the way of sports, unless we have to include such sports on the Sabbath day. When we want to engage in skiing, to find men to enter the Olympics, it appears that we have to do it on the Sabbath day. When we dedicate a park or playground in this city, we think we have to do it on the Sabbath day. Our hunting and fishing season must begin on the Sabbath day.

These things are displeasing in the sight of God, and I speak not merely for the Latter-day Saints, but for all good Christian people. If they believe in the words of Chirst, in the words of the scripture, then they ought to sanction what I am saying, and when we turn from the commandments the Lord has given unto us for our guidance then we do not have a claim upon his blessings.

(Joseph Fielding Smith, an Apostle, *CR*, October, 1935, pp. 14-15.)

Live The Sabbath Day Within The Framework Of The Doctrine & Covenants

In this, our day, the Lord has put great emphasis on observance of the Sabbath day. When the Saints first went to Independence, Missouri, he gave them a list of standards which must be observed by those who are to build up and live in that Zion. One of them upon which he put great emphasis was observance of the Sabbath day. He said:

> And that thou mayest more fully keep thyself unspotted from the world, thou shalt go to the house of prayer and offer up thy sacraments upon my holy day;
>
> For verily this is a day appointed unto you to rest from your labors, and to pay thy devotions unto the Most High;
>
> ...remember that on this, the Lord's day, thou shalt offer thine oblations and thy sacraments unto the Most High, confessing thy sins unto thy brethren, and before the Lord.
>
> And on this day, thou shalt do none other thing, only let thy food be prepared with singleness of heart that thy fasting may be perfect, or, in other words, that thy joy may be full. *(D&C 59:9-10, 12-13.)*

Because we live in a Sabbath-breaking society, we must—if we would magnify our callings in the priesthood—live in the world but not be of the world, for the Lord has said, "...the inhabitants of Zion shall...observe the Sabbath day to keep it holy." *(D&C 68:29.)*

We need not shop on the Sabbath day. There will be no shopping in the city of Zion on the Sabbath.

We need not attend recreational events, nor hunt or fish on the Sabbath.

If we are really intent on magnifying our callings in the priesthood, we will on the Sabbath day live within the framework of the instructions given by the Lord in that section of the Doctrine and Covenants.

(Marion G. Romney, Second Counselor in the First Presidency, *CR-E*, May, 1974, p. 80.)

What We May Do On The Sabbath Day

The Lord has told us what we may do in the house of prayer; and what we may do in the house of prayer we may do, I take it, in our homes. We may seek learning. We may read good books. We may acquaint ourselves with languages, tongues, and people.

I call your attention again to the fact that the only places of gathering to which we are authorized to go, the only gatherings we are authorized to attend, are the meetings in the house of prayer. No other gathering is authorized on the Sabbath.

I think we may listen to good music in the home. I do not think we may go joyriding, nor to beach parties nor on picnics! Nowadays, as this conference is witnessing throughout this valley and in adjacent areas, you may have what we may call movies right in your home. We shall have them tomorrow, Sunday. I think there is a great difference between looking at a good movie in your home and going to a movie house, a very great difference. But the home movies we look at should be of a kind that teach things specified in the revelations, as would be in order in the house of prayer.

Of course, I do not suppose there is any need of my even mentioning, though perhaps it might be well for me to mention, that horse racing on Sunday is not a proper place for a Latter-day Saint to be. They have a good deal of it, they tell me, in the southern part of the state. I have been in touch with some of the officers and know how difficult they think it is to handle. If you Latter-day Saints cannot stay away from horse racing and betting on Sunday, I am not sure how much the Lord is going to listen to your prayers about some other things that you very much desire. Of course, we may not gamble at any time or in any place.

(*J. Reuben Clark Jr.*, First Counselor in the First Presidency, *CR*, October, 1950, pp. 107-111.)

Refrain From Buying On The Sabbath Day

Unless the world alters the course of its present trends (and that is not likely); and if, on the other hand, we continue to follow the teachings of the prophets, we shall increasingly become a peculiar and distinctive people of whom the world will take note. For instance:...

As the Sabbath increasingly becomes a day of merchandising, those who obey the precept of the law written by the finger of the Lord on Sinai and reinforced by modern revelation will appear more unusual....

We can refrain from buying on the Sabbath day. With six other days in the week none of us needs to buy furniture on Sunday. None of us needs to buy clothing on Sunday. With a a little careful planning we can easily avoid the purchase of groceries on Sunday.

(Gordon B. Hinckley, an Apostle, *CR-E*, November, 1974, p. 100.)

The Sabbath Day Is More Than Just A Day Of Rest

What is the purpose of the Sabbath Day? Is it a day for rest alone, or for relaxation and recreation? Or does it have a deeper meaning?

There are many who just "rest" on the Sabbath, and who seldom if ever attend church services. But they do read Sunday papers, watch TV, eat heavy dinners, and nap on the front room couch. Is this what the Lord expects?

And there are many who golf or ski on Sunday or fish or hunt and come home tired at night to sleep and thus recoup their energies. Have they pleased the Lord?

One man said: "Sunday is just a day of rest, and the important thing is to get some relaxation and rest from the normal routine."

Another said: "If going to church is unpleasant, stay away."

And still another: "Sunday is no different from Monday in the eyes of the Lord. Do on Sunday what you would on Monday."

Views such as those are what have made Sunday a day of fun and recreation for much of the world and drawn them away from the Lord. But is that God's idea of the Sabbath?

The Lord did set apart the Sabbath from Mondays and all other days. He did call it "My holy day." He did declare it a day of rest, but He did not stop there, for He made it a day of worship as well. He made it a time for building His kingdom.

It is just as much a violation of the Sabbath to refuse to worship as it is to resume our usual employment on that day.

It is just as much a violation of the Sabbath to spend the day in recreation as to spend it in making money.

Sunday is for rest—plus—and that plus includes going to the house of prayer "on My holy day" and there offering up our sacraments and oblations to the Lord, confessing our sins to our brethren and making the necessary adjustment in our lives—upward.

It includes building the kingdom of God by our good works.

Rest alone on the Sabbath is a violation of the spirit of the Sabbath.

Skiing and similar activities on Sunday are violation of the Sabbath.

Failure to attend church services without a reasonable excuse is a violation of both the law and the spirit of the Sabbath.

Failure to truly worship God on that day is a violation of the principle of Sabbath observance.

Sunday should be given over to sincere worship of the Lord, to building His kingdom, to increasing our faith, to teaching our children the principles of the gospel; to bringing about closer family solidarity; to making reconciliation with those whom we have offended, this before we "bring our gift to the altar;" and to "keeping ourselves unspotted from the sins of the world."

And what else did the Lord say? "And on this day thou shalt do none other thing, only let thy food be prepared with singleness of heart." *(D&C 59)*

If we are sincere followers of the Savior, we do not have the option of doing anything that pleases our vanity on His holy day, for He has commanded us in firm language what we are to do, and that is, to worship Him!

(Editorial, *CN*, February 22, 1975, p. 16.)

Concerning T. V. Viewing On The Sabbath

[Comments on this subject were made by *Spencer W. Kimball*, President of the Church, in the June, 1975 *Ensign*, on page 6.]

CHAPTER 46

SEX EDUCATION

Sex Education Is The Responsibility Of Parents

The following statement concerning sex education in the schools is repeated in order that members of the Church who are not aware may be informed of the view of the First Presidency on the subject:

> We believe that serious hazards are involved in entrusting to the schools the teaching of this vital and important subject to our children. This responsibility cannot wisely be left to society, nor the schools; nor can the responsibility be shifted to the Church. It is the responsibility of parents to see that they fully perform their duty in this respect.
>
> *(PB*, June, 1971.)

Students Should Discuss Sex Education With Their Parents

Nearly all students are exposed to sex education in the public schools. Therefore, they should know how the First Presidency feels about this:

> We believe that serious hazards are involved in entrusting to the schools the teaching of this vital and important subject to our children. This responsibility cannot wisely be left to society, nor the schools; nor can the responsibility be shifted to the Church. It is the responsibility of parents to see that they fully perform their duty in this respect.

Talk to your parents. Ask them your questions. It will honor them, and you will discover that they are the persons who can best answer your candid and honest questions. When sex education is presented in school, discuss it with your parents and together keep things in perspective.

(Policies & Procedures, *NE*, November, 1971, p. 47.)

Some Teachers Rob The Creative Act Of All Sanctity

Some teachers have tried to lay bare to our youth the mysteries of life, and so have robbed the creative act of all the sanctity with which from the beginning God has enshrouded it. These have given no restraining righteous principle in its place. So, with too many, modesty has become a derided virtue, and the sex desire has been degraded to the level of hunger and thirst.

Heber J. Grant, J. Reuben Clark Jr., David O. McKay
The First Presidency *(CR,* October, 1942, pp. 9-10.)

The False Concepts Of Sex Education

These deceptive and shadowed objectives of well-propagan-dized programs are moving at a very rapid clip. The first to which I refer is sex education or family life education, which is placing emphasis on raw sex in the school classroom, creating widespread contention, causing deep concern among parents and leaders.

The programmers of this type of sex education, aware of resistance, are fortified with worked-out methods to deal with parental and community opposition. This matter needs the serious concern of an aroused public to deny the use of such materials and more firmly establish sound moral teachings in the fields of phys-iology and hygiene, as now provided by public school law.

The National Education Association and American Medical Association's endorsement of a maturation educational program seems to have stepped up the activity of such organizations as the Sex Information and Education Council of the United States (known as SIECUS) and the School Health Education Studies (known as SHES), with others, particularly those that are integrated in family life education courses.

With ominous precision, reputable publishing houses are competing in this untapped market with expertly prepared materials, films, and teaching aids of all sorts. Herein, because of its sensational marketable value, is a formidable danger.

False images in the life of the very young will result from their idea to teach facts of reproduction before youth are emotionally involved. The misguided fostering of sex education in the class-room on the basis that it will lessen sex ignorance and reduce illegitimate pregnancy, venereal disease, and related problems has no basis for sound conclusions. Actual experience has proven the results to be just the opposite.

(Alvin R. Dyer, a Counselor in the First Presidency,
CR, April, 1969, pp. 54-55.)

In schoolrooms the children are taught what is popularly called "the facts of life." Instead of bringing about the alleged purpose of the teaching, that is, the strengthening of the morals of youth, this teaching seems to have had directly the opposite effect. The teaching seems merely to have whetted curiosity and augumented appetite. Never before, in my lifetime, has immorality had the tolerance and the prevalence it has today among youth and the middle-aged.

(*J. Reuben Clark Jr.*, Second Counselor in the First Presidency, *RSM*, December, 1952, p. 794.)

CHAPTER 47

SEXUAL MORALITY AND IMMORALITY
(See: Abortion; Adultery; Birth Control;
Dress Standards; Homosexualtiy; Marriage; Sex Education.)

Immorality Handled By Church Courts

Cases handled by Church Courts...include...fornication, adultery, homosexual acts, or other infractions of the moral code....
(GHI, 1968, p. 122.)

Illicit Non-Marital Sexual Relationships Stand In Enormity Next To Murder

The doctrine of this Church is that sexual sin—the illicit sexual relations of men and women—stands, in its enormity, next to murder.

The Lord has drawn no essential distinctions between fornication, adultery, and harlotry or prostitution. Each has fallen under His solemn and awful condemnation.

You youths of Zion, you cannot associate in non-marital, illicit sex relationships, which is fornication, and escape the punishments and the judgments which the Lord has declared against this sin. The day of reckoning will come just as certainly as night follows day. They who would palliate this crime and say that such indulgence is but a sinless gratification of a normal desire, like appeasing hunger and thirst, speak filthiness with their lips. Their counsel leads to destruction; their wisdom comes from the Father of Lies.

You husbands and wives who have taken on solemn obligations of chastity in the holy temples of the Lord and who violate those sacred vows by illicit sexual relations with others, you not only commit the vile and loathsome sin of adultery, but you break the oath you yourselves made with the Lord Himself before you went to the altar for your sealing. You become subject to the penalties which the Lord has prescribed for those who breach their covenants with Him.

Of the harlots and those who visit them, God speaks in terms of divine contempt. They are they who have bargained away an eternity of bliss for the momentary pleasures of the flesh.

The Lord will have only a clean people. He has said, "I, the Lord, will contend with Zion, and plead with her strong ones, and chasten her until she overcomes and is clean before me." *(D&C 90:36)*

But they who sin and repent, and, they repenting, God will forgive them, for the Lord has said, "Behold, he who has repented of his sins, the same is forgiven, and I, the Lord, remember them no more." *(D&C 58;42)*

By virtue of the authority in us vested as the First Presidency of the Church, we warn our people who are offending, of the degradation, the wickedness, the punishment that attend upon unchastity; we urge you to remember the blessings which flow from the living of the clean life; we call upon you to keep, day in and day out, the way of strictest chastity, through which only can God's choice gifts come to you and His Spirit abide with you.

How glorious is he who lives the chaste life. He walks unfearful in the full glare of the noonday sun, for he is without moral infirmity. He can be reached by no shafts of base calumny, for his armor is without flaw. His virtue cannot be challenged by any just accuser, for he lives above reproach. His cheek is never blotched with shame, for he is without hidden sin. He is honored and respected by all mankind, for he is beyond their censure. He is loved by the Lord, for he stands without blemish. The exaltations of eternities await his coming.

Heber J. Grant, J. Reuben Clark Jr., David O. McKay
The First Presidency
(CR, October, 1942, pp. 11-12.)

The Church Is Dedicated To One Moral Standard

In The Church of Jesus Christ of Latter-day Saints there is but one standard of morality. No young man has any more right to sow his wild oats in youth than has a young girl. He who is unchaste in young manhood is untrue to a trust given to him by the parents of the girl, and she who is unchaste in maidenhood is untrue to her future husband and lays the foundation of unhappiness in the home, suspicion, and discord. Do not worry about these teachers who encourage promiscuity and self-gratification. Just keep in mind this eternal truth, that chastity is a virtue to be prized as one of the life's noblest achievements.

In this day when modesty is thrust into the background, and chastity is considered an outmoded virtue, I appeal to parents especially, and to my fellow teachers, both in and out of the

Church, to teach youth to keep their souls unmarred and unsullied from this and other debasing sins, the consequences of which will smite and haunt them intimately until their conscience is seared and their character becomes sordid. A chaste, not a profligate, life is the source of virile manhood. The test of true womanhood comes when the woman stands innocent at the court of chastity. All qualities are crowned by this most precious virtue of beautiful womanhood. It is the most vital part of the foundation of a happy married life and is the source of strength and perpetuity of the race.

(David O. McKay, President of the Church, *CR,* April, 1967, pp. 7-8.)

The Lighted Way Eventually Brings Couples To A Virtuous Union

[Comments on this subject were made by *Spencer W. Kimball,* President of the Church, in the April, 1974, General Conference, and can be found in the *Ensign,* May, 1974, p. 6.]

Living A Life Of Moral Purity Brings Joy And Happiness

It is the duty of parents and of the Church not only to teach but also to demonstrate to young people that living a life of truth and moral purity brings joy and happiness, while violations of moral and social laws result only in dissatisfaction, sorrow, and, when carried to extreme, in degradation.

(David O. McKay, President of the Church, *CR,* April, 1967, p. 6.)

Abstain From Petting And Other Improper Sexual Relationships

[Comments on this subject were made by *Spencer W. Kimball,* President of the Church, in the April, 1974, General Conference, and can be found in the *Ensign,* May, 1974, p. 7.]

Men And Women Who Change Their Sex Status Will Answer To Their Maker

[Comments on this subject were made by *Spencer W. Kimball,* President of the Church, in the October, 1974, General Conference, and can be found in the *Ensign,* November, 1974, p. 8.]

Better Dead Clean, Than Alive Unclean

Youth, if you want to be guided by wisdom, stay close to your parents. Listen to the counsel of your father and your mother and lean heavily upon the experience of their lives, because they are entitled to inspiration in the rearing of their family. Young men, may I plead with you to keep yourself morally clean? Revere womanhood. May I remind you of what our youth repeated some years ago as a slogan in the MIA. It was a quotation from a portion of a message of the First Presidency particularly to servicemen in military service during some of these strenuous, difficult times through which you and others like you have lived. This is what the First Presidency wrote:

"How glorious and near to the angels is youth that is clean. This youth has joy unspeakable here and eternal happiness hereafter. Sexual purity is youth's most precious possession. It is the foundation of all righteousness. Better dead clean, than alive unclean."

(Harold B. Lee, an Apostle,
IE, June, 1954, pp. 409-410.)

The Lord Does Not Approve Of Masturbation Or Homosexuality

[Comments on this subject were made by *Spencer W. Kimball*, an Apostle, at Brigham Young University on January 5, 1965: see the *B.Y.U. Extension Publication* for that date. See also: *The Miracle of Forgiveness*, pp. 77-78.]

CHAPTER 48

SUICIDE

Concerning The Holding Of Funerals For Those Who Committed Suicide

Holding of funerals for suicides:

"Where a person dies under unusual circumstances, the place and nature of the services are matters for the family to decide in consultation with the bishop."

(GHI, 1968, p. 161)

To Take One's Own Life Is Self-Murder, A Dreadful Sin

We are asked:

"If a member of the Church should commit suicide because of unrequited love, or other exciting cause, would it be proper for the authorities of the ward to have a public funeral service in such a case as a mark of respect to the family, who may be faithful members of the Church?"

Every member of the Church should be made to understand that it is a dreadful sin to take one's own life. It is self-murder, and, therefore, anyone committing this crime should not expect a public and honorable funeral. There is a wide distinction between the condition of one who dies a natural death and one who dies by his own hand. No one should be led to believe that if he commits this sinful act he will still receive the same respect and honor at his burial from the Priesthood and people of God that others do who die as faithful members of the Church. No encouragement of this kind should be given to anyone who has an inclination to commit suicide. For this reason a person who commits suicide should be buried privately and without ostentations, and certainly the funeral services should be conducted without the authorities of the Church lending their presence to the funeral. All should be taught that it is a sin of great magnitude to take the life which the Creator has given to them.

An epidemic of suicides prevailed at one time in Paris, and various devices were suggested to check its course. The last method adopted was to expose the naked body of the suicide in the public morgue. It is said that this was so disgraceful and had such an effect upon the public mind that the number of suicides immediately fell off, and the tendency was checked. In many countries and among many religious sects suicides (unless a jury brings in a verdict that the person who has taken his own life was insane) are not permitted to be buried in what is called consecrated ground—that is, to be buried in the same cemetery with those who die natural deaths.

> (*George Q. Cannon*, First Counselor in the
> First Presidency, *JI*, June 1, 1893, p. 352.)

People Are No More Justified In Killing Themselves Than They Are In Killing Others

Suicide, or self-murder, is becoming an event of startling frequency in our country. At no time since the people came to these valleys has there been so many suicides in proportion to the population as of late. In fact, in early days, it was a crime almost unknown to the people; and if a self-murder occurred, it shocked the community and excited deep and wide-spread comment. But now there is scarcely a daily paper without an account of some person having attempted self-destruction. A mania for self-killing appears to be going through the country. No doubt the commission of this act by one suggests the crime to others. Weak-minded people, or those who have a love for notoriety, brood over the killing of which they have heard, until their minds become morbid and partly insane upon the subject, and in a moment of temptation they destroy themselves.

The frequency with which this crime is committed calls loudly upon those in authority in the community to take some measures to check the mania. It should receive immediate attention. The seal of public condemnation should be put upon suicide. Those who have an inclination of this kind should be made to understand that in killing themselves, they gain an infamous notoriety and bring upon themselves public dishonor and the same condemnation that is attached to murder of every kind.

This crime is increasing rapidly in the United States and other nations. It seems to be one of the results of Satan's increased influence over the children of men. Having no tabernacle himself, he would like to prompt every child of God to destroy his body.

When a human being becomes possessed of the devil, the tabernacle is soon wrecked; for neither he nor his companion spirits know to what use to put a fleshly tabernacle except to destroy it.

Man did not create himself. He did not furnish his spirit with a human dwelling place. It is God who created man, both body and spirit. Man has no right, therefore, to destroy that which he had no agency in creating. They who do so are guilty of murder, self-murder it is true; but they are no more justified in killing themselves than they are in killing others. What difference of punishment there is for the two crimes, I do not know; but it is clear that no one can destroy so precious a gift as that of life without incurring a severe penalty.

By the people of mediaeval times the remains of those who were guilty of this offense were treated as the remains of other murderers. In England, it was the practice to dig the grave of the suicide in a place where four roads met. The body was consigned to the hole, and a stake was driven through it into the ground, and it was then covered up. This was a barbarous method of treating the lifeless remains of a human being; but it clearly expresses the horror that was entertained by the people of those days of this dreadful crime. It doubtless was designed to be barbarous in order to impress the minds of the people with the awful consequences of such an act, and to show the execration with which the memories of suicides would be held by surviving generations. To this day places of this kind, where the bodies of suicides were buried are known and pointed out by the common people. The remembrance of the manner in which they destroyed themselves, and their burial places, are perpetuated from generation to generation, and such spots are dreaded and shunned, especially in the night.

This custom of refusing Christian burial to self-murderers prevails upon the continent of Europe. The Catholic church in Europe rigidly excludes murderers from burial in what is known as consecrated ground. This is the rule also where the Greek church, the Lutheran church and the church of England have control. The mortal remains of no suicide is permitted to be buried in ground which has been consecrated as the last resting place of those who lead proper lives. In this way these churches show their condemnation of this crime. I think the Latter-day Saints should do no less. There is no people who are taught as we are to place a high value upon life. We are taught to look upon murder as a most frightful crime. The sacredness and importance of human life are impressed upon us by every revelation which God has given concerning man and his future destiny. The Spirit of God impresses man to look with abhorrence upon the shedding of blood; and no man, who is possessed of it, will take the life of an animal, a foul, a fish, or even an insect, unnecessarily.

In order to palliate the crime of self-murder there is a disposition often shown to attribute the act to insanity or aberation of mind. This is especially so where the individual who destroys himself or herself has been respected, or where they have respectable connections. In this way it is thought the feelings of surviving relatives will be saved. Doubtless there are many cases of self-murder which are due to insanity; but that this mania can be greatly controlled and checked, experience has abundantly proven. At one time, in the city of Paris, the mania for self destruction became almost an epidemic. The authorities, being alarmed at the increase of the crime, took the subject into consideration, and, finally, decided to expose the body of every suicide, stripped of every vestige of clothing, to the gaze of all the public, who chose to visit the morgue, or dead-house. It seemed a brutal thing to do, but the epidemic needed a strong remedy. It had the desired effect. Suicides almost ceased. Even abandoned women shrank from committing self-murder in view of such a penalty--the exposure of their persons after death to the vulgar gaze. This experiment plainly proves that there can be checks used to prevent this crime.

I do not believe that many would commit suicide among us if it were known beforehand that such indignities as I have referred to would be heaped upon their lifeless remains. But if officers and members of our Church meet together, and some of our Elders, with eloquent words, bear testimony to the moral worth and the excellent traits of character of the one who has violently taken his or her own life, and then a cortege is formed to accompany the body, with solemn pageantry, to the cemetery, to consign it to a resting place amidst the honored dead whose lives have been just and pure, what is there to make the living think that self-murder is a dreadful sin against God and against humanity?

Many perhaps will think this language harsh. Sympathy for the families of those who commit this deed would prompt words of comfort, because of the dreadful trial to which they are subjected; but this crime is becoming too common to admit of this method of dealing with it. Justice to the living—justice to the rising generation, demands that it shall receive the condemnation which it deserves. It is murder, and men and women can not be justified in staining their hands even with their own blood or in taking their own lives.

The Church of Jesus Christ of Latter-day Saints should set

its seal of reprobation and condemnation upon this dreadful act. Instead of honoring them who commit it by making their funerals distinguished, and treating them as though they were dead heroes or heroines, and making no distinction between them and those who have worn themselves out in the service of their God, let them be buried in secret and without display, and in ground far removed from the burial places of those who have lived lives of honor and purity.

(*George Q. Cannon*, First Counselor in the First Presidency,
JI, September 15, 1886, pp. 274-275.)

Only A Fool Would Ever Consider Taking His Own Life

[Comments on this subject were made by *Spencer W. Kimball*, an Apostle, in his book: *The Miracle of Forgiveness*, 1969, pp. 99, 130.]

CHAPTER 49

TAXES

Priesthood Leaders Are To Be On Guard Against Persons Opposing Federal Tax Laws

Officials of the Internal Revenue Service have called attention to the fact that certain individuals, who claim Church membership, are making it appear as though their opposition to the Federal tax laws is Church sponsored. We call attention to what was said by the President of the Church at a recent General Priesthood Meeting on this subject:

> Now there is another danger that confronts us. There seem to be those among us who are as wolves among the flock, trying to lead some who are weak and unwary among Church members, according to reports that have reached us, who are taking the law into their own hands by refusing to pay their income tax because they have some political disagreement with constituted authorities. *(Harold B. Lee* in *Conference Report of The Church of Jesus Christ of Latter-day Saints*, Oct. 1972, p. 127.)

We ask priesthood leaders to be on guard against such persons. They are not to be invited to speak in priesthood or sacrament meetings, firesides, or other Church meetings in attempting to spread their propaganda. Priesthood leaders should also teach the necessity of abiding the law according to the revelations. The Lord has said:

> Let no man break the laws of the land, for he that keepeth the laws of God hath no need to break the laws of the land.
> Wherefore, be subject to the powers that be, until he reigns whose right it is to reign, and subdues all enemies under his feet. *(D&C 58:21-22.)*

(*PB*, April, 1973, p. 1.)

The Power To Tax Is The Power To Destroy

And in Article IX of the same Bill of Rights is written:

> The enumeration in the Constitution, of certain rights, shall not be construed to deny or disparage others retained by the people.

This is an absolute recognition by the government of the inherent right of free agency of man. He should be deprived of as little of his freedom as possible. None, as a matter of fact, without his consent—that is, the consent of the majority. Even then, the limitations placed upon man's free agency should be confined to those essentials of government by which our security is insured, and the individuals permitted to live lives of liberty and to pursue happiness as they would.

The difficulty with all governments, and one to which our own has fallen heir, is that the majority, by virtue of its right to place limitations on man's free agency, has undertaken to infringe upon the rights reserved to the individual, for the direct and immediate benefit of the majority individually rather than for the establishment of law and order. For example: the Constitution expressly prohibits taking of personal property for public purposes without just compensation. Under the guise of taxation, the Constitution is violated and property is taken from one and given to another. This demonstrates clearly the power to tax is the power to destroy. That is the course which we now pursue. Even here it is a question of the proper use of our free agency. The Constitution defines our rights. Our difficulties today come as a result of the use we make of our own free agency in preserving and protecting these rights, which should be unalienable, as declared....

I for myself have long since determined that a safe criterion by which movements political, social, or religious can be judged meritoriously is by their impact upon our Godly attribute of free agency.

(*Henry D. Moyle*, an Apostle,
RSM, 1957, 44:577-578.)

The Spendthrift Policies Of Government Aid Revolutionists

At a recent business conference, the chairman is quoted as having said, with reference to our tax structure, which he said could be improved, but that taxes would continue to be high for a "long time:" "Better, then, to face up to this fact, and then go ahead with business expansion plans. As a short range effect, business will be helping to get and keep the economy on its feet and the principles of private enterprise more firmly entrenched."

The ultimate principle behind this is just as sinister as the "no-trouble" concept. It reduces itself to this: Accept the spendthrift policies of government, and make no fight against them, take no aggressive stand, and, of course, no agressive measures, but make all the money you can, and so furnish to the revolutionary crew [Communists and Socialists] more taxes with which to carry out all their perverting plans and policies.

It is reported further that business and industry are at the moment much perturbed lest there should be a violent depression that shall bring on trouble; so we must do more pump priming. Here again we are to yield all that is asked—go ahead somehow and make money, more money, and more money, for the revolutionists to spend, tying us down, in the thought that this will forestall the evil day.

(*J. Reuben Clark*, First Counselor in the
First Presidency, *CN*, September 25, 1949, p. 2.)

CHAPTER 50

TITHING

Pay One Tenth Of All Income Annually

Inquiries are received at the office of the First Presidency from time to time from officers and members of the Church asking for information as to what is considered a proper tithe.

For your guidance in this matter, please be advised that we have uniformly replied that the simplest statement we know of is the statement of the Lord himself, namely, that the members of the Church should pay "one-tenth of all their interest annually," which is understood to mean income. No one is justified in making any other statement than this.

We feel that every member of the Church is entitled to make his own decision as to what he thinks he owes the Lord and to make payment accordingly.

Sincerely yours,
Joseph Fielding Smith, Harold B. Lee, N. Eldon Tanner
The First Presidency *(CL*, March 19, 1970.)

Those Without Income Are Exempt From Paying Tithing

Church members should pay one-tenth of their interest (income) annually into the tithing funds of the Church.

Those without income (including wives who have no separate income from their husbands), and those entirely dependent on relief, are exempt from the payment of tithing.

Missionaries on full-time missions are not required to pay tithing on money received from their families or others for their support. Additional personal income should be tithed.

(GHI, 1968, p. 102.)

What Should Be Tithed

In a very early period of the history of this Church, when in its infancy, the Lord said unto us, in a revelation which is contained in the *Doctrine and Covenants*, "He that is Tithed shall not be burned." In several of the revelations the subject of Tithing is referred to in a general way; but the special revelation on that subject was given at Far West, Missouri, in July, 1838, in answer to the question, "O Lord, shew unto thy servants how much thou requirest of the properties of thy people for Tithing." And by this revelation we learned that we were required to consecrate all of our surplus property for the purposes mentioned therein, and after doing that, to pay annually one-tenth of our increase. This means increase from every source. For instance, if a man depend only upon the labor of his own hands, then one-tenth of his earnings would be his lawful Tithing. But if in addition to this he possess teams or employ other labor, then the increase of such labor should also be Tithed. Again, if he should be engaged opening up farms, building or making other improvements, thus accumulating a surplus around him, one-tenth of the increase of such property would be due, as Tithing, as well as a tenth of his labor combined. Then again, should part of his surplus property be in such a condition as to enable him to invest it in any branch of business, one-tenth of the profits arising therefrom is due as Tithing; or should he have money loaned out on interest, on every dollar so accumulated the sum of ten cents belongs to the Lord, in accordance to his law regulating the Tithing of his people; and so on, this law strictly applying to our income derived from every source.

It is not, as some verily suppose, the Tithing of what you may have left after deducting all of your expenses; or in other words, after spending all you can. There are some calling themselves Latter-day Saints who try to appease their conscience in the belief that Tithing means the tenth of what may be left after deducting all expenses, which would amount to this: "What we cannot spend we will give a tenth of that as our Tithing." How much, my brethren and sisters, do you think the Lord would get if all of us felt and acted so? This is not the law of Tithing; all who aim to comply with it after this manner deviate from its true reading. We are required to pay the tenth of our increase, or interest, or income, which is our Tithing, and which is necessary for the general welfare in building Temples, sustaining the Priesthood, administering to the poor, etc., while we retain the nine-tenths for the sustenance of ourselves and families, etc.

(*Erastus Snow*, an Apostle,
JD, 1878, 19:336.)

Specifics About Tithing Different Types Of Income

Frequently we hear the expression "I can't afford to pay tithing." Persons who make such statements have not yet learned that they can't afford not to pay tithing. There are many members who from experience can and do testify that nine-tenths carefully planned, budgeted, and spent wisely, with the blessings of the Lord, will go much farther than ten-tenths spent haphazardly without planning and without the Lord's blessings.

The payment of tithing is a test of our faithfulness and loyalty. President Joseph F. Smith, many years ago, counseled:

> By this principle (tithing) the loyalty of the people of this Church shall be put to the test. By this principle it shall be known who is for the kingdom of God and who is against it.
> (Joseph F. Smith, *Gospel Doctrine*, Deseret Book Co., 1939, p. 225.)

Often the question is asked, "What is a tithe?" Joseph L. Wirthlin, a former Presiding Bishop of the Church, gave a clear definition when he explained:

> The very word itself denotes one-tenth. A tithe is one-tenth of the wage earner's full income. A tithe is one-tenth of the professional man's net income. A tithe is one-tenth of the farmer's net income, and also one-tenth of the produce used by the farmer to sustain his family which is a just and equitable requirement, as others purchase out of their income such food as is needed to provide for their families. A tithe is one-tenth of the dividends derived from investments. A tithe is one-tenth of net insurance income less premiums if tithing has been paid on the premiums. *(Conference Report*, April 1953, p. 98. Italics added.)

The law of tithing has come from the Lord as a commandment, and when we keep that law and commandment we are entitled to the blessings that are promised, for the Lord has said:

> I, the Lord, am bound when ye do what I say; but when ye do not what I say, ye have no promise. *(D&C 82:10.* Italics added.)
>
> *(Henry D. Taylor,* an Assistant to the Council of the Twelve Apostles, *CR-E,* May, 1974, p. 107.)

CHAPTER 51

WAR
(See: Military Service)

International Disputes Should Be Settled Through Peaceful Negotiations

Therefore, renounce war and proclaim peace....*(D&C 98:16.)*
Thus the Church is and must be against war. The Church itself cannot wage war, unless and until the Lord shall issue new commands [see *D&C 98:34-38*, which states that the third offense and God's approval brings justification for going to war]. It cannot regard war as a righteous means of settling international disputes; these should and could be settled—the nations agreeing—by peaceful negotiation and adjustment.

Heber J. Grant, J. Reuben Clark Jr., David O. McKay
The First Presidency *(CR*, April, 1942, pp. 93-95.)

In War The Righteous Suffer With The Wicked

The whole world is in the midst of a war that seems the worst of all time. This Church is a worldwide Church. Its devoted members are in both camps. They are the innocent war instrumentalities of their warring sovereignties. On each side they believe they are fighting for home, and country, and freedom. On each side, our brethren pray to the same God, in the same name, for victory. Both sides cannot be wholly right; perhaps neither is without wrong. God will work out in His own due time and in His own sovereign way the justice and right of the conflict, but He will not hold the innocent instrumentalities of the war, our brethren in arms, responsible for the conflict. This is a major crisis in the world-life of man. God is at the helm.

But there is an eternal law that rules war and those who engage in it. It was given when, Peter having struck off the ear of Malchus, the servant of the High Priest, Jesus reproved him, saying:

> Put up again thy sword into his place: for all they that take the sword shall perish with the sword. *(Matt. 26:52.)*

The Savior thus laid down a general principle upon which He placed no limitations as to time, place, cause, or people involved.

He repeated it in this despensation when He told the people if they tried to secure the land of Zion by blood, then "lo, your enemies are upon you." This is a universal law, for force always begets force; it is the law of 'an eye for an eye, a tooth for a tooth' *(Ex. 21:24; Lev. 24:20);* it is the law of the unrighteous and wicked, but it operates against the righteous who may be involved.

Mormon, recording the war of revenge by the Nephites, against the Lamanites, pronounced another great law:

> But, behold, the judgments of God will overtake the wicked; and it is by the wicked that the wicked are punished; for it is the wicked that stir up the hearts of the children of men unto bloodshed.
> *(Mormon 4:5)*

But, we repeat, in this war of the wicked, the righteous suffer also. Moroni, mistakenly reproving Pahoran 'for sitting upon his throne in a state of thoughtless stupor, while his enemies were spreading the work of death around him, yea, while they were murdering thousands of his brethren,' said to Pahoran:

> Do ye suppose that, because so many of your brethren have been killed it is because of their wickedness? I say unto you, if ye have supposed this ye have supposed in vain; for I say unto you, there are many who have fallen by the sword; and behold it is to your condemnation;
> For the Lord suffereth the righteous to be slain that his justice and judgment may come upon the wicked; therefore ye need not suppose that the righteous are lost because they are slain; but behold, they do enter into the rest of the Lord their God. *(Alma 60:7, 12-13)*

In this terrible war now waging, thousands of our righteous young men in all parts of the world and in many countries are subject to a call into the military service of their own countries. Some of these, so serving, have already been called back to their heavenly home; others will almost surely be called to follow. But 'behold,' as Moroni said, the righteous of them who serve and are slain 'do enter into the rest of the Lord their God,' and of them the Lord has said "those that die in me shall not taste of death, for it shall be sweet unto them." *(D&C 42:46.)* Their salvation and exaltation in the world to come will be secure. That in their work of destruction they will be striking at their brethren will not be held against them. That sin, as Moroni of old said, is to the condemnation of those who 'sit in their places of power in a state of thoughtless stupor,' those rulers in the world who in a frenzy of hate and lust for unrighteous power and dominion over their fellow men, have put into motion eternal forces they do not comprehend and cannot control. God, in His own due time, will pass sentence upon them.

Vengeance is mine; I will repay, saith the Lord. *(Romans 12:19)*

Heber J. Grant, J. Reuben Clark, Jr., David O. McKay
The First Presidency (*CR*, April, 1942, pp. 95-96.)

Three Conditions Which Justify Entrance Into War

I still say that there are conditions when entrance into war is justifiable, and when a Christian nation may, without violation of principles, take up arms against an opposing force. Such a condition, however, is not a real or fancied insult given by one nation to another. When this occurs proper reparation may be made by mutual understanding, apology, or by arbitration.

Neither is there justifiable cause found in a desire or even a need for territorial expansion. The taking of territory implies the subjugation of the weak by the strong—the application of the jungle law.

Nor is war justified in an attempt to enforce a new order of government, or even to impel others to a particular form of worship, however better the government or eternally true the principles of the enforced religion may be.

There are, however, two conditions which may justify a truly Christian man to enter—mind you, I say enter, not begin—a war: (1) An attempt to dominate and to deprive another of his free agency, and, (2) Loyalty to his country. Possibly there is a third, viz., Defense of a weak nation that is being unjustly crushed by a strong, ruthless one.

Paramount among these reasons, of course, is the defense of man's freedom. An attempt to rob man of his free agency caused dissension even in heaven....To deprive an intelligent human being of his free agency is to commit the crime of the ages.

So fundamental in man's eternal progress is his inherent right to choose, that the Lord would defend it even at the price of war. Without freedom of thought, freedom of choice, freedom of action within lawful bounds, man cannot progress. The Lord recognized this, and also the fact that it would take man thousands of years to make the earth habitable for self-governing individuals. Throughout the ages advanced souls have yearned for a society in which liberty and justice prevail. Men have sought for it, fought for it, have died for it. Ancient freemen prized it, slaves longed for it, the Magna Charta demanded it, the Constitution of the United States declared it.

This love of liberty which God has planted in us constitutes the bulwark of our liberty and independence. It is not our frowning battlements, our bristling seacoasts, our army, and our navy. Our defense is in the spirit which prizes liberty as the heritage of all men, in all lands, everywhere. Destroy this spirit, and we have planted the seeds of despotism at our very doors. *(Abraham Lincoln)*

A second obligation that impels us to become participants in...war is loyalty to government.

> We believe that governments were instituted of God for the benefit of man; and that He holds men accountable for their acts in relation to them, both in making laws and administering them, for the good and safety of society.
>
> We believe that no government can exist in peace, except such laws are framed and held inviolate as will secure to each individual the free exercise of conscience, the right and control of property, and the protection of life. *(D&C 134:1-2)*

The greatest responsibility of the state is to guard the lives, and to protect the property and rights of its citizens; and if the state is obligated to protect its citizens from lawlessness within its boundaries, it is equally obligated to protect them from lawless encroachments from without—whether the attacking criminals be individuals or nations.

(David O. McKay, Second Counselor in the First Presidency, *CR,* April, 1942, pp. 72-73.)

Concerning The War In Vietnam

I have spoken previously from this pulpit about the war in Vietnam. With your indulgence I should like again to say a few words on this, because I know that it is a subject on the minds and in the hearts of thousands of our people who have sons there. The welfare of their loved ones is the constant burden of their thoughts and prayers. Even for those of other nations, the war is a matter of deep concern.

One cannot have been to Vietnam as I have on a number of occasions, and felt in some small measure the dreadful sorrow of the land, without making a plea for peace a part of his daily prayers. This war, like others, is fraught with terrible evil and unspeakable tragedy. I minimize none of these.

But notwithstanding the evil and the tragedy, I see a silver thread shining through the dark and bloody tapestry of conflict. I see the finger of the Lord plucking some good from the evil designs of the adversary. I see coming out of this conflict, as I have witnesses in other conflicts in Asia, an enlargement of the Lord's program....I am convinced that there are many and will be many in that land who someday will respond to the message of the restored gospel. I do not know when that day will come, but I am confident that it will come, and that the efforts of your sons who are there in military service will make that day possible.

(Gordon B. Hinckley, an Apostle,
CR, April, 1968, pp. 21-22.)

Defend The Constitutional Government

At the close of the first World War, Nov. 11 was made a national holiday marking the signing of the truce which ended that four-year conflict. Its designation was Armistice Day.

After the second World War there were new victories to be celebrated and new heroes to be honored. The 1918 armistice was eclipsed by the peace of 1945. After that came the Korean conflict, and now that in Vietnam.

Many military men were involved in every war, and they too are honored quite as much as the heroes of earlier times. So the day became known as Veterans' Day, for men of all wars.

Some have urged that recognition of this day be discontinued. But should it? Do we not owe a sacred obligation to our heroic men who served in every war, those who died for us, or were wounded, crippled or made blind, as well as those who served without injury?

The Savior taught that there is no greater evidence of love than for one man to give his life for another. Our valiant veterans fought and many died for us. This all must admit. Their love of country and fellowmen cannot be discounted, and must never be.

Their cause was our cause. We are safe and well at home because of their defense of us.

Our way of life in which we are free to grow, develop, advance, and perfect ourselves, is the life for which they fought. They did not die to protect criminals in their crimes, rioters in their defiance of law and order, nor arsonists in their destructive methods. They did not die to protect snipers who shoot down firemen seeking to control the dastardly work of arsonists, nor those who murder police officers doing their duty.

Those veterans fought for life, not death: for lawful and honorable peace, not peace at any price which is no peace at all. They fought for the right to marry well, to have virtuous children, and to live in law-abiding communities where women and children are safe on the streets and can live without fear.

They fought for the right to worship God according to the dictates of their own conscience. They fought to preserve goodness, not evil; to promote the common wealth, not the avarice of predators.

God gave us a free government which allows for all the good things of life. Our Church is committed to the protection of good government. We believe in being subject to duly elected rulers, and we are pledged to obey the law.

It is part of our religion to do so. Criminality in all its forms is opposed to true Christianity. No one can be an arsonist and a true Christian at the same time, nor will a true Christian riot against law and order, nor shoot down police and firemen, nor in any other way seek to destroy "the establishment."

"The establishment" as we know it—our Constitutional Government—is God-given. To fight against it is literally to fight against the purposes of the Almighty.

And to fight for that government is to defend that which is divinely given.

So when men enter the military service and defend this land— and its flag—they are in a righteous service.

And so it is that the First Presidency, in addressing the youth of this land have said:

> We believe our young men should hold themselves in readiness to respond to the call of their government to serve in the armed forces.

Latter-day Saints are not slackers. They are not conscientious objectors, and they are not pacifists in the usually accepted definition.

Latter-day Saints are loyal citizens of the countries in which they live, and "believe in being subject to kings, presidents, rulers, and magistrates, in obeying, honoring and sustaining the law."

Therefore they honor the veterans of our wars—men who risked their lives—for the sake of their fellow men—that right may prevail in the world.

(Editorial, *CN*, November 7, 1970.)

CHAPTER 52

WELFARE AND WORK
(See: Right to Work Laws)

Strive For Greater Productivity In Your Employment

In this holiday season we urge members of the Church everywhere to contemplate the words of the Savior:

> Inasmuch as ye have done it unto the lest of these my brethren, ye have done it unto me. *(Matthew 25:40)*

There continues to be much hungering and suffering generally in the world. In the months ahead there could be more.

We therefore suggest that you be even more mindful of the needy in your area as well as throughout the world. Specifically we suggest that you and your family observe more diligently these teachings of the Church...

Strive for greater productivity in your employment. Give more than your employer requires. The Lord said to Adam "By the sweat of thy face shalt thou eat bread, until thou shalt return unto the ground" *(Moses 4:25)* and the same applies to all of Adam's descendants. It is a blessing that we are required to work, and we should do it willingly and without complaint....

These are times to remember, perhaps more than ever before, that inner strength, happiness, and peace come through keeping the commandments of Him whom we honor at Christmas time.

Spencer W. Kimball, N. Eldon Tanner, Marion G. Romney
The First Presidency
(CL, December 16, 1974.)

Aim Of The Church Is To Help People Help Themselves

Our primary purpose was to set up, in so far as it might be possible, a system [the Church Welfare Program] under which the curse of idleness would be done away with, the evils of a dole abolished, and independence, industry, thrift, and self respect be once more established amongst our people. The aim of the Church

is to help the people to help themselves. Work is to be re-enthroned as the ruling principle of the lives of our Church membership.
(Heber J. Grant, President of the Church,
CR, October, 1936, p. 3.)

The Objective Of The Church Welfare Plan Is To Build Character

My experience has taught me, and it has become a principle with me, that it is never any benefit to give, out and out, to man or woman, money, food, clothing, or anything else, if they are able-bodied, and can work and earn what they need, where there is anything on the earth, for them to do. This is my principle, and I try to act upon it. To pursue a contrary course would ruin any community in the world and make them idlers. (*Discourses of Brigham Young* [Deseret Book Co., 1943], p. 274.)....

This is the essence of the Church security program, not merely that men should be fed and clothed, we know that this is important, but that the eternal man should be built up by self-reliance, by creative activity, by honorable labor, by service; a generation raised in idleness cannot maintain its integrity. (*Richard L. Evans, Improvement Era*, vol. 39 [1936], p. 768.)

From the beginning the long-range objective of the Welfare Plan was to build character in the members of the Church, both givers and receivers alike, thus rescuing all that is finest down deep inside of them and bringing to flower and fruitage the ladened richness of the spirit, which after all is the mission and purpose and reason for the being of this Church. (*Albert E. Bowen, Church Welfare* [Deseret Sunday School Union, 1946], p. 44.)

You in the Church must realize now that in order to put these divinely inspired admonitions into practice as they have come from heaven-inspired leaders, the members of the Church have been given the family home evening plan for family instruction and involvement. Linked with that, he has given us the plan of temporal salvation in the churchwide welfare program, where everyone is to give in labor, money, or service to the full extent of his ability and then receive from out of the bounties, of which each one who needs has been a producer, and then without embarrassment or reticence, he receives according to his need.

Beyond this the Lord has directed the establishment of children and youth activities and of instruction to mothers and fathers in the auxiliaries and priesthood quorum organizations of the Church, where every means is provided to give to all, as an outside observer said, speaking of the youth activities provided by the

Church, "the opportunity to participate in so many good things that they have little or no time for the evil activities."

(Harold B. Lee, President of the Church, *CR*, October, 1972, pp. 61-62.)

Decreasing Work Week May Not Be Beneficial To Mankind

[Comments on this subject were made by *Spencer W. Kimball*, President of the Church, in the October, 1974, General Conference, and can be found in the *Ensign*, November, 1974, p. 6.]

The Church Welfare Program Was Instituted By Revelation

The present-day Church welfare program was instituted by revelation from God to his mouthpiece, the prophet and earthly president of The Church of Jesus Christ of Latter-day Saints. It was inaugurated by the First Presidency at a general conference of the Church held in October, 1936, thirty-seven years ago. It is significant that the man who served for a quarter century as the first managing director of the General Church Welfare Committee is today the Lord's mouthpiece on earth, President Harold B. Lee, and that President Marion G. Romney, who was so closely associated with him in that endeavor, now stands as a counselor at his side.

At the April 1937 general conference of the Church, President J. Reuben Clark, Jr., of the First Presidency, asked: "What may we as a people and as individuals do for ourselves to prepare to meet this oncoming disaster, which God in his wisdom may not turn aside from us?" President Clark then set forth these inspired basic principles of the Church welfare program:

> First and above and beyond everything else, let us live righteously....
> Let us avoid debt as we would avoid a plague; where we are now in debt, let us get out of debt; if not today, then tomorrow.
> Let us straitly and strictly live within our incomes, and save a little.
> Let every head of every household see to it that he has on hand enough food and clothing, and, where possible, fuel also, for at least a year ahead. You of small means put your money in foodstuffs and wearing apparel, not in stocks and bonds; you of large means will think you know how to care for yourselves, but I may venture to suggest that you do not speculate. Let every head of every household aim to own his own home, free from mortgage. Let every man who has a garden spot, garden it; every man who owns a farm, farm it. (*Conference Report*, April, 1937, p. 26.)

(Ezra Taft Benson, an Apostle, *CR*, October, 1973, p. 90.)

Church Members Should Strive To Be Self-Sustaining

Pursuant to the foregoing principles and instructions, "...welfare workers ... [must] earnestly teach and urge Church members to be self-sustaining to the full extent of their powers. No true Latter-day Saint will, while physically able, voluntarily shift from himself the burden of his own support. So long as he can, under the inspiration of the Almighty and with his own labors, he will supply himself with the necessities of life. We should not forget these principles when we administer the Church Welfare Program.
(Marion G. Romney, Second Counselor in the
First Presidency, *CR*, October, 1973, p. 106.)

The Family, Instead Of The Church Or Government, Should Take Care Of Its Own Members

Now, second, the family should do all they can do. Those who have mothers and fathers who are confined should care for them by furnishing those soul needs such as love, care, and tenderness. If you recall the words of the epitaph:

> Here lies David Elginbrod;
> Have mercy on him, God,
> As he would do if he were God
> And you were David Elginbrod.

So we might also declare to you, try to understand them, try to anticipate their needs. Before you turn the financial responsibility of them over to the Church, state, or government, use every resource you or any member of your family has. Nursing home care provided by the Church was up 411 percent last year.

I believe the Savior would be pleased if we would bring these souls back into our homes, if possible, and if not, to pay the expenses from members of the family. I don't know of any mother or father in the Church who turned their children over to society during those prolonged sicknesses or during those first years of life when it took 24 hours a day to care for the infant child.

Now, third, after the individual and family have used all their resources, then the Church is called in to assist. Let me go back to one thought that came to me. I just talked to a young man the other day, and he said that in his family a grandfather had been very critically ill, had been bedfast and the family tended him during those long hours and, as it were, the man had to wear a diaper. The family changed the diaper regularly. Is that more than he would have done for them? No. We must not forget our family members.

(Vaughn J. Featherstone, Second Counselor in the
Presiding Bishopric, CR-E, November, 1974, p. 30.)

Concerning Public Welfare Systems

These systems rely for their financial resources upon public treasuries which are fed out of the taxation of the people. The donor thus becomes not a voluntary giver but a compelled giver. Between him and the beneficiaries of his contribution there is no bond, hence the character building value which attends voluntary responses to the cry of need is lost. He has paid his taxes and is through, experiencing none of the exhilaration of spirit which floods the being of the voluntary donor to the relief of distress.

On the other side the beneficiary of aid paid under the mandate of law is all too likely to forget the sense of gratitude which should well up in the heart of one who receives voluntarily rendered succor. Instead he is all too apt to fall into the habit of thinking that he is getting only what is of personal right his and in that spirit to become demanding and grasping for more and greater bestowals at the expense of a proper sense of thankfulness.

(Albert E. Bowen, an Apostle,
Church Welfare Plan, 1946, p. 16.)

Work Is A Physical And Spiritual Necessity

When our Father sent our first parents out from Eden, he pronounced, as I read it, the principle of work: "In the sweat of thy face shalt thou eat bread...." *(Gen. 3:19.)* "...cursed is the ground for thy sake," he said. *(Gen. 3:17.)*

For thy sake. Work is a principle, a privilege, a blessing—not a curse—but an absolute essential, a physical and spiritual necessity.

Much restlessness and difficulty on the part of young people comes because they have often been overly insulated from challenging and meaningful assignments, with an overemphasis on leisure and on working less and less. Even if a person has all the wealth he wants, he still needs to work for the sake of his soul—and the same is true of those who have learned to live on very little. Work is a physical and spiritual necessity.

Anyone, young or old, would be restless if he didn't have a useful part in helping to bring good things about; a rewarding and meaningful work to do.

Some don't know where things come from as well as they once did. It's so easy to go to the shop or the market without being aware of the toil of plowing and planting, of making and producing, or what it takes to bring things about. Someone has to do everything—not only the easy and glamorous things, but every routine and tedious task. Someone has to do everything.

We need to give our young people the economic facts of life—as well as the moral and spiritual facts; what it means to produce; what it means to meet a payroll; what it means to provide for a family; what it means to save—what it means to stay solvent. I think those who provide productive, wholesome work for other people are in a way heroic. Thank God for them.

(*Richard L. Evans*, an Apostle,
IE, December, 1970, p. 88.)

Proper Recreation Is Not Idleness

No people believe more than do the Latter-day Saints in wholesome recreation. Certainly all work and no play is not good. But proper recreation is not idleness for it is just what the word says: re-creation—renewing—rebuilding one's strength and energies for further work ahead.

(Editorial, *CN*, August 31, 1974, p. 16.)

CHAPTER 53

WITCHCRAFT AND EVIL PRACTICES
(See: Astrology)

The Evils Of Witchcraft And Other Superstitions

After all the horrors, persecutions, and cruelties that have been brought about by the senseless belief in witchcraft, it seems strange in this age of enlightenment that men or women, especially those who have received the gospel, can be found anywhere who believe in such a pernicious superstition. The Bible and history alike conclusively brand this superstition as a child of evil. In ancient times, God required the Israelites to drive the Canaanites from their land, and witchcraft was one of the crimes which he laid at the door of the Canaanites and for which they were adjudged unworthy of the land which they possessed....

Witchcraft has not infrequently been the last resort of the evildoer. Men bereft of the Spirit of God, when the voice of the Lord has ceased to warn them, have frequently resorted to witchcraft in the endeavor to learn that which heaven withheld; and the people of God from very early days to the present have been troubled with superstitious and evil-minded persons who have resorted to divination and kindred devices for selfish purposes and scheming designs. In the Middle Ages it rested like a nightmare upon all Christendom....

Let it not be forgotten that the evil one has great power in the earth and that by every possible means he seeks to darken the minds of men and then offers them falsehood and deception in the guise of truth. Satan is a skillful imitator, and as genuine gospel truth is given the world in ever-increasing abundance, so he spreads the counterfeit coin of false doctrine. Beware of his spurious currency; it will purchase for you nothing but disappointment, misery, and spiritual death. The father of lies he has been called, and such an adept has he become, through the ages of practice in his nefarious work, that were it possible he would deceive the very elect.

Those who turn to soothsayers and wizards for their information are invariably weakening their faith. When men began to forget the God of their fathers who had declared himself in Eden and subsequently to the later patriarchs, they accepted the devil's substitute and made for themselves gods of wood and stone. It was thus that the abominations of idolatry had their origin.

The gifts of the Spirit and the powers of the holy priesthood are of God; they are given for the blessing of the people, for their encouragement, and for the strengthening of their faith. This Satan knows full well. Therefore he seeks by imitation miracles to blind and deceive the children of God. Remember what the magicians of Egypt accomplished in their efforts to deceive Pharaoh as to the divinity of the mission of Moses and Aaron. John the Revelator saw in vision the miracle-working power of the evil one. Note his words: "And I beheld another beast coming up out of the earth; ... and he doeth great wonders, so that he maketh fire come down from heaven on the earth in the sight of men, And deceiveth them that dwell on the earth by the means of those miracles," etc. *(Rev. 13:11, 13-14.)* Further, John saw three unclean spirits whom he describes as "the spirits of devils, working miracles." *(Rev. 16:14.)*

That the power to work wonders may come from an evil source is declared by Christ in his prophecy regarding the great judgment: "Many will say to me in that day, Lord, Lord, have we not prophesied in thy name? and in thy name have cast out devils? and in thy name done many wonderful works? And then will I profess unto them, I never knew you: depart from me, ye that work iniquity." *(Matt. 7:22-23.)*

The danger and power for evil in witchcraft is not so much in the witchcraft itself as in the foolish credulence that superstitious people give to the claims made in its behalf. It is outrageous to believe that the devil can hurt or injure an innocent man or woman, especially if they are members of the Church of Christ, without that man or woman has faith that he or she can be harmed by such an influence and by such means. If they entertain such an idea, then they are liable to succumb to their own superstitions. There is no power in witchcraft itself, only as it is believed in and accepted.

(Joseph F. Smith, President of the Church, *JI*, September, 1902, pp. 560-563.)

Superstitious Practices Are Inspired Of The Devil

It is needless to assert that to those who are intelligent and not bound by old notions and superstitions, there is no truth in what people call witchcraft. Men and women who come under the influence of a belief therein are bewitched by their own foolishness and are led astray by pretenders and mischief-makers who "peep and mutter." It is really astonishing that there should be any to believe in these absurdities. No man or woman who enjoys the Spirit of God and the influence and power of the holy priesthood can believe in these superstitious notions; and those who do will lose, indeed have lost, the influence of the Spirit of God and of the priesthood and are become subject to the witchery of Satan, who is constantly striving to draw away the Saints from the true way, if not by the dissemination of such nonsense, then by other insidious methods.

One individual cannot place an affliction upon another in the way that these soothsayers would have the people believe. It is a trick of Satan to deceive men and women and to draw them away from the Church and from the influence of the Spirit of God and the power of his holy priesthood, that they may be destroyed. These peepstone men and women are inspired by the devil and are the real witches, if any such there be. Witchcraft and all kindred evils are solely the creations of the superstitious imaginations of men and women who are steeped in ignorance and derive their power over people from the devil, and those who submit to this influence are deceived by him. Unless they repent, they will be destroyed. There is absolutely no possibility for a person who enjoys the Holy Spirit of God even to believe that such influences can have any effect upon him. The enjoyment of the Holy Spirit is absolute proof against all influences of evil; you never can obtain that Spirit by seeking diviners and men and women who "peep and mutter." That is obtained by imposition of hands by the servants of God and retained by right living. If you have lost it, repent and return to God, and for your salvation's sake and for the sake of your children, avoid the emissaries of Satan who "peep and mutter" and who would lead you down to darkness and death.

It is impossible for anyone possessing the spirit of the gospel and having the power of the holy priesthood to believe in or be influenced by any power of necromancy.

(*Joseph F. Smith*, President of the Church,
IE, September, 1902, pp. 896-898.)

CHAPTER 54

WOMENHOOD AND MOTHERHOOD
*(See: Abortion; Birth Control; Children: Needs, Responsibilities,
and Discipline; Divorce; Home and Family Life;
Husbands and Fathers; Marriage)*

The Holy Calling And Divine Service Of Motherhood

Amongst His earliest commands to Adam and Eve, the Lord said: "Multiply and replenish the earth." He has repeated that command in our day. He has again revealed in this, the last dispensation, the principle of the eternity of the marriage covenant. He has restored to earth the authority for entering into that covenant, and has declared that it is the only due and proper way of joining husband and wife, and the only means by which the sacred family relationship may be carried beyond the grave and through eternity. He has declared that this eternal relationship may be created only by the ordinances which are administered in the holy temples of the Lord, and therefore that His people should marry only in His temple in accordance with such ordinances.

The Lord has told us that it is the duty of every husband and wife to obey the command given to Adam to multiply and replenish the earth, so that the legions of choice spirits waiting for their tabernacles of flesh may come here and move forward under God's great design to become perfect souls, for without these fleshly tabernacles they cannot progress to their God-planned destiny. Thus, every husband and wife should become a father and mother in Israel to children born under the holy, eternal covenant.

By bringing these choice spirits to earth, each father and each mother assume towards the tabernacled spirit and towards the Lord Himself by having taken advantage of the opportunity He offered, an obligation of the most sacred kind, because the fate of that spirit in the eternities to come, the blessings or punishments which shall await it in the hereafter, depend, in great part, upon the care, the teachings, the training which the parents shall give to that spirit.

No parent can escape that obligation and that responsibility, and for the proper meeting thereof, the Lord will hold us to a strict accountability. No loftier duty than this can be assumed by mortals.

Motherhood thus becomes a holy calling, a sacred dedication for carrying out the Lord's plans, a consecration of devotion to the uprearing and fostering, the nurturing in body, mind and spirit, of those who kept their first estate and who come to this earth for their second estate "to see if they will do all things whatsoever the Lord their God shall command them." *(Abraham 3:25)* To lead them to keep their second estate is the work of motherhood, and "they who keep their second estate shall have glory added upon their heads for ever and ever." (op. cit.)

This divine service of motherhood can be rendered only by mothers. It may not be passed to others. Nurses cannot do it; public nurseries cannot do it; hired help cannot do it—only mother, aided as much as may be by the loving hands of father, brothers, and sisters, can give the full needed measure of watchful care.

The mother who entrusts her child to the care of others, that she may do non-motherly work, whether for gold, for fame, or for civic service, should remember that "a child left to himself bringeth his mother to shame." *(Prov. 29:15)* In our day the Lord has said that unless parents teach their children the doctrines of the Church "the sin be upon the heads of the parents." *(D&C 68:25)*

Motherhood is near to divinity. It is the highest, holiest service to be assumed by mankind. It places her who honors its holy calling and service next to the angels. To you mothers in Israel we say God bless and protect you, and give you the strength and courage, the faith and knowledge, the holy love and consecration to duty, that shall enable you to fill to the fullest measure the sacred calling which is yours. To you mothers and mothers-to-be we say: Be chaste, keep pure, live righteously, that your posterity to the last generation may call you blessed.

Heber J. Grant, J. Reuben Clark, Jr., David O. McKay
The First Presidency, (*CR*, October, 1942, pp. 12-13.)

The Three Realms Of Women's Influence

I do not know that there is any objection to women entering the fields of literature, science, art, social economy, study and progress, and all kinds of learning, or participating in any and all things which contribute to the fulness of her womanhood and increase her upbuilding influence in the world; but I do know that there are three areas or realms in which women's influence should always be felt. No matter what changes take place, these three realms should be dominated always by the beauty, the virtue, and the intelligence of womankind. The first is the realm of home building. Next to that is the realm of teaching, and the third is the realm of compassionate service.

It is not necessary to convince us of the potency of home influence in shaping character. There are certain trusts to which it is only necessary to call attention and minds instinctively assent to them. All else may be forgotten, but the experiences of childhood will remain undimmed on the walls of memory.

The highest ideal for our young girls today, as for our mothers and grandmothers and great-grandmothers who crossed the plains, is love as it may be expressed in marriage and home building, and this virtue in which love finds true expression is based upon the spiritual and not the physical side of our being.

One of the greatest needs in the world today is intelligent, conscientious motherhood. It is to the home that we must look for the inculcation of the fundamental virtues which contribute to human welfare and happiness.

Womanhood should be intelligent and pure, because it is the living life fountain from which flows the stream of humanity. She who would pollute this stream by smoking tobacco, using poisonous drugs or by germs that would shackle the unborn is untrue to her sex and an enemy to the strength and perpetuity of the race.

The laws of life and the revealed word of God combine in placing upon motherhood and fatherhood the responsibility of giving to children not only a pure, unshackled birth, but also a training in faith and righteousness. They ought to be taught "...to understand the doctrine of repentance, faith in Christ the Son of the living God, and of baptism and the gift of the Holy Ghost by the laying on of the hands when eight years old, ..." To those who neglect this in precept and example, the *Doctrine and Covenants* says, "...the sin be upon the heads of the parents...." *(D&C 68:25.)*

Next to motherhood and teaching, woman attains her highest glory in the realm of compassionate service....

The desire to render service to the wounded, sick, and dying gave to the world one of the most potent organizations among nations today. I refer to the International Red Cross Association. Its beneficent tree, which now sheds its fruit on all lands, sprang from the seed of love and compassion in the heart of Florence Nightingale.

Let me emphasize that woman's realm is not man's realm, though equally important and extensive, though women excel in many vocations which years gone by were considered man's activity alone. The greatest harmony and happiness in life will be found when womankind is helped and honored in the spheres in which

God and nature destined her most effectively to serve and bless mankind. I have named three realms for women. There are many more, but the more that men honor her in those realms, the happier will be men and women and children throughout the world.

There is nothing in life so admirable as true manhood; there is nothing so sacred as true womanhood.

A beautiful, modest, gracious woman is creation's master-piece. When to these virtues a woman possesses as guiding stars in her life righteousness and Godliness and an irresistable impulse and desire to make others happy, no one will question that she be classed among those who are the truly great.

(David O. McKay, President of the Church, *IE,* August, 1965, pp. 676-677.)

The Numerous Capabilities Of Women

We wish, in our Sunday and day schools, that they who are inclined to any particular branch of study may have the privilege to study it. As I have often told my sisters in the Female Relief societies, we have sisters here who, if they had the privilege of studying, would make just as good mathematicians or accountants as any man; and we think they ought to have the privilege to study these branches of knowledge that they may develop the powers with which they are endowed. We believe that women are useful, not only to sweep houses, wash dishes, make beds, and raise babies, but that they should stand behind the counter, study law or physic, or become good bookkeepers and be able to do the business in any counting house, and all this to enlarge their sphere of usefulness for the benefit of society at large. In following these things they but answer the design of their creation. These, and many more things of equal utility are incorporated in our religion, and we believe in and try to practice them.

(Brigham Young, President of the Church, *JD,* 1869, 13:61.)

The Relationship Of A Wife To Her Husband

In defining the relationship of a wife to her husband, the late President George Albert Smith put it this way:

In showing this relationship, by a symbolic representation, God didn't say that woman was to be taken from a bone in the man's head that she should rule over him, nor from a bone in his foot that she should be trampled under his feet, but from a bone in his side to symbolize that she was to stand by his side, to be his companion, his equal, and his helpmeet in all their lives together.

I fear some husbands have interpreted erroneously the statement that the husband is to be the head of the house and that his wife is to obey the law of her husband. Brigham Young's instruction to husbands was this:

> Let the husband and father learn to bend his will to the will of his God, and then instruct his wives and children in this lesson of self-government by his example as well as by his precept. *(Discourses of Brigham Young* [Deseret Book Co., 1925], pp. 306-307.)

This is but another way of saying that the wife is to obey the law of her husband only as he obeys the laws of God. No woman is expected to follow her husband in disobedience to the commandments of the Lord.

(Harold B. Lee, First Counselor in the First Presidency,
E, February, 1972, p. 48-50.)

The Many Roles Of Mothers

Girls, prepare yourselves to assume the roles of mothers by gaining knowledge and wisdom through a good education. We teach that the glory of God is intelligence, and so we must all be aware of what is going on around us and be prepared to thwart Satan in his attempts to divert us from our divine destiny. With knowledge, wisdom, determination, and the Spirit of the Lord to help us we can succeed.

We also believe that women should involve themselves in community affairs and in the auxiliary organizations of the Church, but always remember that home and children come first and must not be neglected. Children must be made to feel that mother loves them and is keenly interested in their welfare and everything they do. This cannot be turned over to someone else. Many experiments have been made and studies carried out which prove beyond doubt that a child who enjoys mother's love and care progresses in every way much more rapidly than one who is left in institutions or with others where mother's love is not available or expressed.

(N. Eldon Tanner, First Counselor in the First Presidency,
CR, October, 1973, p. 127.)

Motherhood Is The Noblest Calling In The World

President David O. McKay put it beautifully when he said, speaking of mothers,

> This ability and willingness properly to rear children, the gift to love, and eagerness, yes, longing to express it in soul development, make motherhood the noblest office or calling in the world. She who can paint a masterpiece or write a book that will influence millions deserves the admiration and the plaudits of mankind; but she who rears successfully a family of healthy, beautiful sons and daughters, whose influence will be felt through generations to come, whose immortal souls will exert an influence throughout the ages long after paintings shall have faded, and books and statues shall have decayed or shall have been destroyed, deserves the highest honor that man can give, and the choicest blessings of God. In her high duty and service to humanity, endowing with immortality eternal spirits, she is co-partner with the Creator himself. *(Gospel Ideals,* Salt Lake City; Improvement Era, 1953 pp. 453-54.)

(H. Burke Peterson, First Counselor in the Presiding Bishopric, *CR-E,* May, 1974, pp. 31-32.)

Mothers Should Receive Confirmation From The Holy Ghost Before Seeking Employment Outside The Home

Brothers and sisters, do without if you need to, but don't do without mother. Mother is more important in the home than money or the things money can buy. Our Father in heaven wants you to be in your home to guide these spirits as no one else can, in spite of material sacrifices that may result. He created you to learn to be a good mother—an eternal mother. It is your first and foremost calling. No baby-sitter, no grandmother, no neighbor, no friend, no Relief Society sister, older brother or sister, or even a loving dad can take your place.

Again we say, unless the Holy Ghost has given you a confirmation that it is all right, don't go out of your home for hire.

(H. Burke Peterson, First Counselor in the Presiding Bishopric, *CR-E,* May, 1974, p. 32.)

Satanic Beliefs Which Lure Mothers Out Of The Home

One of the great tragedies of our day is the confusion in the minds of some which would cause mothers to go to work in the marketplace. Satan, that master of deceit, would have us believe that when we have problems with our children, the answer may be a nicer home in a finer neighborhood, that they might have their own bedroom, or better quality clothes, and maybe their own car. Satan would have us believe that money or the things money can buy are more important in the home than mother.

Now there are some mothers with school-age children who are the bread-winners of their family and they must work; they are the exception. Fathers and mothers, before you decide you need a second income and that mother must go to work out of the home, may I plead with you: first go to the Lord in prayer and receive his divine approbation. Be sure he says yes. Mothers with children and teenagers at home, before you go out of your homes to work, please count the cost as carefully as you count the profit. Earning a few dollars more for luxuries cloaked in the masquerade of necessity—or a so-called opportunity for self-development of talents in the business world, a chance to get away from the mundane responsibilities of the home—these are all satanic substitutes for clear thinking. They are counterfeit thoughts that subvert the responsibilities of motherhood. As you count the costs of mother working out of the home, please consider the following:

—A mother gone when her children need her most or one who is too tired from a day spent in employment. Far better for a boy or girl to go to school in last year's shirts or hand-me-down dresses that are clean even though not in the height of fashion and come home to find mother there, than for a boy or girl to go to school in finer and newer clothes and come home to a new TV or a baby-sitter because Mother is away working.

(H. Burke Peterson, First Counselor in the Presiding Bishopric, *CR-E,* May, 1974, p. 32.)

Present Day False Allurements vs. The True Responsibilities And Influence Of Women

From the beginning God has made it clear that woman is very special, and he has also very clearly defined her position, her duties, and her destiny in the divine plan. Paul said that man is the image and glory of God, and that woman is the glory of the man; also that the man is not without the woman, neither the woman without the man in the Lord. (See *1 Cor. 11:7, 11.)* You will note that significantly God is mentioned in connection with this great partnership, and we must never forget that one of woman's greatest privileges, blessings, and opportunities is to be a co-partner with God in bringing his spirit children into the world.

It is of great concern to all who understand this glorious concept that Satan and his cohorts are using scientific arguments and defarious propaganda to lure women away from their primary responsibilities as wives, mothers, and homemakers. We hear so much about emancipation, independence, sexual liberation, birth control, abortion, and other insidious propaganda belittling the role of motherhood, all of which is Satan's way of destroying woman, the home, and the family—the basic unit of society.

It is so important that our young girls keep themselves from this kind of pollution. The girls of today will be the women of tomorrow, and it is necessary that they prepare for that role. Can you imagine the kind of world we will have in the future if the girls of today are weakened morally to the extent that virtue will not be taught in their homes, and their children, if any, are not nurtured within the walls of homes sanctified by the holy laws of matrimony?

Marriage is ordained of God, and we must do everything we can to strengthen the ties that bind, to strengthen our homes, and to prepare ourselves by exemplary living to teach our children the ways of God, which is the only way for them to find happiness here and eternal life hereafter.

As we enumerate the many important responsibilities a woman has in connection with her duties as a wife, a mother, a homemaker, a sister, a sweetheart, or a good neighbor, it should be evident that these challenging responsibilities can satisfy her need to express her talents, her interests, her creativity, dedication, energy, and skill which so many seek to satisfy outside the home. It is impossible to estimate the lasting influence for good a woman can have in any of these roles. Let me remind us all of her primary responsibilities.

First of all, as I mentioned before, she is a co-partner with God in bringing his spirit children into the world. What a glorious concept! No greater honor could be given. With this honor comes the tremendous responsibility of loving and caring for those children so they might learn their duty as citizens and what they must do to return to their Heavenly Father. They must be taught to understand the gospel of Jesus Christ and to accept and live his teachings. As they understand the purpose of life, why they are here and where they are going, they will have a reason for choosing the right and avoiding the temptations and buffeting of Satan, who is so very real and determined to destroy them.

A mother has far greater influence on her children than anyone else, and she must realize that every word she speaks, every act, every response, her attitude, even her appearance and manner of dress affect the lives of her children and the whole family.

It is while the child is in the home that he gains from his mother the attitudes, hopes, and beliefs that will determine the kind of life he will live, and the contribution he will make to society.

President Brigham Young expressed the thought that mothers are the moving instruments in the hands of Providence and are the machinery that give zest to the whole man, and guide the destinies and lives of men and nations upon the earth. He further said:

> Let mothers of any nation teach their children not to make war, and the children would not grow up and enter into it. *(Discourses of Brigham Young* p. 199.)

When the Lord God said, "It is not good that the man should be alone; I will make him an help meet..." he meant just that, and so presented Eve to Adam. *(Gen. 2:18)* We are taught that a man should leave his father and mother, and cleave unto his wife, and that they should be one flesh, and thus is described the relationship that should exist between husband and wife. *(Gen. 2:24)* It is said that behind every good man there is a good woman, and it is my experience and observation that this is generally true.

It is interesting to note that when executives of companies look for new employees, or are planning promotions for their experienced ones, they always want to know what kind of wife a man has. This seems to be very important. In the Church when men are being considered for new priesthood offices, the question is always raised about the worthiness of the wife and whether or not she can give him full support.

Women, you are of great strength and support to the men in your lives, and they sometimes need your help most when they are least deserving. A man can have no greater incentive, no greater hope, no greater strength than to know his mother, his sweetheart, or his wife has confidence in him and loves him. And men should strive every day to live worthy of that love and confidence.

President Hugh B. Brown once said at a Relief Society conference:

> There are people fond of saying that women are the weaker instruments, but I don't believe it. Physically they may be, but spiritually, morally, religiously, and in faith, what man can match a woman who is really converted to the gospel! Women are more willing to make sacrifices than are men, more patient in suffering, more earnest in prayer. They are the peers and often superior to men in resilience, in goodness, in morality, and in faith. *(Reflief Society Conference,* Sept.19, 1965.)

And girls, don't underestimate your influence on your brothers and your sweethearts. As you live worthy of their love and respect you can help greatly to determine that they will be clean and virtuous, successful and happy. Always remember that you can go much further on respect than on popularity. I was reading the other day of a report of a conversation between two young prisoners of war in Vietnam. One said:

> I am sick of war, bombers, destruction, prison camps, and every thing and everybody.
> I feel much like that myself. Said the other. But there is a girl back home who is praying that I will come back. She cares, and it really helps me endure all these atrocities.

(N. Eldon Tanner, First Counselor in the First Presidency, *CR,* October, 1973, p. 124-125.)

CHAPTER 55

WORD OF WISDOM
(See: Cola Drinks; Drugs)

Saints Are Not To Use Tobacco, Liquor, Or Harmful Drugs

The world is smitten, nigh unto death, with great and grievous tribulations, following the commission of cardinal sins.

Over the earth, and it seems particularly in America, the demon drink is in control. Drunken with strong drink, men have lost their reason; their counsel has been destroyed; their judgment and vision are fled; they reel forward to destruction.

Drink brings cruelty into the home; it walks arm in arm with poverty; its companions are disease and plague; it puts chastity to flight; it knows neither honesty nor fair dealing; it is a total stranger to truth; it drowns conscience; it is the bodyguard of evil; it curses all who touch it.

Drink has brought more woe and misery, broken more hearts, wrecked more homes, committed more crimes, filled more coffins, than all the wars the world has suffered.

Therefore, we thank the faithful Saints for their observance of the Word of Wisdom, for their putting aside of drink. The Lord is pleased with you. You have been a bulwark of strength to this people and to the world. Your influence has been for righteousness. The Lord will not forget your good works when you stand before Him in judgment. He has blessed and will continue to bless you with the blessings He promised to those who obey this divine law of health. We invoke the mercies of the Lord upon you that you may continue strong in spirit, to cast off temptation and continue teachers to the youth of Zion by word and deed.

But so great is the curse of drink that we should not be held guiltless did we not call upon all offending Saints to forsake it and banish it from their lives forever.

God has spoken against drink in our day, and has given to this, the Lord's own Church, a specific revelation concerning it, as a word of wisdom by revelation—

> That inasmuch as any man drinketh wine or strong drink among you, behold it is not good, neither meet in the sight of your Father...
> And, again, strong drinks are not for the belly, but for the washing of your bodies.—*(D&C 89:5,7)*

This declares the divine wisdom. It is God's law of health, and is binding upon each and every one of us. We cannot escape its operation, for it is based upon eternal truth. Men may agree or disagree about this word of the Lord; if they agree, it adds nothing; if they disagree, it means nothing. Beyond His word we cannot reach, and it is enough for every Latter-day Saint, willing and trying to follow divine guidance.

For more than half a century President Grant has on every appropriate occasion admonished the Saints touching their obligation to keep the Word of Wisdom. He has told them what it means to them in matters of health, quoting the words of the Lord thereon. He has pointed out that treasures of knowledge, even hidden knowledge, would come to those who lived the law. He has, over and over again, shown what it would mean financially to every member who would keep the law, what it would mean financially to our people, and what it would mean financially to a nation. He has told us what it would mean in ending human woes, misery, sorrow, disease, crime, and death. But his admonitions have not found a resting place in all our hearts.

We, the First Presidency of the Church of Jesus Christ of Latter-day Saints, now solemnly renew all these counsels, we repeat all these admonitions, we reinvoke obedience to God's law of health given us by God Himself.

We repeat here the directions heretofore given by President Grant: We ask that every General Authority, every stake and ward officer, every officer of Priesthood quorums, every auxiliary officer in ward, stake, or general board, every president of mission, every regular or stake missionary, in short, every officer in every Church organization, strictly to keep the Word of Wisdom from this moment forward. If any feels too weak to do this, we must ask him to step aside for some one who is willing and able so to do, for there are thousands of Latter-day Saints who are willing to obey the commandments and who are able to carry on the work of the Lord.

We ask all Church presiding officers immediately to set their official houses in order.

The Lord will not otherwise fully prosper us in our service in His cause, wherefore we shall stand accused before Him that we walked not in the lead of His flock in the full stature of worthy, righteous example. Furthermore, we make a like call upon all these officers to keep also the law of tithing, to live the law of strictest chastity, and to observe and do the commandments of the Lord.

That in these dire days, we may, each in his own place, enjoy the abundant physical blessings of the righteous life, we call upon all true Latter-day Saints, in or out of office, to keep this law of health,—completely to give up drink, to quit using tobacco, which all too often leads to drink, to abandon hot drinks and the use of harmful drugs, and otherwise to observe the Word of Wisdom. We urge the Saints to quit trifling with this law and so to live it that we may claim its promises.

Upon you parents, laden with the divinely imposed responsibility of guiding pure, eternal spirits through the early years of their earth existence, we urge a faithful performance of your sacred duty, to teach this law of health to your children both by precept and example. Of a surety the Lord will not hold us guiltless if we fail one whit in guarding, protecting, and guiding these precious souls on their way to exaltation.

Parents, these are not the times for weak attempts and half measures, but for the full strength of righteous, prayerful, God-fearing effort to walk ourselves, and to lead our children, along the paths of sobriety and chastity.

How great are the blessings promised to those who observe the law:

> And all saints who remember to keep and do these sayings, walking in obedience to the commandments, shall receive health in their naval and marrow to their bones;
> And shall find wisdom and great treasures of knowledge, even hidden treasures;
> And shall run and not be weary, and shall walk and not faint.
> And I, the Lord, give unto them a promise, that the destroying angel shall pass by them, as the children of Israel, and not slay them.
> (D&C 89:18-21)

When, as the Lord Himself has declared, plague, pestilence, famine, and death shall be poured out upon the nations for their wickedness, and when these shall break over our heads and our loved ones are smitten nigh to death, when hearts are torn and the anguish of grief almost overwhelms us, who can fathom the joy or measure the blessing of that father and mother who can stand before the Lord and say: "We have kept Thy commandments. We and ours have lived Thy law. Vouchsafe Thy promised blessings unto us. We remember Thy word, 'I, the Lord, am bound when ye do what I say.' Let Thy healing power rest upon our afflicted ones 'that the destroying angel shall pass by them, as the children of Israel, and not slay them.' "

As with a person, as with a people, so it is with a nation. A drunken nation cannot expect that God will withhold His judgments, nor ward off the ravages of the destroyer. A drunken nation is a seedbed for disaster—political, physical, moral, and spiritual. A drunken nation may not, even in its hours of direct distress, pray to God for help, with that simple assurance and unpolluted faith which bring aid and comfort to those who abide the law of sobriety and keep His commandments.

Rulers of nations may not suppose that their peoples will be less drunken than are they themselves. We call upon the rulers of all nations to show their peoples by their examples how to live the sober and virtuous life. We call upon them to bring into their counsels, the reenthroned reason of undrunken minds. Then will wisdom and vision return, and peace will leave her hiding place to bless the world. We exhort men and rulers the world over to learn the blessings which come to those who live God's full law of health, that they may, under His hands and by His power, help to bring salvation, temporal and spiritual, to the whole human race.

Heber J. Grant, J. Reuben Clark, Jr., David O. McKay
The First Presidency
(*CR*, October, 1942, pp. 8-10.)

Avoid Beverages Having The Appearance, Smell, And Taste Of Those We Have Been Counseled Not To Use

The Word of Wisdom, section 89 of the *Doctrine and Covenants*, remains as to terms and specifications as found in that section. There has been no official interpretation of that Word of Wisdom except that which was given by the Brethren in the very early days of the Church when it was declared that "hot drinks" meant tea and coffee.

While the use of beverages where the dilatorius effects have been removed might not be considered breaking the Word of Wisdom, it is well to avoid in all cases the appearance of evil by refraining from the use of drinks which have the appearance, the smell, and the taste of that which we have been counseled not to use.

Spencer W. Kimball, N. Eldon Tanner, Marion G. Romney
The First Presidency

[Compilers Note: The above is a statement contained in a letter, dated April 17, 1975, from the First Presidency, which was related to this compiler who had requested the expressed position of the Church on specific types of so-called "decaffeinated coffee drinks."]

Do Not Waste Food; Guard Your Health

In this holiday season we urge members of the Church everywhere to contemplate the words of the Savior:

Inasmuch as ye have done it unto the least of these my brethren,
ye have done it unto me. *(Matthew 25:40)*

There continues to be much hungering and suffering generally in the world. In the months ahead there could be more.

We therefore suggest that you be even more mindful of the needy in your area as well as throughout the world. Specifically we suggest that you and your family observe more diligently these teachings of the Church: ...

Do not waste food. While millions in the world hunger, other millions eat too much and otherwise waste food. Teach your children to use food frugally....

Guard your health. Get adequate exercise and rest. Observe the Word of Wisdom. Eat wisely. Avoid excesses. Teach your children good health habits....

These are times to remember, perhaps more than ever before, that inner strength, happiness, and peace come through keeping the commandments of Him whom we honor at Christmas time.

Spencer W. Kimball, N. Eldon Tanner, Marion G. Romney
The First Presidency
(CL, December 16, 1974.)

Concerning Church Members Who Dispense Alcoholic Beverages

Involvement by members of the Church in handling, sale or serving of alcoholic beverages should be discouraged. Cautious consideration should be exercised before persons so involved are called to Church positions.

(GHI, 1968, p. 163.)

Saints Urged To Defeat Alcoholic Bill

The First Presidency has urged members of the church in the State of Washington to oppose passage of a referendum which would permit 19-year-olds to purchase and consume alcoholic beverages.

In a letter Oct. 21 to church officers in the 19 stakes and two missions in the State of Washington, the First Presidency told the more than 72,800 church members living in the state:

> We deplore the efforts of those who attempt to broaden the sale and use of spirituous beverages, particularly among young people.
>
> We are fully aware of the many problems that result in legally making liquor available to young men and women who generally are more prone to form new habits, good and bad, than older adults.
>
> To lower the age for liquor consumption will only add to the mounting problems of health, crime, accidents, and broken homes which already beset our society.
>
> For these reasons, we encourage members of the church, as citizens, to vote against Referendum 36, and, as citizens, to take steps calculated to prevent the passage of this referendum.

The letter was signed by President Harold B. Lee and his two counselors, President N. Eldon Tanner and President Marion G. Romney.

(CN, October 27, 1973, p. 12.)

How The Word Of Wisdom Became A Commandment

The reason undoubtedly why the Word of Wisdom was given—as not by "commandment or restraint" was that at that time, at least, if it had been given as a commandment it would have brought every man, addicted to the use of these noxious things, under condemnation; so the Lord was merciful and gave them a chance to overcome, before He brought them under the law. Later on, it was announced from this stand, by President Brigham Young [*JD*, 1859, 7:337; & *JD*, 1867, 12:117], that the Word of Wisdom was a revelation and a command of the Lord. I desired to mention that fact, because I do not want you to feel that we are under no restraint. We do not want to come under condemnation.

(Joseph F. Smith, President of the Church,
CR, October, 1913, p. 14.)

Dispense With Multitudinous Food Dishes

The Americans, as a nation, are killing themselves with their vices and high living. As much as a man ought to eat in half an hour they swallow in three minutes, gulping down their food like the canine quadruped under the table, which, when a chunk of meat is thrown down to it, swallows it before you can say "twice." If you want a reform, carry out the advice I have just given you. Dispense with your multitudinous dishes, and, depend upon it, you will do much towards preserving your families from sickness, disease and death.

(*Brigham Young*, President of the Church,
JD, 1869, 13:154.)

The Church Is Concerned About The Waste Of Food

[Comments on this subject were made by *Spencer W. Kimball*, President of the Church, in the October, 1974, General Conference, and can be found in the *Ensign*, November, 1974, p. 6.]

The Practice Of Professional Firms Serving Liquor As A Part Of Their Entertainment Is Deplorable

[Comments on this subject were made by *Spencer W. Kimball*, President of the Church, in the October, 1974, General Conference, and can be found in the *Ensign*, November, 1974, pp. 5-6.]

SELECTED BIBLIOGRAPHY

Andrus, Hyrum L., *Doctrines of the Kingdom* (Bookcraft, Inc., Salt Lake City, Utah, 1973), 576 pp.

Benson, Ezra Taft, *God, Family, Country: Our Three Great Loyalties* (Deseret Book Company, Salt Lake City, Utah, 1974), 422 pp.

Book of Mormon, The (The Church of Jesus Christ of Latter-day Saints, 1968 ed.), 568 pp.

Bowen, Albert Ernest, *Church Welfare Plan* (Deseret Sunday School Union of The Church of Jesus Christ of Latter-day Saints, Salt Lake City, Utah, 1946), 151 pp.

Brigham Young University Speeches of the Year; Provo, Utah. An annual publication.

Brigham Young University Extension (Service) Publication; Provo, Utah, January 5, 1965.

Burton, Alma P., *Doctrines From The Prophets* (Bookcraft, Inc., Salt Lake City, Utah, 1970), 476 pp.

Church News (of The Church of Jesus Christ of Latter-day Saints), section of the Deseret News: a daily newspaper (Salt Lake City, Utah, 1943-1975).

Circular Letters of the First Presidency. These are policy letters written by the First Presidency of The Church of Jesus Christ of Latter-day Saints, which are distributed to General Authorities, Stake and Mission Presidents, and Bishops and Branch Presidents. (Available at the Church Historian's Office, Salt Lake City, Utah, particularly the years 1890-1975.)

Clark, James R., *Messages of the First Presidency* (Bookcraft, Inc., Salt Lake City, Utah, 1965), Volumes 1-5.

Conference Reports (Annual and Semi-annual of The Church of Jesus Christ of Latter-day Saints, 1897-1975).

Daily Universe, The (Newspaper of Brigham Young University, Provo, Utah).

Deseret News (Daily newspaper, Salt Lake City, Utah, particularly the years 1900-1975).

Deseret Sunday School Union Board of The Church of Jesus Christ of Latter-day Saints, *Christ's Ideals for Living* (Wheelwright Lithographing Company, Salt Lake City, Utah, 1955), 464 pp.

Doctrine and Covenants, The (The Church of Jesus Christ of Latter-day Saints, 1968 ed.), 312 pp.

Dunn, Paul H., *Discovering the Quality of Success* (Deseret Book Company, Salt Lake City, Utah, 1973), 140 pp.

Ensign, The (Monthly magazine of The Church of Jesus Christ of Latter-day Saints, 1970-1975).

Evans, Richard L., *An Open Door* (Publishers Press, Salt Lake City, Utah, 1967), 217 pp.

Evans, Richard L., *Thoughts For One Hundred Days* (Publishers Press, Salt Lake City, Utah, 1966), 227 pp.

First Presidency of The Church of Jesus Christ of Latter-day Saints, The, *Gospel Doctrine: Selections from the Sermons and Writings of Joseph F. Smith* (Deseret News Press, Salt Lake City, Utah, 1971), Volumes 1-2.

First Presidency of The Church of Jesus Christ of Latter-day Saints, The, *Immortality and Eternal Life: Selections from the Writing and Messages of President J. Reuben Clark, Jr.* (Deseret News Press, Salt Lake City, Utah, 1969), 338 pp.

Friend, The (Monthly magazine of The Church of Jesus Christ of Latter-day Saints, 1970-1975).

General Handbook of Instructions (The Church of Jesus Christ of Latter-day Saints, 1968), 206 pp.

Gospel in Principle and Practice, The (Brigham Young University Press, Provo, Utah, 1966), Volumes 1-2.

Holy Bible, The (Old and New Testaments—King James Edition, Missionary copy bound for The Church of Jesus Christ of Latter-day Saints, 1969 ed.).

Improvement Era, The (Monthly magazine of The Church of Jesus Christ of Latter-day Saints, 1897-1970).

Instructor, The (Monthly magazine of The Church of Jesus Christ of Latter-day Saints, 1930-1970).

Journal History of the Church (Items about The Church of Jesus Christ of Latter-day Saints; a historical collection since the mid-1800's: available at the Church Historian's Office, Salt Lake City, Utah).

Journal of Discourses (Contains talks given by General Authorities and other Church leaders of the L.D.S. Church between the years 1851-1886).

Juvenile Instructor (Monthly magazine of The Church of Jesus Christ of Latter-day Saints, 1866-1929).

Kimball, Spencer W., *Faith Precedes the Miracle* (Deseret Book Company, Salt Lake City, Utah, 1972), 364 pp.

Kimball, Spencer W., *The Miracle of Forgiveness* (Bookcraft, Inc., Salt Lake City, Utah, 1969), 376 pp.

Lee, Harold B., *Stand Ye In Holy Places* (Deseret Book Company, Salt Lake City, Utah, 1974), 398 pp.

Lee, Harold B., *Ye Are The Light Of The World* (Deseret Book Company, Salt Lake City, Utah, 1974), 364 pp.

Lund, John Lewis, *The Church and the Negro* (U.S.A., 1967), 129 pp.

McConkie, Bruce R., *Doctrines of Salvation: Sermons and Writings of Joseph Fielding Smith* (Bookcraft, Inc., Salt Lake City, Utah, 1954), Volumes 1-3.

McConkie, Bruce R., *Mormon Doctrine* (Bookcraft, Inc., Salt Lake City, Utah, 1966), 856 pp.

Messenger, The (A policy bulletin of The Church of Jesus Christ of Latter-day Saints, 1956-1964).

Millennial Star, The (Monthly magazine of The Church of Jesus Christ of Latter-day Saints, Great Britain, 1840-1970).

New Era, The (Monthly magazine of The Church of Jesus Christ of Latter-day Saints, 1970-1975).

Newquist, Jerreld L., *Gospel Truth: Discourses and Writings of President George Q. Cannon* (Deseret Book Company, Salt Lake City, Utah, 1957), Volumes 1-2.

Newquist, Jerreld L., *Prophets, Principles and National Survival* (Publishers Press, Salt Lake City, Utah, 1964), 579 pp.

Pearl of Great Price, The (The Church of Jesus Christ of Latter-day Saints, 1968 ed.), 65 pp.

Petersen, Mark E., *Patterns for Living* (Bookcraft, Inc., Salt Lake City, Utah, 1962), 325 pp.

Pratt, Orson, edited by, *The Seer* (Liverpool, England, 1853-1854), Volumes 1-2, 320 pp.

Priesthood Bulletin, The (A policy bulletin of The Church of Jesus Christ of Latter-day Saints, 1965-1975).

Relief Society Magazine, The (Monthly magazine of The Relief Society of The Church of Jesus Christ of Latter-day Saints, particularly 1914-1964).

Richards, Franklin D., and Little, James A., *A Compendium of the Doctrines of the Gospel* (1898 edition).

Richards, LeGrand, *A Marvelous Work And A Wonder* (Deseret Book Company, Salt Lake City, Utah, 1969 ed.), 452 pp.

Roberts, Brigham H., *A Comprehensive History of the Church* (Brigham Young University Press, Provo, Utah, 1956), Volumes 1-6.

Salt Lake Tribune, The (Daily newspaper, Salt Lake City, Utah).

Smith, Joseph, *(The Documentary) History of the Church* (Deseret Book Company, Salt Lake City, Utah, 1946-1951), Volumes 1-7.

Smith, Joseph F., *Gospel Doctrine* (Deseret Book Company, Salt Lake City, Utah, 1919), 553 pp.

Smith, Joseph Fielding, *Answers to Gospel Questions* (Deseret Book Company, Salt Lake City, Utah, 1957), Volumes 1-6.

Stewart, John J., *Mormonism and the Negro* (Community Press Publishing Company, Orem, Utah, 1960), 54 pp. With this publication is bound *The Church and the Negroid People*, by William E. Berrett.

Stewart, John J., *The Glory of Mormonism* (Mercury Publishing Company, Salt Lake City, Utah, 1963), 256 pp.

Talmage, James E., *Jesus The Christ* (Deseret Book Company, Salt Lake City, Utah, 1961 ed.), 804 pp.

Talmage, James E., *The Articles of Faith* (Deseret Book Company, Salt Lake City, Utah, 1961 ed.), 536 pp.

Teachings of the Living Prophets (Brigham Young University Press, Provo, Utah, 1970), 323 pp.

Turner, Rodney, *Woman and the Priesthood* (Deseret Book Company, Salt Lake City, Utah, 1972), 333 pp.

Widtsoe, John A., *Discourses of Brigham Young* (Deseret Book Company, Salt Lake City, Utah, 1954), 497 pp.

Widtsoe, John A., *Priesthood and Church Government* (Deseret Book Company, Salt Lake City, Utah, 1967 ed.), 397 pp.

INDEX

A

Abortion, 19-21; amenable to laws of repentance, 19; an evil act, 20; Church opposed to, 19; Church members submitting to, will be disciplined, 19; conditions, might be justified, 19, 20; evil of premeditated, 20; free, a part of the immoral sex revolution, 106; is one of the most revolting and sinful practices in this day, 21; mentioned, 268; position of Church on, 19.

A Compendium of the Doctrines of the Gospel, 136.

Adultery, 23-24; Church courts to handle, 24, 227; death the ancient penalty for, 24; scriptures on, 23-24; thou shalt not commit, 23.

Alcohol, use of, in the home by parents gives license to children to do the same, 111.

Alcoholic, concerning Church members who dispense, beverages, 275; Saints urged to defeat, bill, 275; the ill effects of men under the, influence, 271.

Amusements, innocent, are proper kinds of, 46; not to be encouraged on the Sabbath day, 213-214.

Animals, a sin in neglecting stock, 162; no religion in abusing, 162-163; should not be killed except for food, 161-162.

Answers to Gospel Questions, 41-42, 67-68, 85-87.

Anti-Communist Organizations, Church members free to join, 203.

Articles of Faith, The, 65-66.

Ashton, Marvin J., 110-111.

Astrology, 25-26; God did not devise the cult of, 26; God's laws prohibit the superstitions of, 26.

B

Babies, fasting when nursing, not required, 140.

Ballard, Melvin J., 96.

Bankruptcy, even in, a person should endeavor to pay all his debts, 98; when, is justified, 96.

Bars, are hell-holes of Satan, 151.

Beauty, importance of, in keeping up homes, farms, and places of business, 125.

Bennion, Lowell L. 92-93.

Benson, Ezra Taft, 35, 68-69, 80, 141, 144-145, 253.

Beverages, concerning Church members who dispense alcoholic, 275; should avoid, which have the appearance, smell, and taste of those we have been counseled not to use, 274.

Birth Control, antagonistic to the best interests of home and state, 28; attitude of Church on, 27; based on vanity, passion, and selfishness, 28; blessed are those who do not practice, 32; brings no promise of salvation, 29-30; husbands use of self-control and, 27, 33; is an abomination, 31; is sinful, 32; mentioned, 268; the only legitimate practice of, 33; those who practice, will reap the whirlwind of God, 34; where parents enjoy health, contrary to Church teachings, 27.

Birth Control and Population Explosion, 27-39.
Birthrate, decreasing, a treat to the perpetuity of any nation, 101.
Books, circulation of pornographic, has reached an alarming stage, 205.
Bowen, Albert E., 255.
Brigham Young University Extension Publication, 230.
Brigham Young University Speeches of the Year, 204.
Brockbank, Bernard P., 150-151.
Brown, Hugh B., 67.
Burglary, criminal conviction of, justifies excommunication, 89.
Burton, Theodore M., 145-146, 198-199.

C

Caffeine, a drug, 73, amount of, in Cola drinks, 74.
Camping Trips, on Sunday not approved, 213.
Cannon, George Q., 231-235.
Capital Crime, Church revelations make death the penalty for, 41.
Capital Punishment, 41-43; a divine law never revoked, 41; eternal significance of, 42-43.
Card Playing, 45-51; affects spiritual sensitivity, 50; an excessive pleasure, 45; a vice, 45-46; a waste of time, 47-48; concerning, in the home, 48; encourages trickery and cheating, 47; evils of, 45-46; persistent, begets spirit of gambling, 48; should be stopped by Latter-day Saints, 49-50; with gambling cards discouraged, 50, 51.
Cards, non-gambling, not objectionable, 51.
Character, determined by one's amusements, 45.
Charity Support, 53.
Chastity, is in this day considered an outmoded virtue, 228; is the most vital part of a happy marriage, 229.
Checkers, does not intoxicate players like card playing, 47.
Chess, does not intoxicate players like card playing, 47.
Children, are entitled to three fundamental things, 55; destroying of unborn, most despicable of sins, 21; important that, feel that mother loves them, 265; need both parents, 167; parental example to, 55-56; parents should not compel, to fast, 140; reprove, betimes with sharpness, 59; responsibilities to parents, 56-57; should be corrected through kindness, 57-58; should be given responsibilities, 57; should never neglect parents, 57.
Children: Needs, Responsibilities, and Discipline, 55-60.
Christianity, will never be reunited as one church through the wisdom of men, 113-115.
Church (L.D.S.), has no civil political functions, 61; mission of, is to establish peace, 197, 198.
Churches, councils alone will not bring unity among, 113.
Church and State, 61-63; concerning the separation between, 61-63.
Church News, 25-26, 33, 35-39, 42-43, 53, 57, 59-60, 73-74, 78-79, 97-98, 102, 106-107, 109, 111-112, 113-114, 120, 121, 127-128, 155-156, 197-198, 202-203, 205, 220-221, 238-239, 249-250, 256, 275-276.
Church Welfare Plan, 255.
Church Welfare Program, aim of, is to help people help themselves, 251-252; instituted by revelation, 253; objective of, is to build character, 252.

Circular Letters of the First Presidency, 27, 65, 103, 117, 123, 139, 144, 149, 157-158, 191-193, 201-202, 205-206, 213-214, 241, 251, 275.

Citizens, duty of, to exercise voting franchise, 201; Latter-day Saints should be loyal, to the countries in which they live, 250.

Citizenship (American), communism hostile to, 76.

Civil Laws, 65-66; Church members should wield influence in encouraging good, 65; Church members to be obedient to, unless directed otherwise by God, 65-66.

Civil Rights, 67-69; Church for full, 67; communist influence in, movement, 68-69; Negroes should have full, 191; Negroes should receive all privileges and, under the Declaration of Independence, 67.

Clark, J. Reuben, Jr., 75-76, 78-79, 83, 96, 158-159, 218-219, 224-225, 238-239.

Clawson, Rudger, 33.

Cleanliness, importance of, in keeping up homes, farms, and places of business, 125.

Closed Shops, Church is against, 209-211; are un-American and undemocratic, 212.

Coca-Cola, amount of caffeine in, 74; Church does not own stock in, company, 72; leave alone, 71-72.

Cola Drinks, 71-74; amount of caffeine in, 74; Church has never officially taken a position on, but advises against drinks containing harmful, habit-forming drugs, 71.

Communism, cannot live with Christianity, 79; Church members free to join anti-, movements, 203; debases and enslaves the individual, 76; destroys free-agency, 77; goal is to destroy constitutional government, 79; hostile to American citizenship and Church membership, 76; influence of, in Civil Rights movement, 68-69; is based upon intolerance and force, 75; is not the United Order, 75; play-on-words and propaganda of, 77-78; Satan's counterfeit for the gospel, 76; the Civil Rights movement a, program for revolution in America, 68-69.

Communism and Socialism, 75-80.

Communists, masters of deceit, 80.

Conference Reports, 20, 23-24, 34-35, 50, 55, 56-57, 58-59, 61-63, 65, 67, 68-69, 71-72, 76-78, 79-80, 82, 90, 92-93, 95-97, 99-102, 109-111, 113, 121-122, 143, 144-145, 153-155, 166-167, 171-175, 177-182, 183-184, 189-190, 197, 199-200, 203, 211-212, 217-218, 219, 223-224, 227-229, 245-249, 251-254, 261-262, 265, 267-270, 271-274, 276.

Constitutional Government (U.S.), 81-83; began under the direction of God, 82, 83; defend, 249-250.

Constitution of the United States, allegiance to, is basic to our freedom, 83; although inspired not perfect, 82; Church stands for, 211; founded in the wisdom of God, 81; written by men who accepted Christ, 87.

Creation, concerning the biblical, story, 135-136.

Cremation, 85-87; Church discourages, 85; Church never taken a definite stand on, 85; does not nullify resurrection, 85-87; left to the decision of the family, 85; makes unnecessary dedicatory prayers, 85; no part of the gospel, 85; one reason why the world practices, 86.

Crime, 92-95; conviction of a, involving moral turpitude justifies Church excommunication, 89; one factor contributing to the growth of, 90; relationship of pornography to, 206.

D

E

Fishing, should not engage in, on the Sabbath day, 215.

Food, Church concerned about waste of, 275, 277; dispense with multitudinous, dishes, 276-277; do not waste, 275; prepare, with singleness
of heart on Sabbath day, 221; teach children to use, frugally, 275.

Food Storage, 143-146; concerning sharing, with others in time of need,
145-146; essentials, 144-145; maintain a year's supply of, 143, 144;
those that have land should produce some food items for, 143.

Fornication, handled by Church courts, 24, 227; no fine distinction between
adultery and, 24.

Free Agency, people cannot be affected by astrology because of, 25, 26.

Friend, The, 105.

Fuel, where possible have, enough for a year's supply, 253.

Funerals, concerning the holding of, for those who committed suicide, 231.

G

Gambling, 147-151; Church opposed to, in any form, 147; non-, card games
not objectionable, 50-51; Saints should not use cards which are used
for, 50; the spirit in which things are done determines whether we are,
or are entering into legitimate business enterprises, 150.

Gambling Casinos, are hell-holes of Satan, 151; Saints should not work or
participate in, 149.

Games of Chance, Church opposed to any, 147; not approved Church entertainment, 147-149.

General Handbook of Instructions, 24, 85, 89, 139-140, 147, 213, 227,
231, 241, 275.

Girls, appropriate dress standards for, 103-107; beware of, who place low
premiums on missionary service, 185; instruct young, in the art of
housekeeping, 156; prepare yourselves to be mothers by gaining knowledge and wisdom, 265.

Glory of Mormonism, The, 195-196.

Government, Church does advocate principles of good, 203; Church separation from, 61-63; debt spending may bring bondage to all, 97; mission
of, is to protect rather than to dictate, 120; overloaded with agencies, 97.

Government Leaders, allegiance should be to Constitution rather than to,
83; pray for, 81-82.

Governments, those, not ordained of God will crumble, 81.

Grant, Heber J., 71-72, 95-96, 251-252.

H

Habits, bad, reduces one's freedom to slavery, 111.

Hallucinations, turn on to inspiration, not to, 112.

Happiness, only through obedience to the gospel will mankind find, 197.

Harlots, God speaks of, in terms of divine contempt, 227.

Health, guard your, by adequate exercise, rest and avoiding excesses, 275.

Hiking, on Sunday not approved, 213.

Hinckley, Gordon B., 219-220, 248-249.

Hitchhikers, improper parental example results in, who have no particular
destination except away from truth, 111.

Home, importance of spirituality in the, 154-155; improper parental example
in, cause of wandering youth, 111; is the strength of a republican

nation, 153; is where a baby first experiences security and love, 153; keep, ties strong, 153; let love abound in, 153; make, an anchor for children in this day of turmoil, 154; mothers should receive confirmation from the Holy Ghost before seeking employment outside, 266; no other success can compensate for failure in, 100-101; own your own, 96, 253; parents should make, a heaven on earth, 171-172; safety of our nation depends upon the purity and strength of, 156; Satanic beliefs that lure mothers out of, 266-267; should provide children with spiritual enlightenment, 120; the chief school of human virtues, 100; utilize Sabbath day in promoting family association in, 213.

Home and Family Life, 153-156.

Homebreaking, is sin, 175.

Homes, keep, cleaned, orderly and beautiful, 125.

Homosexuality, 157-159; a sin in the same degree as adultery, 157; a sin of Sodom and Gomorrah, 158; every form of, is sin, 158; handled by Church courts, 24, 227; in men and women is to be forsaken, 157; Lord does not approve of , 230.

Homosexuals, convince, through kind persuasion of possible forgiveness, 157-158.

Honesty, teach children, 89.

Horoscope, suggestions are outlandish, 25.

Hunting, of animals should not be for sport but for food, 161-162.

Hunting and Treatment of Animals, 161-163.

Husbands, are to be faithful to their wives, 175; how, can make home a happy place, 168; instruct wives by example and precept, 265; not justified in resorting to physical force against wives, 166-167; should be true to wives and children, 166; should not abuse their wives, 166; should treat wives kindly, 165.

Husbands and Fathers, 165-168.

Hypnotherapy, the value of, 170.

Hypnotism, 169-170; demonstrations should not be sponsored or encouraged by Church leaders, 169; limits free agency, 169-170; the value of, 170.

I

Idleness, a generation raised in, cannot maintain its integrity, 252; proper recreation is not, 256.

Immorality, abstain from, 227-230; handled by Church courts, 227.

Income, live within your, 253; specifics about tithing different types of, 242-243; those people without, exempt from paying tithing, 241.

Infanticide, is a crime, 34.

Improvement Era, The, 47-48, 57, 72, 83, 119-120, 129-135, 140, 147-149, 150, 167, 169-170, 187-188, 212, 214-216, 230, 255-256, 258-259, 262-264.

Instructor, The, 117-119.

Integrity, teach children, 89.

Internal Revenue Service, mentioned, 237.

International Red Cross Association, sprang from the seed of love and compassion, 263.

Ivins, Anthony W., 97.

J

Jesus Christ Superstar, Church leaders should not permit use of, rock opera at Church sponsored meetings, 188; is a profane and sacreligious attack upon true Christianity, 189; strips Jesus Christ of His divine attributes, 189.

John Birch Society, Church is not opposed to, 203.

Jokes, filthy, mentioned as part of the immoral sex revolution, 107.

Journal History of the Church, 82-83.

Journal of Discourses, 21, 34, 55-56, 57-58, 78, 81-82, 89, 91-92, 120-121, 135-136, 162-163, 165, 166, 203-204, 241-242, 264, 276-277.

Juvenile Instructor, 45-47, 48-49, 161-162, 165, 216, 231-235, 257-258.

K

Killing, of animals should not be except for food, 161-162; of human beings is a crime punishable by death, 41; people not justified in, themselves, 232-235.

Kimball, Heber C., 162-163.

Kimball, Spencer W., 21, 24, 34, 50, 57, 89, 96, 100, 109, 122, 125, 144, 158, 172, 173, 175, 182, 183, 203, 206, 217, 221, 229, 230, 235, 253, 277.

Knowledge, wisdom is the right application of, 118.

L

Labor, entitled to a fair return for its work, 209; may not legally engage in sabotage, 209; must have some organization, 209; must not deny right to work, 209; must operate within limitations, 209; not compelled to work, 209; should eliminate strikes and boycotts from methods of warfare, 210; when in, Church members should assume a conservative attitude, 210.

Land, Saints that have, should produce food for storage, 143.

Law, administration of, has become a science for protecting the criminal from just punishment, 90.

Lee, Harold B., 34-35, 79, 105-106, 113, 153-154, 172-173, 204, 230, 252-253, 264-265.

Life, a dreadful sin to take one's own, 231-232; living a, of moral purity brings joy and happiness, 229; only a fool would ever consider taking his own, 235; our birth into this, had a relationship to the, heretofore, 194; purpose of, is to create eternal family units, 171; when a mother feels, it is her infant's spirit entering its body preparatory to existence, 21.

Liquor, Saints are not to use, 271-274; the practice of professional firms serving, as a part of their entertainment is deplorable, 277.

Lord's Day, is a holy day and not a holiday, 213.

Love, helps children to progress rapidly, 265; let, abound in home, 153.

L.S.D., a vicious drug, 110.

Lyman, Francis M., 169-170.

M

Man, child of God, 134; did not originate from lower animal forms, 133-134; earth events prior to its habitation by, 136, 137; first being that came upon the earth, 136; origin of, 129-134.

Y